The Shakespeare play as poem

IN MEMORIAM

Y. H. SUBRAHMANYAM,

MY FATHER

The Shakespeare play as poem

a critical tradition in perspective

S. VISWANATHAN
Reader in English Literature, University of Hyderabad

CAMBRIDGE UNIVERSITY PRESS

CAMBRIDGE
LONDON   NEW YORK   NEW ROCHELLE
MELBOURNE   SYDNEY

Published by the Press Syndicate of the University of Cambridge
The Pitt Building, Trumpington Street, Cambridge CB2 1RP
32 East 57th Street, New York, NY 10022, USA
296 Beaconsfield Parade, Middle Park, Melbourne 3206, Australia

First published 1980

Phototypeset in V.I.P. Palatino by
Western Printing Services Ltd, Bristol
Printed in Great Britain at the
University Press, Cambridge

British Library Cataloguing in Publication Data
Viswanathan, S
The Shakespeare play as poem.
1. Shakespeare, William – Criticism and
interpretation – History – 20th century
I. Title
822.3'3   PR2969   79-41618

ISBN 0 521 22547 7

Contents

Acknowledgements

I record my gratitude to Professor R. A. Foakes for his advice and encouragement with regard to this and other work by me; and to the 'readers' and the editorial staff of Cambridge University Press and to Mr Michael Black. I am grateful for their valuable suggestions for improvement. My debt to the Shakespeare critics and scholars, whom I undertake to criticise in this volume, especially to Wilson Knight, L. C. Knights and Wolfgang Clemen, is deep and beyond repayment.

Preface

This study examines some aspects of a dominant school, if not the dominant trend, of Shakespeare criticism in the twentieth century; namely the poetic interpretation of Shakespeare, sometimes referred to as the school of Knight and Knights, or more loosely as the school of the 'imagists'. The advent of this critical approach is not merely a matter of reaction against the character-criticism of Bradley and Coleridge and its extreme manifestations in the nineteenth-century commentators like Anna Jameson and Mary Cowden Clarke. Early twentieth-century developments in Shakespeare scholarship as well as in Shakespeare criticism, related to developments in modern literary criticism and literature in general, made available new perceptions about what may be called the ontological status or mode of existence and also the function of Shakespearian drama. The rise of the poetic approach has more to do with these developments than with a revolt against Bradley. Placed in this context, the school of the poetic interpreters can be seen to have a double relationship, not only of rivalry, antagonism and at times conflict with the school of theatrical and historical scholarship and interpretation, but of more or less tacit and unconscious collaboration, even of indebtedness.

There is no denying the basic difference between scholarship and criticism – between the scholarly-interpreter's 'then-meaning' and the critic-interpreter's 'now-meaning'. As the following study tries to show, one regrets that the critic-interpreter does not make as much use of historical scholarship as he might. Yet when the study of Shakespeare is viewed historically, it appears that the poetic interpretation has, in a number of ways, been indirectly fostered by scholarship in this century. There are many instances of the 'imaginative intuition' of the critic and the 'practical sagacity' of the scholar (to use the phrases employed by C. H. Herford in *A Sketch of Recent Shakespearian Investigation* (1922)) providing mutual corroboration. At any rate, the poetic critics' basic attitudes and assumptions, and their idea of what Shakespearian drama is, are such that their rise and currency can be seen to be promoted by the contributions of the scholar-interpreters, especially when a historical if not a historicist view is taken of the contributions of these critic-interpreters and of the causes and consequences of their critical ventures. So the interplay between the commentaries of these critics and the findings of historical scholars and scholar-interpreters claims particular attention.

Chapter 1 considers the circumstances in Shakespeare studies in which the poetic interpretation arose, and attempts to place the school of Wilson Knight and L. C. Knights in the history of Shakespeare criticism. The chapter shows how earlier scholarly discoveries and critical findings made the time ripe for interpretation of the plays through their poetry.

The overall context of the poetic approach to Shakespeare goes far beyond Shakespeare studies, so the relevant backgrounds and governing influences in the modern literary and cultural scene have to be reckoned with. I outline this general ethos in chapter 2.

Through the perspective thus gained, the interpretative commentaries of Wilson Knight, L. C. Knights, Spurgeon and other 'poetic' critics are studied in chapters 3, 4, 5 and 6. Given the importance of his commentaries, Wilson Knight's 'spatial' interpretation is dealt with in two chapters, 3 and 4. I turn to the no less important and influential studies of the plays by L. C. Knights in chapter 5. In the sixth chapter I study the methods of Caroline Spurgeon and such successors as Wolfgang Clemen, and the inter-communication between imagistic analysis and historical scholarship. The last chapter contains my concluding observations.

Abbreviations and usages

Standard abbreviations of journal and yearbook titles have been used where appropriate, besides abbreviations for some frequently cited titles by Wilson Knight, L. C. Knights, Caroline Spurgeon and Wolfgang Clemen. Citations are from the editions specified.

BJRL	*Bulletin of the John Rylands Library*
CL	G. Wilson Knight, *The Crown of Life* (London, 1948, reprint of the first edition of 1947)
Clemen	Wolfgang Clemen, *The Development of Shakespeare's Imagery* (London, 1951)
CQ	*Critical Quarterly*
EC	*Essays in Criticism*
ELH	*Journal of English Literary History*
E&S	*Essays and Studies*
ES	*English Studies*
GL	*The Golden Labyrinth: A Study of British Drama* (London, 1962), reissued 1965
JAAC	*Journal of Aesthetics and Art Criticism*
JEGP	*Journal of English and Germanic Philology*
IT	G. Wilson Knight, *The Imperial Theme* (London, 1954 reprint of the 1951 edition)
MLN	*Modern Language Notes*
MLQ	*Modern Language Quarterly*
MLR	*Modern Language Review*
MP	*Modern Philology*
N&Q	*Notes and Queries*

PMLA	*Publications of the Modern Language Association of America*
PQ	*Philological Quarterly*
RES	*Review of English Studies*
SAB	*Shakespeare Association Bulletin*
SEL	*Studies in English Literature 1500–1900*
SF	G. Wilson Knight, *The Sovereign Flower* (London, 1958)
SP	*Studies in Philology*
Spurgeon	Caroline F. E. Spurgeon, *Shakespeare's Imagery and What It Tells Us* (Cambridge, 1965 paperback edition, first edition, 1935)
SQ	*Shakespeare Quarterly*
SR	*Sewanee Review*
SS	*Shakespeare Survey*
SST	L. C. Knights, *Some Shakespearean Themes* (London, 1959)
SST&AH	L. C. Knights, *Some Shakespearean Themes and An Approach to 'Hamlet'* (Harmondsworth, 1966)
ST	G. Wilson Knight, *The Shakespearian Tempest* (London, 1960 reprint of the 1953 edition, first edition 1932)
TS	*Theatre Survey*
UTQ	*University of Toronto Quarterly*
WF	G. Wilson Knight, *The Wheel of Fire* (London, 1959 reprint of the second edition of 1949, first edition 1930). It is the 1959 version to which I refer unless otherwise stated.

Quotations from the text of Shakespeare are from Peter Alexander's Tudor edition of Shakespeare's *Complete Works* (London, 1951).

1

Modern Shakespeare criticism: a pattern in the carpet

Some of the richest harvest of criticism in our 'age of criticism' has been gathered in the field of Shakespeare commentary. Modern Shakespeare criticism constitutes the most impressive and substantial part of the whole body of Shakespeare criticism through the centuries. In its range and depth, in its multiplicity of approaches and methods, modern Shakespeare criticism shows great complexity and sophistication, and uses speculative instruments drawn from different branches of knowledge. Not only does the literary criticism of the age find its true image in its Shakespeare criticism; creative literature, indeed the entire intellectual and cultural spirit of the age is also reflected there. If modern literary criticism consists of a number of schools using conflicting modes of approach to the study of literature, and hence deserves to be called 'a veritable Tower of Babel',[1] so more obviously does modern Shakespeare criticism; the variety and, at times, the clash of critical voices and 'languages' are most readily perceived here. Three distinct trends, schools or movements can be isolated in modern Shakespeare commentary, and a threefold classification of critics into historical, theatrical and poetic can be made.[2] The

---

[1] René Wellek, *Concepts of Criticism* (New York and London, 1963), p. ix.
[2] Other modes of classification have been employed. Alan S. Downer, 'The Life of our Design', *Shakespeare: Modern Essays in Criticism*, edited by L. F. Dean (New York, 1961), p. 19, divides critics into 'the Shakespeare-as-a-poet' ones and 'the Shakespeare as-a-dramatist' ones. Anne Ridler calls the two groups the 'theatrical' and the 'linguistic', Anne Ridler, ed., *Shakespeare Criticism: 1935–1960* (London, 1963), pp. vii-ix. Allardyce Nicoll, *Shakespeare* (London, 1952), p. 49, distinguishes between the school of romantic criticism of which Coleridge is father, and which considers Shakespeare's works as divorced from their age and original theatre, and the school which concerns itself with the

2 The Shakespeare play as poem

poetic interpretation of Shakespeare might be called the trend of
twentieth-century Shakespeare criticism, and in this book I am
concerned with the contribution of this school, especially of some
of its leading exponents,[3] and the interrelations between it and
other schools of Shakespeare criticism.

For the sake of perspective, any study of this dominant school
of Shakespeare criticism in this century should start with an
account of the other main approaches. I will attempt to indicate
the general outlines of the theory, explicit or implicit, behind
these approaches to Shakespeare, and of the methods generally
adopted. Such a chart will give us a historical angle of vision,
from which it becomes clear that the developments in other
schools fostered a climate congenial to the emergence and vogue
of poetic criticism. What is more, the relation between the poetic
school and the historical school, and the poetic school and the
theatrical school, is not one of simple rivalry or opposition, but
rather one of unconscious collaboration. Behind the surface

Elizabethan Shakespeare. He also divides critics into 'Bradleyites' concerned
with the conventions of the Elizabethan stage (p. 52). Kenneth Muir 'Fifty years
of Shakespearian Criticism', *Shakespeare Survey*, 4 (1951), uses categories such as
'Bradley and Bradleyites', 'Approaches to Shakespeare', 'Disintegration and
Reintegration', 'Scholarship and Criticism', 'Realism and Convention', and
'Imagery, Symbolism and liberty of interpreting'. L. D. Lerner, in the introduction to *Shakespeare's Tragedies: An Anthology of Modern Criticism* (Harmondsworth, 1963), sees approaches to Shakespeare in the present century in terms
of Aristotle's six elements of drama – plot, character, diction, thought, music,
and spectacle (p. 10).
[3] I have given detailed attention to only a few of the critics. J. Middleton Murry,
William Empson, Derek A. Traversi and Robert B. Heilman merit study on the
lines pursued here. A response to the poetic-dramatic constituents of the plays
has become a characteristic of competence in the commentator or scholar,
thanks to the impact of the poetic interpreters.
The contributions of Murry and Empson are substantial, individual and
influential. No adequate consideration can be attempted in the compass of this
study. Two general observations are worth making. There is an evolution in
Empson's commentaries and to an extent in Murry's, towards greater use of
historical findings, and thus towards greater interplay between historical scholarship and critical insight. In his later essays and books (*The Structure of Complex
Words* (London, 1951) and *Milton's God* (London 1961)), Empson employs
methods of character-criticism in conjunction with semantic analysis, and specu-
lates about the likely response of the original audience of the plays ('Hamlet
When New', *Sewanee Review*, 61 (1953), 15–42, 185–205), thus ostensibly restoring plays to their theatrical context; but his reconstructions are often too mod-
ernistic and speculative.

appearance of antagonism, there has been a dialogue and fruitful meeting-ground. To call attention to this does not blur basic differences or take refuge in historical determinism or inevitability, but promotes awareness that our apprehension of Shakespeare today consists of a synthesis achieved both by scholarship and by criticism. What might strike the reader as a pattern of reaction and revolt against convention is rather one of continuity and adaptation, or at least one of challenge and response. Such is the relation of the poetic school with the other schools of modern Shakespeare criticism.

The two other major schools (I will comment on minor categories later) are evidently those of the historical critics and the theatrical critics. Because of the over-general nature of these terms, further division of these categories will be useful: such divisions can be made partly from a chronological, and partly from a methodological point of view.

Certain general characteristics of the whole historical school may first be identified. A number of interpreters who use the findings of historical scholarship about the background and conventions of the Elizabethan age (there is hardly any aspect which has not been enquired into) are customarily brought together under this category. This was a major trend until the twenties and the thirties, and it is only natural that the findings of historical scholarship have been assimilated and reapplied by other critical schools. But the historical critics proper make it a principle of interpretation that Shakespeare's art is determined rather than conditioned by the background of his age and culture. Now that our historical knowledge about almost every epoch of literature of the past and about the Elizabethan era in particular is so considerable, it is axiomatic that the age conditions, to some extent, govern the writer and his work. What one needs to remember now is not so much how Shakespeare is best approached as 'the Elizabethan Shakespeare' in his original context as how, for all that he was 'the soul of the age', he is, after all, 'for all time'. We have to remember that the great writer in both subtle and obvious ways transcends the age, and questions, directly or obliquely, its commonplace assumptions. The crucial question is whether the historical sense of the reader should inform his apprehension of the work of Shakespeare or of any classic, or whether historical knowledge intervenes at a subsequent stage, after the reader's personal response to the work, with his modern consciousness uncorrupted by historical conditioning.[4] In any case, making due allowance for Shakespeare's essential universality as we apply historical data to interpretation calls for the exercise of the commentator's critical sense, perception and tact and not a rigid adherence to historical principles. There is the further issue of deciding upon the kinds and degrees of relevance of numerous backgrounds or even resolving contradictions among them.

If we are to discuss the theory of modern historical criticism of Shakespeare, we need first to subdivide this group into categories. First, I distinguish between those pure historical scholars whose research simply produces information or legitimate conjectures, and those who apply these findings to interpretation. It is with the second group that we are concerned.

Among them are those who interpret or criticise the plays in terms of what they consider to be the expectations and response of the original Elizabethan audiences, and their taste and cultural calibre. Others proceed on assumptions about the 'primitive' structure and conventions of Elizabethan drama, and explain problems of the plays in these terms. There are those who interpret Shakespearian drama in the light of their knowledge of social and economic conditions in late sixteenth- and early seventeenth-century England. We also have writers who base their interpretation of plays on their idea of the intellectual and cultural climate of the age, or on its elements such as medieval and Renaissance concepts, assumptions about 'the Elizabethan world-picture', Elizabethan psychology, pneumatology, demonology and superstitions, popular cultural traditions, Christian religious and theological beliefs, ethical and homiletic teachings, and structures of ideas. Other critics examine the plays in the light of the large body of knowledge which has now been

---

[4] Discussed in chapter 5 (pp. 151–3), especially in connection with L. C. Knights's 'Historical Scholarship and the Interpretation of Shakespeare', *SR* 63 (1955), 223–40 and John Lawlor's reply, *SR*, 64 (1956), 186–206.

gathered about medieval and Renaissance, or native and neoclassical, literary and dramatic theories, practices and conventions,
or the concepts of 'kinds' and genres available in the Elizabethan
age. Some commentators relate the plays, their characters and
situations, to the life of Shakespeare, to people he knew or events
he lived through, providing counterparts in Elizabethan England. Those who see topical references in Shakespeare occupy a
common ground between this category and the approach
through social and economic findings. We have interpretations
based on findings about the extent and nature of Shakespeare's
education, reading and learning; just as we have interpretations
which relate the plays to their plot-sources, direct as well as
secondary, and to sources of individual passages, ideas and
images. To the same broad subdivision belong commentators
who trace influences of various kinds, such as the influence of the
Bible, the Homilies, the Emblem-books, and proverb-lore; the
influence on Shakespeare of his predecessors and of contemporary poets and playwrights, and the influence of thinkers such
as Montaigne and Machiavelli. Among the historical critics must
be placed 'the disintegrators', with their conviction about the
many hands involved in Shakespearian drama. It is here too that
the bibliographical critics belong. Then we have the linguistic
critics. The approach advocated by the Neo-Aristotelian critics is
also related to historical scholarship. Allied in one respect to
these, but distinct from them, is the group of 'plot' and 'structure'
analysts.

The rise of something like a historical sense, can be traced back
to the Shakespeare criticism of Dryden and Johnson. It is a kind of
historical sense which manifests itself in Dryden's insistence on
the greater refinement and superiority of his own age over the
Elizabethan, which was, from his point of view, though one of
the 'giant race before the Flood', also one of barbarians with
'uncharter'd freedom'. This prejudiced picture of the Elizabethan
age and its taste has endured in some quarters from Dryden's day
to this. Yet however inadequately or falsely conceived the historical sense of critics like Dryden and Johnson might be, they did
have one. Johnson's commentary on Shakespeare is remarkable
among other things for this evidence of historical consciousness.

In the eighteenth century, that period of pioneer Shakespearian editing and scholarship, editors could exhibit a historical sense especially in their annotation. In the latter half of the century the first foundations of systematic Elizabethan and Shakespearian scholarship can be said to have been laid. The names of Steevens and Malone claim our respect.[5] Malone's pioneering work gave a new direction and bearing to Shakespeare studies. The lead given by the late-eighteenth-century scholar-editors was not pursued properly by critics for more than half a century, and it was fairly late in the nineteenth century before it developed on a recognisable scale. This gap in the evolution of modern Elizabethan and Shakespearian scholarship is sad; especially when we remember that it coincided with the Romantic period, a period of major shifts of focus in Shakespeare criticism, and in which a general love and enthusiasm for the Elizabethan age and its literature was part of the Romantic cult. It is a matter of regret that Coleridge and Hazlitt, Lamb and De Quincey, could not make contact with the tradition of scholarship established before their time by Malone, Capell and Steevens. Coleridge was in principle indifferent to, and at times deliberately opposed to, the findings of scholarship, as in the case of Malone's chronology of Shakespeare's plays. It is a nice point to decide whether the Romantics' extreme universalisation of Shakespeare and their treatment of the plays in a timeless context, divorced from his age and theatre, arise from or lead to the lack of a continuing tradition of scholarship. The roots of modern historical scholarship about Shakespeare and the Elizabethan age lie, like the roots of modern literary scholarship in general, in the latter half of the nineteenth century; it was this age which saw the elevation of Shakespeare to a school and later a college and university text, his aggrandisement as national institution and symbol. Yet even A. C. Bradley, in his *Shakespearian Tragedy* (London, 1904, 1957) seems deliberately to have shut himself off

---

[5] J. Isaacs, 'Shakespeare Criticism, From Dryden to Coleridge', *A Companion to Shakespeare Studies*, ed. Harley Granville-Barker and G. B. Harrison (Cambridge, 1934); Arthur Brown, *Edmond Malone and English Scholarship* (London, 1963); S. K. Sen, *Capell and Malone, and Modern Critical Bibliography* (Calcutta, 1960) and O. Hood Phillips, *Shakespeare and the Lawyers* (London, 1972), pp. 142–4.

from the Elizabethan scholarship of his day, and made only fitful contact with it in some of his occasional essays.[6]

The systematic application of historical findings to the interpretation of secular literature is a characteristic twentieth-century development. It is customary to see the rise of the historical criticism of Shakespeare in the various modes outlined above as one of the two chief ways of reacting against the Romantic, nineteenth-century, unhistorical or a-historical criticism of Shakespeare, the main representative of which was A. C. Bradley; the other mode of reaction being 'the New Criticism' or the poetic interpretation of Shakespeare. On closer examination, we see that historical criticism looks like a reaction mainly because the pioneering critics of this school in the early decades of the twentieth century found in Bradley an easy target to attack, since he happened to be the leading Shakespearian immediately preceding them. When we examine the basic premises of the post-Bradleyan critics, and their ulterior conception of the Shakespeare play, or the framework of their approaches to it, we find that these are so radically different from those of Bradley, that the question of reaction is scarcely appropriate, where there is so little contact.[7]

[6] A. C. Bradley, 'Shakespeare's Theatre and Audience' in *Oxford Lectures on Poetry* (London, 1909), 'Monosyllabic Lines and Words in English Verse and Prose' and 'Scene Endings in Shakespeare and in *The Two Noble Kinsmen*' in *A Miscellany* (London, 1929), and 'The locality of *King Lear*, Act 1 Scene II', *Modern Language Review*, 4 (1909), 238–40. Katharine Cooke, *A. C. Bradley and His Influence in Twentieth-Century Shakespeare Criticism* (Oxford, 1972), pp. 72–3 and *passim*, comments on Bradley's response to scholarship, and his occasional academic research. Among Bradley's MSS. preserved in Balliol College Library is a notebook listing Shakespeare's words beginning with 'A', Katharine Cooke (p. 72) adds 'their purpose quite obscure'. Possibly Bradley thought of compiling a concordance improving on Bartlett.

Katharine Cooke shows that Bradley was a regular theatre-goer. In his approach to Shakespeare he was not anti-theatrical, still less anti-poetic. Wilson Knight has made plain that he considered his 'spatial' interpretation a continuation and extension of Bradley's response. Bradley was associated in 1906–7 with Gilbert Murray and Granville-Barker in the cause of the establishment of a National Theatre as a Shakespeare memorial. 'Soon after Barker joined forces with Archer, a meeting was held at Spenser Wilkinson's house to plan a strategy to enlist supporters; in attendance were Gilbert Murray (1866–1957), A C. Bradley (1851–1935), Hamilton Fyfe (1869–1951), Wilkinson, Barker, and Archer' (George B. Bryan, 'Lady Randolph Churchill and the National Theatre', *Theatre Survey*, 15 (1974), 144).

[7] R. S. Crane, *The Languages of Criticism and the Structure of Poetry* (Toronto, 1953), p. 26 makes this point.

Once the foundations of historical scholarship in Shakespeare
studies had been laid in the second half of the nineteenth century, attention was directed to the Elizabethan audiences which,
in one view, conditioned or determined the nature of Shakespearian drama. Robert Bridges[8] isolated what he thought to be
faults and defects in the plays: improbabilities of plot and inconsistencies of characterisation, lack of taste evidenced in 'bad jokes
and foolish verbal trifling', 'extreme badness of passages',
'scenes which offend our feelings'. He attributed these defects to
Shakespeare's willingness to yield to the demands of his audience, to give the public what it wanted and to play, not so much
to the gallery as to the pit. It is worth recalling that a prejudiced,
because superior, view of the Elizabethan audience was common
in Shakespeare criticism as seen in incidental references in the
eighteenth and nineteenth centuries. For that matter, the opinions expressed by Elizabethan dramatists themselves, and sur-
prisingly by both public-theatre and private-theatre playwrights,
are none too complimentary to their audiences, though Shakespeare seems to have known better than his peers. Some Victorian critics of Shakespeare – Dowden, Swinburne and Louns-
bury, for instance – occasionally noted the bearing of audience
expectation and response on Shakespearian drama, and some
Victorian scholars (like Malone in the eighteenth century) specu-
lated about the nature of Elizabethan audiences.

The contribution of Bridges has been to make the consideration
of the nature and demands of the audience and their influence on
the dramatist into a systematic, though tacit, principle of critical
judgement. Studies of the original audiences for works of literature have proliferated in the twentieth century, and the relation
between writer and audience is now a major focus of interest in
literary criticism, especially in the study of modern literature.[9]
The positive result of Bridges's approach has been to underline
the need for awareness of the nature, taste and response of

[8] Robert Bridges, 'The Influence of the Audience on Shakespeare's Drama'
(1907), *Collected Essays* (Oxford, 1927).
[9] Dorothy Whitelock, *The Audience of 'Beowulf'* (1951); Q. D. Leavis, *Fiction and the
Reading Public* (1932); E. D. H. Johnson, *The Alien Vision of Victorian Poetry* (1952);
R. D. Altick, *The English Common Reader* (1957); Edwin Muir, *The Estate of Poetry*
(1962) are examples of such studies.

audiences. But his reading of the relationship between Shakespeare and his audience cannot be acceptable today. The contemptuous view of the Elizabethan audience current from the eighteenth century onwards reached its culmination in Bridges's condemnation of their bad taste, and his thesis that Shakespeare had to reflect the bad taste of his audience has been thoroughly refuted by a number of modern critics.[10] The main flaw in Bridges's argument was a false image of the Elizabethan audience, built on inadequate or no data, and on age-old prejudice. The composition and taste of Elizabethan audiences had not been properly researched then. Modern Shakespeare scholarship has directed attention to this area and has made available a good deal of information about audiences, the most sensible and conclusive evidence being provided by Alfred Harbage. Yet the older habit of gross underestimation of the general quality of Elizabethan play-goers dies hard and survives to some extent in the twentieth century. One remembers William Archer's strictures on Elizabethan drama and its audience. The counter-stress laid by I. A. Richards and L. C. Knights on the keenness of the Elizabethan ear and sensibility, due to to age-long habits of listening to stories and sermons, and so attesting the persistence of the tradition of oral communication, has at times given the impression of idealising the Elizabethan audience. The result is that, as Harbage put it, 'sometimes distance lends courage also to the idealist, and the Globe is filled with mute inglorious Shakespeares' (*Shakespeare's*

---

[10] G. Wilson Knight, 'Tolstoy's Attack on Shakespeare', *The Wheel of Fire* (2nd edn, London, 1949), pp. 270–97. J. I. M. Stewart, *Character and Motive in Shakespeare* (London, 1949), chapter 2, 'Falstaff on Boar's Hill', pp. 11–39, and Alfred Harbage, *Shakespeare's Audience* (New York, 1941) and *Shakespeare and the Rival Traditions* (1952).

In his first book Harbage shows that the audience at the Globe was a cross-section of the Elizabethan community. Ann Jennaline Cook, 'The Audience of Shakespeare's Plays: A Reconsideration', *Shakespeare Studies*, 7 (1974), 283–305, has questioned the accuracy of this. In his second book, in his over-eagerness to make a case for the soundness of taste of the audiences in the public theatres, Harbage makes too schematic a distinction between the audiences of the public and private theatres. In *Shakespeare and the Rival Traditions* (p.291), Harbage says of Bridges's strictures on Shakespeare's audiences: 'Possibly the most mistaken single utterance ever made about Shakespearian drama came from Robert Bridges'.

Mention may be made of Martin Holmes, *Shakespeare's Public: The Touchstone of his Genius* (London, 1959), where the author tries to reconstruct the probable response of the original audiences.

Audience, p. 138). This reaction against the older prejudice veers to the other extreme.

The importance of audience-participation in drama, indirectly in its making and directly in its staging, can hardly be gainsaid. But Bridges's lopsided emphasis on the influence of the audience was the result of a naïve understanding of the triangular relationship between writer, audience and work. Modern commentators, learning from his example, avoiding his error of emphasis and proceeding upon a more adequate historical reconstruction of the probable response of the original audience, have been able to illuminate a number of plays.[11]

A second approach of historical scholarship is that of critics who deploy the argument about the primitive conventions which inform Shakespearian and Elizabethan drama. At one time in this century these critics had a powerful hold and were looked upon as the chief representatives of historical criticism. They acquired the label of the 'realist school'. Bridges himself is included in this school. His link with these critics is that they, too, assume that Elizabethan audiences were 'primitive' (it is interesting to trace the semantic shift in the word from the more or less pejorative use by Schücking to the more or less commendatory use of Northrop Frye), naïve and gross in their taste. These critics seem to raise the factor of audience-response into a critical principle and base their interpretation partly on Shakespeare's manipulation of it.

Inconsistencies and improbabilities in plot, situation and atmosphere, as well as lack of motivation in character, were thought not to be faults to be avoided but, on the contrary, the stock-in-trade of the popular dramatist. A liberal admixture of these elements were part of the 'primitive' dramatic conventions and structure which were his heritage and gratified the expectations of his audience. Bridges, approaching from a more or less naturalistic point of view, saw these features as faults and blamed them ultimately on the audience; but E. E. Stoll,[12] the most

---

[11] Moody E. Prior, 'The Elizabethan Audience and the Plays of Shakespeare', *Modern Philology*, 49 (1951–2), 101–23, gives a balanced estimate of the value and limitations of the approach in terms of the probable response of the original audience.

[12] E. E. Stoll, *Shakespeare Studies* (1927); *Poets and Playwrights* (1930); *Art and Artifice in Shakespeare* (1933); *Shakespeare and Other Masters* (1940); *From Shakespeare to*

eloquent pioneer of this mode of criticism, ruled out the naturalistic viewpoint and so did not think these seeming weaknesses a
fault; rather, a necessity of which Shakespeare made a virtue.
Levin Schücking considered them a fault when he came to make a
value-judgement. The outcome of this approach, which is of
general consequence for modern Shakespeare criticism, is that,
between them, Stoll and Schücking highlighted the primitive
elements of structure and convention in Shakespearian and
Elizabethan plays; and alertness to this, in the right proportion,
has deepened our understanding of this drama. Knowledge of
the nature and original function of the dramatic literature of this
age warns us against asking anachronistic questions and applying anachronistic criteria of judgement. In short, this school of
critics emphasised that Elizabethan drama has a quite different
framework of conventions (which may be called 'primitive')
unlike those of modern naturalistic and realistic drama, and that
naturalistic considerations, 'psychological questionings and
realistic misgivings', are anachronistic when applied to it.[13] It is
ironical that this school of criticism has come to be called the
'realist school', a misnomer arising out of the confusing connotations of the word. The main implication in its original use must
have been that these critics try to see Shakespeare's drama as in
itself it really was in its own time, setting and background.[14]

A glance at the circumstances which gave rise to these two
allied approaches – that of Bridges and that of Stoll and Schücking – shows that they are the fruit of new historical perceptions
and findings (in Bridges's case, inadequate or partial findings), in
the light of which a new view of the nature and function of
Shakespearian drama came to be formed.

This hypothesis about Shakespearian drama is totally different from, and opposed to, the latent 'hypothesis' of Bradley and

Joyce (1944) are important among his works. His early essays like *The Ghosts*
(1907); *Shylock* (1911); *The Criminals* (1912) are included in *Shakespeare Studies*. An
influential early essay is 'Anachronism in Shakespeare Criticism', *MP*, 7 (1910),
557–75. *Othello: An Historical and Comparative Study* (1915) and *Hamlet: An Historical and Comparative Study* (1919) are in part incorporated in *Art and Artifice in
Shakespeare*.
[13] Stoll, *Art and Artifice in Shakespeare*, especially chapter 2, 'Othello'.
[14] In this sense these critics can be aligned with the school of historical criticism, as
Kenneth Muir suggests in 'Fifty years of Shakespearian Criticism: 1900–1950'.

the nineteenth-century critics. Bradley and the other 'psychologising'[15] critics wrote as if Shakespearian drama could be
approached as though it were basically little different from the
realistic, psychological novel which was in its heyday in the latter
half of the nineteenth century; hence their attention was fixed on
questions of characterisation. Though Stoll and Schücking seem
to pay a good deal of attention to improbabilities and inconsistencies in characterisation – in so far as they offer to explain them or
explain them away – these critics do not differ from Bradley and
the earlier tradition only or mainly on this issue. What is involved
is a quite different ulterior conception of Shakespearian drama,
seen as governed by a set of primitive conventions. This conception, which lays stress on the non-naturalistic conventional basis
of Shakespeare's drama, concerns not just character but all the
major elements. This is why I suggest that to call this school a
'reaction' against Bradley might imply that all that these critics did
was to provide a new view of character.

The formidable role of E. E. Stoll as scholar-interpreter,
polemicist and critic has been widely acknowledged.[16] For all the
vigorous disagreement aroused by his opinions on particular
situations and characters in the plays, his achievement lies in his
sure grasp of an aspect of Shakespearian drama hitherto neglected: namely, the conventional basis of its techniques and
modes, and their 'primitiveness'. With a refreshing absence of
patronage towards Elizabethan taste, he showed, in book after

[15] R. W. Babcock, *The Genesis of Shakespearian Idolatry: 1766–1799* (1931), p. 155.
[16] L. P. Smith, *On Reading Shakespeare* (New York, 1933), p. 25. J. I. M. Stewart,
Character and Motive in Shakespeare, pp. 79–80. R. W. Babcock, 'Historical Criticism of Shakespeare', *Modern Language Quarterly*, 13 (1952), 6–20, 'Modern Sceptical Criticism of Shakespeare: E. E. Stoll', *SR*, 35 (1927), 15–31, and 'Mr Stoll
Revisited Twenty Years After', *Philological Quarterly*, 27 (1948), 289–313. This
last article is a comprehensive account of the evolution and major shifts of
Stoll's critical attitudes to Shakespeare. Babcock emphasises the change from
the sceptical and rigidly 'objective' early studies to the 'aesthetic' in the later,
shown by the greater stress on the speech-rhythms of characters and the
'musical' methods of Shakespeare. 'Mr Stoll seems to have started as sceptical-
historical, then turned historical-aesthetic and more recently become
aesthetic-historical – to call on Polonius for help – but the sceptical is still with
him today' (p. 290). This later evolution of Stoll's criticism has not been sufficiently noted. The latest role of Stoll as a vigorous controversialist against
imagery analysis is mentioned in chapter 6, on imagistic studies. See also Harry
Levin, 'Induction', *Shakespeare and the Revolution of the Times* (New York, 1976),
pp. 17–20 on Stoll.

book, and article after article, how Shakespeare, working within the limits of 'primitive' conventions, explored and exploited these with dramatic artistry; how such conventions are essential elements and a source of strength in poetic drama; and how the use of poetry can resolve difficulties of dramatic presentation. His insight into the way in which the conventions work together with the poetry is one of his main legacies. Stoll views all the major elements of Shakespeare's drama, not merely character, from the intentionalist and historical angle provided by relating the drama to the conventions and techniques of the time. He directs our attention to variations and control of emphasis by the dramatist; to the effects of sharp contrast deliberately built up at the cost of probability; to the use of such conventions as ghosts, or disguises; to the device of 'the calumniator credited', and by scene-by-scene opportunism; and to the creation of a non-naturalistic poetic and musical ambience through which a convincing dramatic illusion is created. The general effect of Stoll's approach was not just to provide a fresh insight into the modes of Shakespeare's characterisation (that is an incidental effect of his criticism), but, by transferring the accent to situation as the core of drama, to offer a needed corrective to nineteenth-century preoccupation with character.

Schücking's findings are similar to those of Stoll, which is why the two names are usually linked together; but he differs in the matter of interpretation and judgement. Schücking calls attention to the role of primitive stage conventions in the plays, and emphasises their force and meaning: their effect on our understanding of the play. Some of his perceptions about Shakespearian conventions have passed permanently into the general critical consciousness. His probable debt to his countryman and predecessor, Rumelin, has been pointed out by Patrick Murray (*The Shakespearian Scene*, 1969, p. 18). Schücking's approach can be characterised as historical and sociological too,[17] because he gives so much weight to the taste and expectations of the original

---

[17] Levin L. Schücking, co-author of a standard Shakespeare bibliography, later wrote a book called *The Sociology of Literary Taste* (1944), trans. E. W. Dickes, and also a book on the 'baroque' element in Shakespearian tragedy, *The Baroque Character of the Elizabethan Tragic Hero* (1938).

audience. A difference between him and Stoll is that while he explains inconsistencies in terms of convention, he is troubled by them and judges them as faults; for despite his recognition of the force of convention in Shakespeare's drama, his bias is toward naturalism. It is only in his later commentaries that Schücking shows himself aware that Shakespeare makes subtle, and not necessarily naïve, use of techniques which are in their origin and orientation naïve. Perhaps the best-known and most valuable of his individual findings is that revealing the soliloquy as a technique and convention of 'direct self-explanation'[18] (the other devices that he identified and described were those of episodic intensification in plot and depersonalisation of character). Shakespeare's delicate handling of primitive convention to great dramatic effect has been well brought out by critics who have assimilated the principles isolated first by Stoll and Schücking.[19] Among these, special mention may be made of M. C. Bradbrook and S. L. Bethell.[20]

The new awareness in Shakespeare studies, attributable to the influence of Stoll and Schücking, would seem to reside in the perception of the fundamental difference between the non-naturalistic, highly conventionalised medium of Shakespearian drama and the naturalistic mode of modern drama, and other forms of modern literature like the novel or the short story. But the more generally noticed effect of their concentration is their insistence on Shakespeare's theatrical technique and skill at the expense of his literary and dramatic power and their insufficient attention to anchoring his plays in reality. Patrick Murray makes the criticism that Stoll sees in Shakespeare 'not a dramatic artist of the greatest subtlety, power and insight, but a mere provider of exciting spectacle' and that 'Stoll's approach has one feature in

---

[18] Schücking, *Character Problems in Shakespeare's Plays* (London, 1922), chapter 1.

[19] Wolfgang Clemen, *Shakespeare's Soliloquies* (1964), reprinted in *Shakespeare's Dramatic Art* (London, 1972), chapter 4. Nevill Coghill, *Shakespeare's Professional Skills* (Cambridge, 1964), chapter 6, 'Soliloquy', pp. 128–63.

[20] M. C. Bradbrook, *Elizabethan Stage Conditions* (1932), *Themes and Conventions of Elizabethan Tragedy* (Cambridge, 1935; 2nd edn 1980), *English Dramatic Form* (1965) and *Shakespeare the Craftsman* (1969); S. L. Bethell, *Shakespeare and the Popular Dramatic Tradition* (London, 1944).

common with that of many older critics; it fails to take adequate account of the poetry as a vital element in Shakespearian drama' (*The Shakespearian Scene*, p. 10). (A similar complaint is made by Rufus Putney, 'What "Praise to give"?: Jonson vs. Stoll', *PQ*, 23 (1944), 307–19.) The early writings of Stoll and Schücking may have neglected the power of the poetry; but in their later criticism both, especially Stoll, recognised the impact that poetry can have on the drama. The historical judgement that the insistence on the non-realistic nature of Shakespearian drama by the 'realist' school paved the way for the advent of the 'poetic' interpretation has not had due recognition. The irony is that the 'poetic' interpreters thought of themselves as reacting against the historical critics or the 'realists', when it was really the work of this school that brought about the change of climate that incubated the 'poetic' approach. Also, the prevalence in Stoll's and Schücking's time of naturalistic modes of literature facilitated the apprehension of the difference in modes of conception and presentation between it and non-naturalistic drama. A parallel development is the insistence of T. S. Eliot, in his critical essays, on the element of convention in literature in general and drama in particular. Another simultaneous development in the early twentieth century was the acquisition of new information about medieval as well as Elizabethan drama, presented in the work of scholars such as E. K. Chambers. Thus the continuity of dramatic traditions was emphasised, as was – in Stoll's writings – the importance of knowledge about the sources and analogues, literary and popular, of plays.

To sum up: the realist school illuminated Shakespeare criticism as a whole, not just one preoccupation such as character. Yet there is no denying that one of the main practical effects of this school on Shakespeare studies is that character has been approached in a variety of ways other than those based on naturalistic, psychological criteria.

Imbalances and excesses in this school of criticism result from rigid application of its criteria. What later critics (who have learnt from this school) have also learnt to do is to modify these criteria, accepting that Shakespeare's art, Elizabethan art as a whole, though in the main non-naturalistic, contains a considerable admixture of naturalistic modes,[21] and that Shakespeare, while fusing the two modes into a unity, could also individualise and humanise conventions and stock devices.

Modern historical and literary scholarship has made a wealth of detailed knowledge about Elizabethan political, social and economic life accessible to us. A good deal of this knowledge has thrown light on aspects of the plays, such as attitudes taken by the characters or the dramatist himself, or topical allusions and cruces in the matter of explication; it has also enhanced our understanding of the plays as a whole. But commentary on the plays in terms of findings of this kind has not been elevated into a principle of interpretation by any influential critics, except, perhaps, in the case of some Marxist approaches. Rather, this new knowledge has been assimilated into the critical consciousness of the modern Shakespearian, and has been drawn upon judiciously as necessary.[22] The refusal to use this knowledge as a formal method of interpretation is understandable when we remember that internal cultural factors such as theatrical conventions, the general ideological climate and the tastes and beliefs of the age, bear more immediately upon Shakespeare's mind and art than external social, economic and political factors, which are at one remove. Even so, modern criticism credits Shakespeare with a keen political consciousness, drawing attention to his handling of the problems of power, kingship and authority; it also at times tends to assume that Shakespeare shows the need for political and social order and for the avoidance of rebellion by showing this as enjoined by the concept of 'degree' with its assumed theological and spiritual warrant. The historical plays

---

[21] T. S. Eliot, 'Four Elizabethan Dramatists', *Selected Essays* (London, 1934, 2nd edn), p. 114. Eliot's phrase the 'impure art' of Webster, meaning that it contains an intermixture of convention and realism, is applicable to the whole of Elizabethan drama. S. L. Bethell, *Shakespeare and the Popular Dramatic Tradition*, chapter 1 elaborates on the intermixture. Also B. Spivack, *The Allegory of Evil* (New York, 1958), p. 449. Cf. Helen Gardner, *The Business of Criticism* (London, 1963 edn), pp. 136–7 and pp. 146–7.

[22] Edwin Muir, for instance, 'The Politics of *King Lear*' and 'The Natural Man and the Political Man', *Essays on Literature and Society* (London, 1949), pp. 31–48 and 151–65 respectively. L. C. Knights, *Drama and Society in the Age of Jonson* (London, 1937). F. W. Bateson, *English Poetry: A Critical Introduction* (London, 1950).

have been read by Lily B. Campbell as political allegories with contemporary political lessons. Tillyard's reading of the history plays as 'moral history' expressing the 'Tudor myth', including the concept of degree or order, set the standard for a generation, but has now come to be seriously questioned.[23] The unfolding of the topical significances in the plays will be considered later. Attempts to approach Shakespeare's work through the social background of his age have included relating characters in the plays to contemporary social types belonging to various professions and occupations. Not for our times the attempts of nineteenth-century commentators to show Shakespeare as the perfect representative of every profession based on his minute knowledge, shown in the plays.[24] Not for us 'the myth of perfection' about Shakespeare.[25] But Shakespeare's dramatic use of his knowledge of certain professions as they were practised in his own time has been studied, and the study has been used as a means of explication.[26]

One of the distinctive modes of approach to Shakespeare is through new knowledge about his intellectual and cultural

---

[23] Lily B. Campbell, *Shakespeare's Histories: Mirrors of Elizabethan Policy* (San Marino, 1947). Starting from E. M. W. Tillyard, *Shakespeare's History Plays* (London, 1944) and Miss Campbell's book, M. M. Reese, *The Cease of Majesty* (London, 1961); Irving Ribner, *The English History Play in the Age of Shakespeare* (Princeton, 1957); James E. Phillips, *The State in Shakespeare's Politics* (New York, 1940); L. C. Knights, *The Histories*, reprinted in *Shakespeare, The Writer and His Work* ed. Bonamy Dobrée (1964); E. H. Kantorowicz, *The King's Two Bodies: A Study in Medieval Political Theology* (Princeton, 1957), especially chapter 2; E. W. Talbert, *The Problem of Order: Elizabethan Political Commonplaces and an Example of Shakespeare's Art* (Chapel Hill, 1962); H. A. Kelly, *Divine Providence in the England of Shakespeare's Histories* (Cambridge, Mass., 1970); D. M. Riggs, *Shakespeare's Heroical Histories: the Henry VI Plays* (Cambridge, Mass., 1971) and J. W. Lever, *The Tragedy of State* (London, 1971) are among books which have treated the Elizabethan historical dramatists' response to the political theories of the age. R. Ornstein, *A Kingdom for a Stage: The Achievement of Shakespeare's History Plays* (Cambridge, Mass., 1972) marks the culmination of the reaction against Tillyard's interpretation of the histories in terms of the 'Tudor myth'.
[24] T. R. Henn, *The Living Image: Shakespearian Essays* (London, 1972), p. 87, comments on this fallacy   [25] Alfred Harbage 'Shakespeare and the "Myth of Perfection"', *Shakespeare Quarterly*, 15 (1964).
[26] For example, Paul A. Jorgensen, *Shakespeare's Military World* (1956); Sir John Fortescue in *Shakespeare's England* (Oxford, 1916), I, 117–21; John W. Draper, 'Captain General Othello', *Anglia*, 43 (1931), 295–310; Duff Cooper, *Serjeant Shakespeare* (1956); A. F. Falconer, *Shakespeare and the Sea* (London, 1964); George W. Keeton, *Shakespeare's Legal and Political Background* (London, 1967); and Henn, *The Living Image*, pp. 87–116.

milieu. The informing principle behind this approach is the belief that the general cultural setting conditions Shakespeare's drama, and hence can provide insights into the structure and meaning of the plays. It may be convenient to divide this category into a few subcategories: such as interpretations in terms of the 'Elizabethan World Picture'; popular cultural traditions; Elizabethan psychology; ghostlore and ideas of the supernatural; such 'structures of ideas' as common Christian and theological ideas; ethical and homiletic injunctions. The most striking of the subcategories is the interpretation of Shakespeare in terms of Elizabethan beliefs and values, both popular and sophisticated, the general world-view or outlook on life of the Elizabethans, 'the Elizabethan world-picture' as Tillyard called it, the complex of medieval and Renaissance assumptions which composed it. The rise and development of this approach is a characteristic modern development. A compendious survey of aspects of the Elizabethan mind was made by Hardin Craig in his *The Enchanted Glass* in 1936. A development in American philosophy at this time facilitated the emergence of a complete picture of the ruling ideas of the Elizabethan age: the growth of the new branch of knowledge called 'the history of ideas': the pioneer was A. O. Lovejoy. After introducing 'unit-ideas', as the component concepts and assumptions which make up an ideological climate, Lovejoy first traced the history of one such, 'the great chain of being', in his book of that title (published in 1936). This concept was the backbone of the Elizabethan *Weltanschauung*, as was shown by two critics who follow this approach, Theodore Spencer and E. M. W. Tillyard.[27] The considerable vogue for this perspective is attributable to the neatness of the idea of the Elizabethan consciousness and its elements. Latterly, this neatness has come to be questioned.[28] One of the critical disputes in Shakespeare criticism

[27] Theodore Spencer, *Shakespeare and the Nature of Man* Cambridge, 1942). E. M. W. Tillyard, *The Elizabethan World Picture* (London, 1943). The earliest proponents of an important relationship between Shakespeare and the concept of order are Middleton Murry in an article in *The New Adelphi* (1927), 'Shakespeare and Order' (reprinted in *Heaven-and-Earth*, London, 1938), and Alfred Hart, *Shakespeare and the Homilies* (London 1934). Also Douglas Bush, *The Renaissance and English Humanism* (Toronto, 1939), especially p. 3.
[28] Gardner, *The Business of Criticism*, p. 34; Talbert, *The Problem of Order*; Herbert Howarth, 'Put Away the World-Picture', *The Tiger's Heart* (London, 1970),

today is over the admissibility of an Elizabethan world-picture. A second reason for the popularity of this viewpoint is the modern insistence on the continuity of medieval traditions and ways of life into Renaissance England. At times, this amounts to wishing-away the accomplished fact of the Renaissance (somewhat akin to the wishing-away of the Reformation by the Chesterton–Belloc group). This insistence has had a good result, in that readers are aware of the syncretism of traditions and conventions in Elizabethan literature, especially in Shakespeare's drama. It has had a bad result in that there is a tendency to overstress the continuity of the Middle Ages and to forget about its waning, if not its end.[29] Thirdly, disturbing elements such as the influence of Copernicus, Machiavelli and Montaigne, were thought to have broken down the unity of the Elizabethan consciousness and converted it into the fragmented Jacobean consciousness, reflected in Jacobean drama and metaphysical poetry – this was an attractive notion to moderns because of the parallel they sensed between their own situation and that of the Jacobeans, who also lived in a world where traditional values had collapsed. Hence there developed both a pastoral myth of the homogeneous culture of the Elizabethans, who enjoyed a community of values until the Jacobean crisis overtook them, and also a tendency to idealise the Elizabethan world-view and to hanker after it.[30] Fourthly, because of the prevailing requirement in literary-critical writing that the author should exemplify 'an inclusive consciousness'[31] of the age, that the poet should be the antenna of the race, Shakespeare was required to have imbibed the enlightened consciousness of his age in every respect.

165–91; J. W. Lever, *The Tragedy of State* (1971), speaks of 'that hotch-potch of antiquated science, fancy, and folklore dignified by some modern scholars as the Elizabethan World Order', (p. 5) and of 'the so-called "chain of being" being in an advanced condition of rust by the end of the sixteenth century' (p. 5).
[29] Herbert Weisinger, 'The Study of Shakespearian Tragedy since Bradley', *SQ* 6 (1955), makes this complaint.
[30] F. P. Wilson, *Elizabethan and Jacobean* (Oxford, 1945) and Rosemond Tuve, *Elizabethan and Metaphysical Imagery* (Chicago, 1947) emphasise the essential continuity of the two ages, Elizabethan and Jacobean, in intellectual, cultural and literary traditions. The resemblances between our age and the Jacobean era are now seen to be superficial.
[31] The phrase is F. R. Leavis's *New Bearings in English Poetry* (Harmondsworth, 1963, Penguin edn), p. 87.

The question whether the universal genius Shakespeare would have contented himself with blind conformity to the average, or for that matter, the enlightened opinion of his age, has been asked.[32] The rich sense of irony and the complex mind, the essentially dramatic genius of Shakespeare could not but in implicit and subtle ways question received ideas and opinions, contemporary or universal. So, while it can hardly be denied that the idea of 'degree' is an important element of Elizabethan framework of values which pervades the plays, the concept is no master key, no 'open-sesame' to all issues. The concept is not one of Shakespeare's obsessions, though it reached this level of intensity with some critics for some time.[33]

Another branch of historical knowledge which has enriched Shakespearian interpretation and the study of sixteenth- and seventeenth-century literature in general, is study of popular and middle-class English culture of the period. Though the approach has not been erected into a principle of interpretation (a notable exception being the interpretation of a number of comedies as 'festive comedy' by C. L. Barber and Northrop Frye, and some plays as royal entertainments by others), an awareness of popular and middle-class cultural traditions is part of the historical sense of the informed reader or critic of Shakespeare.[34] Traditional seasonal and occasional festive celebrations and observances, or popular entertainment in music, dance and ballad, both in town and in country, are seen to have a bearing on Shakespeare's drama. Interpretation of the plays from this angle has something in common with anthropological and ritualistic

[32] A. P. Rossiter, *Angel with Horns* (London, 1961), p. 59. A. Harbage, *As They Liked It* (1947, paperback edn, 1961), chapter 7, 'The Unreliable Spokesman', points out how utterances on the importance of 'degree' by characters in Shakespeare's plays happen to be from characters who are meant to be wily, scheming politicians. Wilbur Sanders, *The Dramatist and the Received Idea* (Cambridge, 1968) devotes much of his book to showing that Shakespeare cannot be held merely to conform to received opinion.

[33] George Ian Duthie in his *Shakespeare* (London, 1951) tries to make a rule-of-thumb application of the idea to the comedies.

[34] Louis B. Wright, *Middle Class Culture in Elizabethan England* (London, 1935); C. L. Barber, *Shakespeare's Festive Comedy* (Princeton, 1959); Janet Spens, *Shakespeare and the Tradition* (London, 1916), is a pioneer investigation of the relation of the drama of Shakespeare to folk customs and festivals. An important investigation is C. R. Baskervill, 'Dramatic Aspects of Medieval Folk Festivals in England' *Studies in Philology*, 17 (1920), 19–87.

interpretation, which I discuss later (see pp. 32–3). Here too, the modern longing for homogeneity in culture, and for a scale of values commonly shared, and the conspicuous absence of these in modern culture produced an idealisation, a pastoralising of the Elizabethan age and the seventeenth century (till the latter end of which period there was, it was believed, no 'dissociation of sensibility'). The glory of the Elizabethan age was mainly due, it was held, to the unity and continuity between popular, learned and sophisticated cultural traditions, and a shared community of values and of sensibility. There is a measure of truth in this finding, and it is an assumption behind the response to Shakespeare of Leavis and his socio-cultural school of criticism. This element in his approach to Shakespeare, based on this assumption about Elizabethan culture, has not been sufficiently recognised;[35] since it is generally thought that his influence has more to do with the prevailing habit of the 'close reading' of Shakespeare's poetry.[36] An exaggerated sense of the unity of Elizabethan culture is, however, often held; and the cultural stratification of the age, pointed out, for example, by Alfred Harbage, is often ignored.

Some general remarks about the rest of the subcategories can now be made. All these interpretations stem from the discoveries of literary and historical scholarship about the Elizabethan age in particular fields of knowledge or thought which had an impact on the practical, day-to-day life of the Elizabethans. The assumption about Shakespeare's drama which governs these modes of approach is that he must have been familiar with, and also interested in, the main ideas (and in many cases, the main texts) in that particular field of knowledge, and must have incorporated these ideas in the play in discussion.

Attempts have been made to interpret the plays by using the Elizabethan science or pseudo-science of psychology, which was a mixture of physiological, ethical and moral theories. Dowden was the first Shakespearian critic to make a reference to

---

[35] René Wellek, 'The Criticism of F. R. Leavis', *Literary Views: Critical and Historical Essays*, ed. Carroll Camden (1964), especially pp. 190–1, is an example of an acute analysis of Leavis's critical endeavour, which does not make this point.
[36] See pp. 46–8 also.

Elizabethan psychology; the first full-length study of it in relation to Shakespearian drama came in 1927 from Ruth Anderson, a pupil of Hardin Craig. Then in 1930 Miss Lily Campbell put forward an elaborate interpretation of Shakespeare's tragedies as though they had been written as exemplifications of Elizabethan psychological commonplaces. Elizabethan texts of psychology have been cited as authorities warranting such interpretation.[37] Psychological lore has been brought to bear particularly on the treatment of abnormal states of mind represented in the plays. Instances of madness and melancholy have been closely related to Elizabethan psychology. Such studies, when they refrain from imposing a straitjacket of psychological theory on the plays and from treating them and the characters as case-histories, can, at times, illuminate dark places. Louise C. Turner Forest, in her classic attack on the use of Elizabethan psychology as a means of Shakespearian interpretation, has pointed out, though, that there are many contradictions even in the extant evidence about theories of Elizabethan psychology.[38] F. R. Johnson in his rejoinder[39] emphasised that despite the contradictions a common picture does emerge, and all that is needed is a tactful application of whatever Elizabethan psychological theories fit the particular context.[40]

A similar situation exists with regard to Elizabethan attitudes to the supernatural, to ghosts and pneumatology. Dowden and other Victorians (in the first age of psychic research) did pay some attention to this area, but new discoveries in Elizabethan spiritualism, and their application to Shakespearian interpretation are

[37] Edward Dowden, 'The Elizabethan Science of Psychology', *Essays Modern and Elizabethan* (1910), originally published in *The Atlantic Monthly* (1907). Ruth Anderson, *Elizabethan Psychology and Shakespeare's Plays* (1927). L. B. Campbell, *Shakespeare's Tragic Heroes: Slaves of Passion* (London, 1930).

[38] L. C. Turner Forest, 'Caveat for Critics against Invoking Elizabethan Psychology', *Publications of the Modern Language Association*, 61 (1946), 651–72.

[39] F. R. Johnson, 'Elizabethan Drama and the Elizabethan Science of Psychology', *English Studies Today* edited by G. Bullough and C. L. Wrenn (1st series, London, 1951), pp. 111–19.

[40] As shown in, for instance Lawrence Babb, *The Elizabethan Malady* (Michigan, 1951); and J. B. Bamborough, *The Little World of Man* (London, 1952). An attempt has been made to apply the medieval and Elizabethan 'humour' physiology and psychology to the characters of the plays by John W. Draper in his *The Humors and Shakespeare's Characters* (Durham, NC, 1945).

part of modern scholarship. E. E. Stoll, wrote his first book on ghosts in Shakespeare, and showed that the ghost is no mere hallucination, but constitutes an objective reality; Stoll warned against modernising views. Dover Wilson in his interpretation of *Hamlet* was the first twentieth-century critic to outline the different attitudes to ghosts prevalent in the Elizabethan age. Another important contribution was W. C. Curry's *Shakespeare's Philosophical Patterns* (1937) in which, using his knowledge of scholastic medieval notions of evil and of 'the demonic metaphysics' of the Elizabethan age, the author provided striking insights into *Macbeth* and *The Tempest*. A thoroughgoing discussion of medieval-Renaissance notions of spiritlore and pneumatology and of the relevance and applicability of these to Shakespearian drama has recently been offered by Robert H. West in *Shakespeare and the Outer Mystery* (1968). How conflicting if not confusing the arguments drawn from Elizabethan demonology can be is well shown by Robert West. A test-case would be the ghost in *Hamlet*.[41]

I should mention here that striking group of commentators who set forth Christian interpretations of the plays. The rise of this kind of interpretation shows that older ideas about Shakespeare's complete secularity and indifference to religion have been replaced by the general belief that Shakespeare shared and worked into his plays the enlightened moderate religious opinion of the age – such as that of Hooker. These various Christian interpretations consider the plays in the light of medieval and Reformation Christian assumptions, either popularly or esoterically theological. Some of these interpretations have been studied, and their extravagances pointed out, by Ronald M. Frye.[42] He seems to imply that Shakespeare would have been

---

[41] See the contradictory reports of W. W. Greg, John Dover Wilson in R. W. Battenhouse, 'The Ghost in *Hamlet* – A Catholic Lynchpin?', *SP*, 48 (1951), 161–92; Robert H. West, 'King Hamlet's Ambiguous Ghost', *PMLA*, 70 (1951), 1107–17; Sister Miriam Joseph, 'Discerning the Ghost in *Hamlet*', *PMLA*, 76 (1961), 493–502; Correspondence by Paul Siegel, *PMLA* (1963), 148–9; John D. Jump, 'Shakespeare's Ghosts', *Critical Quarterly*, 12 (1970), and Eleanor Prosser, *Hamlet and Revenge* (Stanford, 1967), pp. 106–98, according to which the ghost is a devil (p. 140).

[42] Ronald Mushat Frye, *Shakespeare and Christian Doctrine* (Princeton, 1963). More recently, a forceful argument against 'Evangelizing Shakespeare' has been

familiar only with certain popular theological classics and no others.

There are certain critics who try to apply what they identify as the medieval and Elizabethan ethical background to the judgement of Shakespeare's characters and their actions. Though such an application can be rewarding, it can also give rise to a perverse distortion of universal moral response. What Alfred Harbage, adapting Coleridge's remark, said in *As They Liked It* about Shakespeare always keeping to the high road of universal morals might seem sufficiently obvious, but it is worth re-asserting in the face of attempts to restrict the plays to some narrow concept of a particular ethic. Identification of the influence of the homiletic tradition, especially as exemplified in the Emblem books,[43] has, however, helped readers to grasp certain ideas and images in the plays. An important group of commentators has applied the ethical system of Hooker or Aquinas, or the one behind the medieval Miracle plays and the Moralities, to the analysis of Shakespeare's plays. In addition to these appeals to Elizabethan ethical traditions,[44] we may note the habit among poetic–dramatic critics and some others who do not quite come within the group[45] of talking in terms of the dramatist's moral vision – a moral vision derived from a universal, not historically determined (though influenced) point of view. We have come a long way since Johnson pointed an accusing finger at Shakespeare for

offered by Harry Levin in a review of R. W. Battenhouse, *Shakespearean Tragedy: Its Art and Christian Premises* (1969) in the *Journal of the History of Ideas*, 32 (1971), reprinted in Levin, *Shakespeare and the Revolution of the Times* (New York, 1976), 90–9.

[43] Henry Green, *Shakespeare and the Emblem Books* (London, 1870) and Russell A. Fraser, *Shakespeare's Poetics in Relation to 'King Lear'* (London, 1962).

[44] Virgil K. Whitaker, *Shakespeare's Use of Learning* (1953) and *The Mirror up to Nature* (1965) in which the author demonstrates the moral maturation of Shakespeare in relation to the influence of Hooker's thought. M. D. H. Parker, *The Slave of Life* (London, 1955) and Honor M. V. Matthews, *Character and Symbol in Shakespeare* (Cambridge, 1962).

A good account of twentieth-century findings about the climate of ideas of Shakespeare's times is to be found in J. W. Lever, 'Shakespeare and the Ideas of his Time', *SS*, 29 (1976), 79–91.

[45] Irving Ribner, *Patterns in Shakespearian Tragedy* (1960); Arthur Sewell, *Character and Society in Shakespeare* (1951); D. G. James, *The Dream of Learning* (1951); and *The Dream of Prospero* (1967); Geoffrey Bush, *Shakespeare and the Natural Condition* (1956); Robert Ornstein, *The Moral Vision of Jacobean Tragedy* (Madison, 1960).

not being an overt moralist, a simple didact; or since Bradley found it impossible to see any moral principles of organisation except the broadest neo-Hegelian ones. The modern penchant for discovering moral patterns in the plays, exemplified by L. C. Knights and D. A. Traversi, is at once an outcome and expression of this scholarly preoccupation. The ultimate critical issue here is whether universal, or Elizabethan, or the critic's modern or individual – at times, idiosyncratic – moral standards are to be the criteria; our problems are aggravated by the difficulty of faithfully reconstructing Elizabethan moral values.

One group of critics, who concentrate on medieval and Renaissance, native and neoclassical, literary and dramaturgical (rather than dramatic) conventions and rhetorical traditions and their influence may be said to constitute a distinct species of historical scholarship. The patterns of the native medieval dramatic traditions such as the Mystery and Miracle plays, the Morality plays and the interludes, and those of the allegorical and the romance traditions have also been traced in Shakespeare's drama,[46] have the medieval ethos and ideas of comedy and of tragedy. This is pointed out by Willard Farnham,[47] among others, and by W. W. Lawrence[48] with reference to Shakespeare's 'problem' comedies. He shows that the problems are of our own making, a result of the inappropriate modernisation of ethical issues. Gone are the days of assumed indifference to established canons and habits of classical and neoclassical dramaturgy on the part of Shakespeare and most Elizabethan 'romantic' dramatists. Now, of course, Shakespeare has been made to appear as a 'hard-reading' scholar,[49] who was familiar with neoclassical dramaturgical and

[46] Nevill Coghill on the allegorical element in 'The Basis of Shakespearian Comedy', *Essays and Studies* (1950); Bernard Spivack, *Shakespeare and the Allegory of Evil* (New York, 1958); Matthews, *Character and Symbol in Shakespeare*; R. G. Hunter, *Shakespeare and the Comedy of Forgiveness* (New York, 1965); L. A. Cormican, 'The Medieval Idiom in Shakespeare', *Scrutiny*, 17 (1950–1), 186–202 and 298–317.
[47] *The Medieval Heritage of Elizabethan Tragedy* (Berkeley, 1936); and R. G. Hunter, *Shakespeare and the Comedy of Forgiveness*.
[48] *Shakespeare's Problem Comedies* (New York, 1931).
[49] T. J. B. Spencer, 'The Course of Shakespeare Criticism', *Shakespeare's World* (London, 1965), pp. 172–3 and G. K. Hunter, 'Shakespeare's Reading', *A New Companion to Shakespeare Studies*, edited by K. Muir and S. Schoenbaum (Cam-

dramatic traditions.[50] Shakespeare's debt to the flourishing logical and rhetorical traditions of his time has been brought to light by a number of scholars and these findings have been useful in settling problems of explication, of style and of imagery.[51] The presupposition behind the tracing of such influences is that Shakespeare's education and reading were considerable, and that is the modern consensus.

There is also a critical tendency to relate the plays to biographical findings about Shakespeare, and to interpret them accordingly. The assumption here is that Shakespeare's art, essentially dramatic and objective as it may be, is not altogether impersonal and is, directly or in 'indirect, crooked ways', related to incidents, in his life or characteristics of his personality. Discerning veiled contemporary references or topical significances in the plays is an old enough practice, especially in deciding dates of composition. Several scholars in the twenties and thirties[52] started discovering

---

bridge, 1971), chapter 4, comment on this tendency to assume that Shakespeare had intensive as well as extensive reading habits.

[50] T. W. Baldwin, *Shakespeare's Five-Act Structure* (1947); Madeleine Doran, *Endeavors of Art* (Madison, 1954); Whitaker, *Shakespeare's Use of Learning*.

[51] Sister Miriam Joseph, *Shakespeare's Use of the Arts of Language* (1947); Tuve, *Elizabethan and Metaphysical Imagery*; Brian Vickers, *The Artistry of Shakespeare's Prose* (London, 1968), and *Classical Rhetoric in English Poetry* (1970).

[52] A. L. Rowse, *William Shakespeare* (London, 1963) accounts for too many things in the plays in terms of Shakespeare's life and his life in terms of contemporary history. G. B. Harrison, *Shakespeare at Work, 1592–1603* (Michigan, 1958) is an example of a topicalising commentator. Lillian Winstanley, *Hamlet and the Scottish Succession* (Cambridge, 1921) and *Macbeth, King Lear and Contemporary History Being a Study of the Relations of the Play of Macbeth to the Personal History of James I, the Darnley Murder and the St Bartholomew Massacre and also of King Lear as Symbolic Mythology* (Cambridge, 1922) are examples of a relentless reading into the plays of topical significances. E. M. Albright, 'Shakespeare's Richard II and the Essex Conspiracy', *PMLA*, 42 (1927), 686–728 and J. Dover Wilson, *The Essential Shakespeare* (Cambridge, 1932) and in his New Shakespeare edition of *Hamlet*, postulate a connection between the plays and the Essex conspiracy. Edward Le Comte, 'The Ending of *Hamlet* as a Farewell to Essex', *Journal of English Literary History*, 17 (1950), 87–114 argues first for and then against Shakespeare's portraying Essex in *Hamlet*. Dixon Wector, 'Shakespeare's Purpose in *Timon of Athens*', *PMLA*, 43 (1928), 701–21 finds in the play a parable of the fortunes of Essex. Some scholars also saw behind characters in the plays Shakespeare's rivals or contemporaries in the theatre, such as Ben Jonson and Marston. This habit was parodied by Baldwin Maxwell, 'The Original of Sir John Falstaff: Believe It or Not', *SP*, 27 (1930), 230–2. A topical interpretation of *Love's Labour's Lost* was offered by Frances A. Yates, *A Study of Love's Labour's Lost* (Cambridge, 1936), who has similarly interpreted the last plays in terms of the Prince Henry cult in King James I's court, *Shakespeare's Last Plays* (1975).

topical references in Shakespeare's plays. The game of deciphering and of discovering real-life counterparts and situations was overplayed. Leslie Hotson[53] with his indefatigable literary-detective zeal has been ceaselessly unearthing topical material in the plays. Nor did Dover Wilson, with his quick and sympathetic grasp of trends of historical scholarship let biographical and topical findings go unused. Other critics who employ the 'biocritical' method of approach are Charles Williams and Middleton Murry in places,[54] and most of those critics who have written general surveys of Shakespeare, classifying his life into periods, ever since Dowden's four-period classification. Wilson Knight, for instance, postulates the idea of an inner evolution in Shakespeare, reflected in the plays, and he calls this the 'Shakespeare Progress'. In general, one can see that biographical or topical exegesis (the latter allied to interpretation in terms of political events and social and economic conditions) could occasionally be fruitful, but that excess is likely to follow when either is elevated into a principle of interpretation. Consideration of the evolution of 'the poetic personality' of Shakespeare can certainly offer insights into the plays, as Charles Williams shows in his interpretation of some of the middle-period plays.[55]

However, the habit of secing a simplistic relationship between

Measure for Measure has been interpreted in relation to King James I by D. L. Stevenson, 'The Role of James I in Shakespeare's *Measure for Measure*', *ELH*, 26 (1959), 188–208; J. W. Lever; J. W. Bennett, '*Measure for Measure*', *as Royal Entertainment* (New York, 1966); and Henry Howarth in *The Tiger's Heart: Eight Essays on Shakespeare* (London, 1970). *Macbeth* has been similarly read by J. W. Draper; Henry N. Paul, *The Royal Play of 'Macbeth'* (New York, 1950); and Jane H. Jack, '*Macbeth*, King James and the Bible', *ELH*, 22 (1955), 173–93. J. W. Draper, 'The Occasion of *King Lear*', *SP*, 34 (1937), 176–85 relates the play to the union of England and Scotland under James I, while Glynne Wickham, '*King Lear* as Prologue', *SS*, 26 (1973), 33–48 would relate not only *King Lear* but all the plays after it, including the tragi-comedies, to James I.

On *A Midsummer Night's Dream* contrast Edith Rickert, 'Political Propaganda and Satire in *A Midsummer Night's Dream*', *MP*, 21 (1923–4), with Paul Olson, '*A Midsummer Night's Dream* and the Meaning of Court Marriages', *ELH*, 24 (1957).

[53] *William Shakespeare* (1937), *Shakespeare versus Shallow* (1931), *Shakespeare's Sonnets Dated* (1949), *The First Night of 'Twelfth Night'* (1954) and *Mr W. H.* (1964).

[54] For example, Charles Williams, *The English Poetic Mind* (1932), and his prosometria, *A Myth of Shakespeare* (1928); J. Middleton Murry, *Shakespeare* (London, 1936).

[55] Williams, *The English Poetic Mind*, and *Reason and Beauty in the English Poetic Mind* (Oxford, 1933), pp. 87–90.

the prevailing moods of the plays and the moods of the corresponding periods of Shakespeare's life – especially the postulating
of a 'tragic period' and of a last period ('on the heights') of serene
retirement[56] or senile boredom,[57] once common, and a legacy of
the nineteenth-century romantic notion of all art as self-
expression – has been discredited. This kind of relationship was
once suggested, even by the strictly unspeculative E. K. Chambers, but had been refuted before that by Sidney Lee, later by
G. L. Kittredge, C. J. Sisson and R. W. Chambers,[58] and has
now been laid to rest. However, modern psychological theories
of the deep links between the unconscious and the conscious
enable us to perceive subtle links between elements in the plays
such as imagery, rhythm and atmosphere, or thematic and 'spatial' patterns, and the life and personality, or more acceptably,
the *poetic* personality of Shakespeare.

Any discussion of twentieth-century critical trends relating to
Shakespeare must note the implications of bibliographical
studies for interpretation, especially now that there are two bibliographical schools – 'the new bibliography' and 'the newer
bibliography'. Textual and bibliographical studies have made
great advances, which affect textual and other scholarship rather
than criticism. But critical bibliography closely impinges upon
interpretation – as for instance, in discussions of such cruces as
'solid' or 'sullied' in *Hamlet* (i. ii. 129). Findings in this field can
directly affect the conclusions arrived at by a close 'new critical'
scrutiny of 'the words on the page', especially of imagery and
other local details. As F. W. Bateson has argued in 'Shakespeare's
Laundry Bills', *Shakespeare Jahrbuch*, 98 (1962), 51–63, and other

---

[56] Edward Dowden, *A Shakspere Primer* and *Shakspere: His Mind and Art* (1875).
[57] Lytton Strachey, 'Shakespeare's Final Period' (1904), reprinted in *Books and
Characters* (London, 1922), and *Literary Essays* (London, 1948).
[58] E. K. Chambers in his *Encyclopaedia Britannica* (11th edn) article on Shakespeare.
Sidney Lee, *A Life of William Shakespeare* (1898), revised edn 1925, p. 417. G. L.
Kittredge, *Shakespeare, An Address* (1916). C. J. Sisson, 'The Mythical Sorrows of
Shakespeare', *Proceedings of the British Academy* (1934) reprinted in Peter Alexander, ed., *Studies in Shakespeare* (London, 1964), 9–32. R. W. Chambers, '*Meas-
ure for Measure* and The Jacobean Shakespeare', *PBA*, (1937), reprinted in R. W.
Chambers, *Man's Unconquerable Mind* (London, 1939) as 'The Elizabethan and
the Jacobean Shakespeare'.

essays reprinted in *Essays in Critical Dissent*, interpretative or aesthetic considerations cannot be kept apart from the bibliographical.

Another important group of recent commentators who can be said to form a subcategory of the historical approach, consists of those who use historical linguistics to interpret Shakespeare. It is true that even the most ordinary reading of Shakespeare requires some aid from historical linguistics, which has been provided in editions, glossaries and grammars. But these commentators have developed specific fields of research and applied them to interpretation. H. Kökeritz's[59] reconstruction of Shakespeare's pronunciation has unearthed new homonyms, and puns hitherto unsuspected. William Empson's method of analysis in his *Structure of Complex Words* is in part semantic and hence linguistic, though other speculative instruments are also employed. More recently, Hilda Hulme in her *Explorations in Shakespeare's Language* (London, 1962) and A. C. Partridge in his *Orthography in Shakespeare and Elizabethan Drama* (London, 1964) have used linguistic findings as aids to interpretation. Stylistics, or the application of modern descriptive linguistics to the criticism of Shakespeare has yet to be introduced – through it is an avenue which future criticism will be tempted into taking.

The Chicago group of critics called the neo-Aristotelians can be considered as ultimately part of the school of historical scholarship. They have been among the most vigorous opponents of the 'New Critics'. The Chicago critics' idea of a Shakespearian play is that of a structured and *made* whole, 'a concrete whole or synola',[60] a literary object of which words are but material ele-

---

[59] H. Kökeritz, *Shakespeare's Pronunciation* (New Haven, 1953). Also the important review by E. J. Dobson of the book in *Review of English Studies*, 6 (1955). How Shakespeare's dramatic pointing adds to meaning is the finding of Percy Simpson in his *Shakespearian Punctuation* (Oxford, 1911) and of Peter Alexander in his *Shakespeare's Punctuation* (Oxford, 1945). Cf. Peter Alexander's 'Restoring Shakespeare: The Modern Editor's Task', *SS*, 5 (1952), 1–9.

[60] R. S. Crane, *The Languages of Criticism and the Structure of Poetry*, pp. 81–2 and pp. 150–4.

Ideas of 'structure' and 'action' in the plays have undergone significant shifts. 'Structure' has become a matter of 'theme' and 'imagery'. Similarly a new conception of 'action' as 'patience' (as in Eliot's *Murder in The Cathedral*) or as something depersonalised (as outlined in H. D. F. Kitto's *Form and Meaning in Drama* (London, 1956) and in John Jones's *On Aristotle and Greek Tragedy* (Lon-

ments, to be considered in accordance with the play's genre and its course of action, without any excessive semantic and verbalist preoccupation, or other form of abstraction with which other schools of criticism are charged. It is often held against the neo-Aristotelians that their theories and their adverse comments about other critical standpoints are much more substantial than their output in critical *practice*, especially as applied to Shakespeare, and that it tends towards the simplistic and the naïve in their distrust of subtleties.[61] Insofar as these critics have drawn attention to questions of genres and structural principles based on genre differentiation, their criticism has served to put us in mind of essential factors in the plays. But it seems as though their perceptions are not historical enough; they do not take sufficient note of the fluidity of the Elizabethan age as regards the frequent mixture of genres and the evolution of hybrid forms.[62]

The Chicago group has influenced, directly or indirectly, a significant number of critics who approach the plays in terms of structure, or through plot and action. Among commentators who have developed their ideas of structures the most remarkable is Northrop Frye,[63] and, among those who emphasise the action, the sheer energy and power of Shakespearian tragedy, is John Holloway.[64]

The ideal historical critic of Shakespeare today would have to be a monster of scholarship; the minutiae he would have had to master, legion. 'The armed vision'[65] of the ideal Shakespeare scholar or critic, is frightening to contemplate. When historical scholarship looms so large, we have to remind ourselves that, hard as we may try, we cannot turn ourselves into Elizabethans, and we have been reminded of it.[66] Eliot, whose essays on

don, 1962)) has been put forward. M. Doran has pointed out how cause-and-effect views of action as applied to Elizabethan drama or in romance would be anachronistic. *Endeavors of Art*, pp. 265–79.

[61] John Holloway, 'The New and the Newer Critics' in *The Charted Mirror* (London, 1960), pp. 187–203.

[62] The Elizabethan handling of dramatic genres has been analysed by Madeleine Doran in her *Endeavors of Art*.

[63] He has comments on Shakespearian comedy in his *Anatomy of Criticism* (1957) and a more detailed study of the comedies in *A Natural Perspective* (1965).

[64] *The Story of the Night* (London, 1961).

[65] Stanley Edgar Hyman, *The Armed Vision* (New York, 1952). (Coleridge's phrase.)

[66] Helen Gardner, *The Business of Criticism*, pp. 32–4 and Bonamy Dobrée, 'On (NOT) Enjoying Shakespeare', *ES*, 9 (1956), 47.

Elizabethan drama had a major influence on modern opinion, pointed out how it is more necessary to approximate the Elizabethan writers to our age than to approximate ourselves to their age. In practice, the work of historical scholarship and criticism has led to the inhering of a historical consciousness in the general make-up of the modern scholar and critic, so that it is not so much a question of the quantity of knowledge possessed and applied as a question of general temper and outlook. This is indeed a development for which one cannot but be grateful.

When this eclecticism is generally practised by commentators, even in their choice among categories of critical method, it is natural that several kinds of historical criticism should be combined by the same critic. One mode of historical approach may contradict another: ultimately, it is a question of deciding how much emphasis is to be given to findings under a particular mode. For example, we find an able controversialist like E. E. Stoll[67] questioning the findings of a critic belonging to the same school as himself, such as Schücking, and also the interpretation of character in terms of Elizabethan psychology.

There has also been fruitful cross-fertilisation between one historical school and another, or the historical school and the theatrical. There is some truth in the charge against historical criticism by A. Harbage and Bonamy Dobrée that it tends towards 'an appropriation of Shakespeare by specialists'[68] or 'the subordination of Shakespeare to specialist interests'.[69] Yet thanks to the existence of a variety of historical approaches, no such ultimate appropriation could really be made. Harbage gave us a salutary reminder that the reductiveness of such historical frames of reference will not do – that fiction, after all, does not conform in detail to the philosophy of its age, and that any contemporary system of ideas may be not a cause but only a parallel effect.[70]

---

[67] Stoll in *Hamlet the Man* (English Association Pamphlet no. 91, 1935) and elsewhere has some strictures on Schücking. He attacked some historical critics as 'antiquarians' in *From Shakespeare to Joyce* – chapters 4 and 13, and also in 'Mainly Controversy' in *PQ*, 24 (1945), 289–311.

[68] Harbage, *As They Liked It*, p. v.

[69] Dobrée, 'On (Not) Enjoying Shakespeare', p. 46.

[70] Harbage, *As They Liked it*, chapter 2 'Moral Response', pp. 16–40, especially p. 31.

Harbage relented in his hostility to historical criticism in his *Shakespeare's*

If the expansion of historical scholarship has resulted in new modes of historical criticism of Shakespeare, the arrival of the new sciences of psychology and anthropology, social and cultural, has opened up new avenues of approach (though some have turned out to be blind alleys). The relationship between these sciences and the poetic approach will be discussed in more detail later (see pp. 57–9). Anthropological findings have been drawn on by poetic critics who offer interpretations of the plays in terms of symbol and metaphor, myth and ritual patterns. Critics who exemplify a more recent reaction against the poetic–dramatic approach, against 'the current coin of Shakespeare criticism',[71] and those who, like Francis Fergusson,[72] find ritual rhythms and movements or like Northrop Frye, patterns of myth in the structure of the plays, make use of anthropological insights. Similarly, a general awareness of psychology, rightly or wrongly understood, has been part modern consciousness, and this has influenced premises and modes of proceeding in the poetic school. In addition to occasional interpretative insights via psychology, there have been a few full-fledged psychoanalytical interpretations of the plays.[73] Special notice has to be taken of the application of the Jungian ideas of 'archetypal' or 'primordial' images and patterns to the interpretation of Shakespeare. Literary critics have found Jung's notions more congenial than Freud's, and have cross-bred them with notions of social and cultural anthropology, with remarkable results. F. C. Prescott[74] applied both

Audience, and more so in Shakespeare and the Rival Traditions and Theatre for Shakespeare (Toronto, 1955).

[71] The phrase is John Holloway's. The Story of the Night, p. 1.

[72] Francis Fergusson, The Idea of a Theatre (1949). Robert Hapgood, 'Shakespeare and the Ritualists', SS, 15 (1962), surveys the myth-and-ritual approaches. John Holloway interprets the tragedies from this angle, as Wilson Knight and Tillyard do the last plays. Herbert Weisinger, on the contrary, thinks that in the last plays Shakespeare uses the patterns of myth and ritual as mere machinery, almost in burlesque fashion, and hence wonders whether a myth-and-ritual approach to the plays could help. 'The Myth and Ritual Approach to Shakespearian Tragedy', originally published in The Centennial Review of Arts and Sciences (1957) and reprinted in Perspectives in Contemporary Criticism, edited by Sheldon Norman Grebstein (New York, 1968), pp. 322–36.

[73] Norman N. Holland, Psychoanalysis and Shakespeare (New York, 1964) is a comprehensive and critical account of psychoanalytical approaches to Shakespeare. T. S. Eliot's essay on Hamlet betrays the influence of Freudian ideas.

[74] The Poetic Mind (1922) and Poetry and Myth (1927).

Freudian and Jungian ideas systematically to literary criticism for the first time, and the first full-scale deployment of Jungian concepts in the interpretation of Shakespeare's plays was made by Maud Bodkin.[75] Theories about the ritual origins of Greek drama and literature put forward by eminent classical scholars, though challenged by others, also came to influence critical approaches.

In a sense, the 'theatrical' critics – those preoccupied with Shakespeare as dramatist – constitute a rival school, as developments in theatrical commentaries seem to parallel and thus to promote and confirm the tendencies of poetic commentaries. Twentieth century theatrical critics of Shakespeare may be conveniently divided into two categories: those who try to restore the plays to the original Elizabethan theatrical context by attempting to reconstruct Elizabethan stage conditions; and those who interpret the plays from the point of view of production on the modern stage, but with some approximation to Elizabethan stage conditions.

Writers on the Elizabethan theatre in the early twentieth century such as G. F. Reynolds, E. M. Albright, A. H. Thorndike, T. S. Graves, and C. J. Sisson saw a medieval simplicity and comparative bareness relieved by only a few features of Renaissance ornamentation. A little later, W. J. Lawrence and J. C. Adams visualised the Elizabethan stage as one of Renaissance elaboration, in terms of playing levels and detailed features. In the fifties C. Walter Hodges tried to restore the Globe to its medieval matrix. More recently, the balance of the intermixture of medieval and Renaissance elements in the Elizabethan theatre has been pointed up by Glynne Wickham.

George Kernodle has stressed the elements of pageantry and symbol on the Elizabethan stage, its descent from the *tableux vivants* and its relation to medieval scenic devices such as bowers, fountains, castles, pavilions, arcades and triumphal arches. Others have proposed different origins and antecedents for the Elizabethan theatre. Leslie Hotson has insisted on the analogy with the Spanish stage, and proposed an 'arena stage', with

[75] Maud Bodkin, *Archetypal Patterns in Poetry* (1934).

mansions, the audience sitting on all four sides. Richard Hosley
has, in a series of important articles,[76] exposed the fallacies of
earlier reconstructions of the Elizabethan stage, the false analogy
with the eighteenth- and nineteenth-century multiple stage, and
the myth of the 'inner stage'; and he has emphasised the
medieval affiliations of Shakespeare's stage – for example, in its
use of booths and similar detachable structures. The monumental
volumes of E. K. Chambers and G. E. Bentley[77] on the
Elizabethan and Jacobean stages have all but fully recreated
Shakespeare's theatrical environment. (It may be that the relations postulated by Bentley between the later Shakespeare and
the Blackfriars' Theatre[78] are to be interpreted differently in the
light of the criticisms made by J. A. Lavin.[79])

Discussion of the mode of acting on the Elizabethan stage has
had implications for critical commentary. Attention to stylised,
rhetorical and conventionalised modes of presentation, to acting
conventions and to expression of feeling and passion, and how
these are related to Elizabethan ideas of psychology, decorum
and motivation, and rhetoric has provided support for the non-
naturalistic understanding of Shakespeare's characterisation and
dramatic construction.[80] The rapport between audience and

[76] Richard Hosley 'The Origins of the Shakespearian Playhouse', *SQ*, 15 (1964),
'The Discovery-space in Shakespeare's Globe', *SS*, 12 (1959), 'The Gallery over
the stage in the Public Playhouse of Shakespeare's Time', *SQ*, 14 (1963) and
'The Origins of the So-called Elizabethan Multiple Stage', *The Drama Review*,
12 (1968), 28–50.
[77] E. K. Chambers, *The Elizabethan Stage* (1923), 4 vols, *William Shakespeare* (1930),
2 vols, *Shakespeare: A Survey* (1900, reprinted, London, 1925) and *Shakespeare
Gleanings* (1944). G. E. Bentley, *The Jacobean and Caroline Stage*, 7 vols (Oxford,
1941–68) and *The Profession of Dramatist in Shakespeare's Time* (Princeton, 1971).
[78] 'Shakespeare and the Blackfriars' Theatre', *SS*, 1 (1948).
[79] 'Shakespeare and the Second Blackfriars', *The Elizabethan Theatre III*, edited by
D. Galloway (London and Toronto, 1973).
[80] Bertram Joseph, *Elizabethan Acting* (1951) made a case for stylised acting, but
qualified his views in the second edition (1964) and his other volumes, *The
Tragic Actor* (1958) and *Acting Shakespeare* (1960). An intermixture and gradual
accession in later Elizabethan and Jacobean times of realism in acting is dis-
covered by Marvin Rosenberg, 'Elizabethan Actors: Men or Marionettes?',
PMLA, 69 (1954); R. A. Foakes, 'The Player's Passion: Some Notes on
Elizabethan Psychology and Acting', *E&S*, n.s., 7 (1954); W. A. Armstrong,
'Actors and Theatres', *Shakespeare in his Own Age*, first published in *SS* 17 (1964);
John Russell Brown, *Shakespeare's Plays in Performance* (London, 1966) and
Andrew Gurr, *The Shakespearean Stage, 1574–1642* (Cambridge, 1970, pp. 70–5,
2nd edn 1980); Alfred Harbage in his 'Elizabethan Acting', *PMLA*, 54 (1939)
stressed the element of stylisation, while his *Theatre for Shakespeare* admitted the

actors, through the closeness of spectators on all three sides of the
stage, and the absence of the proscenium arch boxing off the
stage, was such that the words of the actor would come home to
every member of the audience, despite any impediments in
sight-lines. The cumulative effect of findings about the physical
characteristics of the Elizabethan theatre has been to stress the
prime role of the words, the poetry; emphasize that it was a
drama of 'words, words, words', and that stage and acting only
served to accentuate and reinforce their impact. Similarly, the
light thrown on the symbolic and allegorical elements of the
Elizabethan stage illuminates those elements in Shakespearian
drama which have been highlighted by some poetic interpreters.
Wilson Knight in his earliest commentaries set himself against
theatrical critics, but later became an original experimenter in
Shakespearian production, and used his productions to illustrate
his symbolic interpretations.

Among the second category of theatrical critics: that is, those
who relate the plays to the modern stage 'with a difference', the
chief representative is Harley Granville-Barker. The most
influential and substantial commentary on the plays, from the
point of view of how they work on the stage, has been provided
in his *Prefaces to Shakespeare* (in five series, 1927–47). A playwright, actor, producer, and man of the theatre in every sense,
Granville-Barker analysed the actual effects of the plays on the
stage, and his analysis has illuminated other aspects of the plays,
especially their poetry. He comments on the poetry from the
point of view of its theatrical function.[81] His ultimate faith was in
the educative role of drama and the theatre, and this faith is the
basic assumption behind a good part of the poetic interpretation

probability of an intermixture of realism in Elizabethan acting (appendix B in
Theatre for Shakespeare). Alan S. Downer, 'Prolegomenon to a Study of
Elizabethan Acting', *Maske und Kothurn*, 10 (1965), 625–36, is a rare codification
of contemporary references to acting. David Klein (*PMLA*, 71 (1956)) cites a
number of Elizabethan references to acting, which imply an ideal of life-
likeness in acting.

[81] Marion Trousdale, 'The Question of Harley Granville-Barker and Shakespeare
on Stage', *Renaissance Drama*, n.s. 4 (1971), 3–36, thinks that Granville-Barker,
with his stress on the right way of speaking Shakespearian verse on the stage
and on its verbal nuances, sees the plays as the Elizabethans did, as literary
compositions, and regards the dramatic as inseparable from the literary.

of Shakespeare. Another commentator with a similar approach to Shakespeare is Nevill Coghill, experienced as a producer in the amateur, if not the professional, theatre. He has demonstrated how visual meanings reinforce verbal meanings in the stage-realisation of the plays. How an eye for the physical disposition and juxtaposition of characters on the stage can reveal in a flash the dramatic situation and its meaning, as well as the words and their meaning, is made convincingly plain by Maynard Mack, Alan S. Downer, M. L. Rosen, John Russell Brown, J. L. Styan and Glynne Wickham.[82]

The main nineteenth-century approach – character-criticism – has survived in modern Shakespeare criticism in one form or another. Conventional character-criticism has naturally been modified in present-day usage; very rarely has it been retained in its original form. John Palmer (Political Characters in Shakespeare (1945); Comic Characters in Shakespeare (1946)) in his studies of the characters does not engage in speculations about their predramatic past or postdramatic future. H. B. Charlton called himself 'a devout Bradleyite', and there is ground for saying that he carried on the tradition of Bradley. But Charlton introduced certain modifications into character-criticism. His impressions of the characters are governed by a knowledge of the structures of the plays, and the relationship between the plays and their sources. Moreover, Charlton approaches characters from the outside with some objectivity, whereas Bradley's approach is one of psychological inwardness amounting to empathy.

Another significant modification of the idea of character in drama was made by approaching the plays in terms of the moral vision which creates and illuminates their worlds. This approach

---

[82] Coghill, Shakespeare's Professional Skills, especially 'Visual Meaning', 1–31; Maynard Mack, 'The Jacobean Shakespeare', Jacobean Theatre (Stratford-upon-Avon Studies I), edited by J. R. Brown and Bernard Harris (London, 1960); A. S. Downer, 'The Life of Our Design', reprinted in Dean, ed., Shakespeare: Modern Essays in Criticism; M. L. Rosen, Shakespeare and the Craft of Tragedy (Cambridge, Mass., 1960); Russell Brown, Shakespeare's Plays in Performance; J. L. Styan, Shakespeare's Stagecraft (Cambridge, 1967); Glynne Wickham, Shakespeare's Dramatic Heritage (London, 1969) and Michael Goldman, Shakespeare and the Energies of Drama (New York and London, 1972). Also W. M. Merchant, Shakespeare and the Artist (1959), chapter 1.

was exemplified by Arthur Sewell in his *Character and Society in Shakespeare* (1951). The book to which Sewell's was meant to be a complement and a corrective, J. I. M. Stewart's *Character and Motive in Shakespeare*, sought to restore character-criticism modified and strengthened by the aid of Freudian psychology and Frazerian anthropology. Most of these new approaches to character and, through it, to Shakespearian drama, pay due attention to the poetry of the plays and its constituent parts, showing awareness that Shakespeare's drama is primarily *poetic* drama.

Apart from Peter Alexander's and John F. Danby's modified use of character-criticism, two studies, by Una Ellis-Fermor and John Bayley,[83] stress the indispensability of character. The findings of historical scholarship and awareness of the Elizabethan ethos have profoundly altered our view of character in Shakespeare. The knowledge, too, that these are characters in a non-naturalistic poetic drama with whom we have to come to terms makes all the difference to what we think of them. The framework of Elizabethan ideas, moral, social and political, of Elizabethan psychology, theories of motivation and modes of dramatic presentation, make the characters appear in a new light; a dry light perhaps. So Dover Wilson, though in the main he may be said to belong to the character-criticism school, sees character in the light of these historical findings.

The truth is that character-criticism is by no means discarded. Katharine Cooke in *A. C. Bradley and his Influence in Twentieth-Century Shakespeare Criticism*, suggests that the reaction against 'Bradley the character-chaser' is mainly due to two factors. The first is that every reader or commentator finds himself an instinctive 'character-monger' in his response to a Shakespearian play, and so indulges in a sort of unconscious self-castigation by reacting against Bradley (p. 119). The second is that character-criticism is a vein exhausted by Bradley and hence looked upon with

---

[83] Una Ellis-Fermor, *Shakespeare the Dramatist*, edited by K. Muir (London, 1961); John Bayley, *The Characters of Love* (1960). Also, Nicholas Brooke, 'The Characters of Drama', *CQ*, 6 (1964); A. D. Nuttall, 'The Argument about Shakespeare's Characters', *CQ*, 7 (1965); and Robert Langbaum, 'Character *versus* Action in Shakespeare', *SQ*, 8 (1957). Leo Kirschbaum, *Characters and Characterization in Shakespeare* (Detroit/New York, 1962) considers characters, Stoll-like, as 'functions' rather than as 'persons'.

disfavour because it is no longer exploitable (pp. 150–1). But the leading anti-Bradleyan, F. R. Leavis, the inventor of the phrase 'How Many Children Had Lady Macbeth?', has himself practised character-criticism 'with a difference' in relation to *Othello* and *Measure for Measure*, not to speak of the later L. C. Knights's or the later Empson's more tolerant views on character in drama.[84] The Bradleyan approach to character may have gone out of favour, but it has been replaced by other, more valid views.

To sum up, there has been a good deal of intercommunication and cross-fertilisation between the kinds of approach as well as between subcategories. Exclusive commitment to one method only is inappropriate, and the critic whose main speculative instrument is one method is at liberty to employ others. Criticism

[84] 'It is surprising how much, in his essay on *Othello*, Leavis concedes to the Bradleyan approach; he emerges, in his own terms, as an intelligent Bradley . . .', W. J. Harvey, *Character and the Novel* (London, 1965), appendix II 'The Attack on Character', p. 204. Both 'Diabolic Intellect and the Noble Hero: The Sentimentalist's Othello', *Scrutiny*, 6 (1937), 259–83, reprinted in *The Common Pursuit*, and 'The Greatness of *Measure for Measure*', *Scrutiny*, 10 (1941), 234–47 by Leavis are character studies for the most part. It may be instructive to juxtapose the following two statements by two different critics. F. R. Leavis, letter to *TLS*, 9 July 1954, p. 441.
If I agree, or assert (as I do), that in responding to a Shakespeare play that engages us imaginatively we respond *as if* the situations were actual and the characters real, I go on to insist that the 'as if' must be understood to have an essentially qualifying value: it registers the fact that, in responding, we at the same time know that this is *not* actual life, so that our response is, in various ways, different from what it would be in dealing in actual life with such situations as are represented. The value of the 'as if' (to use a shorthand compelled upon me by the need for brevity) varies from play to play, and even from point to point within a play . . . We can determine the precise value on any occasion only by attending sensitively and intelligently to the organization of words that Shakespeare has left us with . . . We judge Othello as we should judge someone we knew in life.
The second statement is by Nuttall, 'The Argument about Shakespeare's Characters', p. 107.
the practice of simply naming the persons of a play without always designating them as 'characters' has long been authorised by usage. It has become part of the shorthand of criticism to omit the designation of logical status once the over-all logical context is clear.
A revealing statement by Empson may also be cited.
I argued in my book *Pastoral* that Satan is not a consistent character, being something more basically dramatic instead; and now I think this wrong. There was a fashion for attacking 'character-analysis', especially in Shakespeare, which I have taken some time to get out of; maybe it has a kind of truth, but it is dangerously liable to make us miss points of character (*Milton's God*, p. 69).
Also correspondence by Empson in *CQ*, 7 (1965), p. 285.

is an instrument of many stops, all of which are meant to be played upon. The quarrel among the adherents of various schools of criticism is only a metaphysical quarrel. When there are so many points of contact, either of agreement or of disagreement, what the critic can do is to express a relative preference for a single method or a set of methods, and he cannot absolutely rule out any other. One can recall the attacks of Logan Pearsall Smith on the historical and theatrical critics (*On Reading Shakespeare* (New York, 1933)); that kind of dismissal of methods of interpretation, except where they are employed extremely deterministically, is not likely to be made today.

2

The rise of the poetic interpretation of Shakespeare: the background and influences

In this chapter, I enquire into those factors in literary criticism in general, in creative literature and in the intellectual and cultural climate of the age, which fostered the growth of this approach. Such an account brings us a historicist perspective from which the poetic interpretation of Shakespeare appears as a phenomenon with a certain inevitability; that perspective will complement the one assumed in the last chapter, in which the more or less unconscious collaboration between historical criticism and the new criticism was pointed out.

What the poetic critics did was to draw our attention to the fact that the essential life-centre of Shakespearian drama, the supreme example of poetic drama, was the verse and its poetic constituents. Hence, primary importance had to be given to their study, and the other conventionally discussed elements, such as character and plot, were to be considered, if at all, in terms of the medium of language and verse through which they find expression.

We start with so many lines of verse on a printed page which we read as we should any other poem. We have to elucidate the meaning (using Dr Richards's fourfold definition) and to unravel ambiguities; we have to estimate the kind and quality of the imagery and determine the precise degree of evocation of particular figures; we have to allow full weight to each word, exploring its 'tentacular roots', and to determine how it controls and is controlled by the rhythmic movement of the passage in which it occurs. In short we have to decide exactly why the lines 'are so and not otherwise'.[1]

[1] L. C. Knights, *Explorations* (London, 1946), p. 16. The quotation is from *How Many Children Had Lady Macbeth?* (first published by the Minority Press in 1932).

It may not be true to say that critics of previous epochs had
ignored the element of poetry in the plays; but it is true that the
modern poetic critics brought a new attitude to verse in Shakespeare and saw in it qualities and functions unsuspected till their
time. The new view of poetry in Shakespearian drama was in
keeping with the modern view of the nature and function of
poetry. In other words, the new approach to Shakespeare in
terms of the poetry of the plays was a natural and inevitable
outcome of the twentieth-century attitude to poetry. Only during
this period could such a view of verse and its function have been
taken. Poetry in Shakespearian drama was not to be considered
an ornamental adjunct, to be relished in quotation out of context,
or in isolation from other elements of drama like character, plot,
situation, or atmosphere. All of these had to be seen in terms of
the poetry, for the plain reason that all these had their being in
poetry.[2] Over and above this implicit idea of how a Shakespeare
play is primarily constituted and how it functions, was the new-
found concern for the impression of the play as a work of literature, as a whole. The insistence on the total response of the reader
to the impact of *all* the elements in the drama acting and reacting
together and forming an organic whole, sprang from a typical
modern article of critical faith. The credo, whose origins can be
traced back to Coleridge and the formulation of his theory of
organic form with reference to Shakespeare, is that a work of
literature is an integrated totality, with interdependent parts
making a whole which is more than the sum of its parts. The fresh
view of the structure of the Shakespearian play which came to be
formed as a result is a remarkable contribution to critical studies.
As commentator, Wilson Knight could apprehend a play as
though it were a shape, and not an activity, as though it were not
merely a sequence of events extended in time, but a spatial whole
like a picture or sculpture. The need for a response to the total
impression made by a work as a whole had been recognised by a
number of critics. Perhaps the first overt formulation of the principle was made by Edgell Rickword in an article in *The Calendar of
Modern Letters* (October, 1926) entitled 'A Note on Fiction'.

[2] L. C. Knights, 'The Question of Character in Shakespeare', *Further Explorations*
(London, 1965), pp. 186–204, especially pp. 196–7.

The shifts of grounds in argument, the new accesses of awareness, and the questioning of old habits of thought in the field of Shakespeare criticism may look like purely intramural changes. But these are only a reflection of changes in the wider circles of contemporary literary criticism, of the twentieth-century modernist (to revive the word and reverse the replacement of 'modernist' by 'modern') literary movement as it manifested itself in poetry, the novel and the drama, of intellectual developments in allied branches of knowledge, and even of changes in the human situation. It may be helpful to outline this background so as to place the rise and evolution of the poetic approach to Shakespeare in perspective.

In the background is the advent of the new poetic, the basis of the twentieth-century poetic revolution brought about by Eliot, Yeats and Pound; the whole new set of literary values brought into currency in the twenties in the fiction of Joyce, Lawrence and Virginia Woolf; and the new experimental drama of Yeats and certain European playwrights; the later revival of poetic drama; the new critical concepts worked out by Eliot, Richards, Empson, and Leavis; the birth and flourishing of the 'new criticism'; the impact of the new sciences and philosophies of the twentieth century such as psychology, social and cultural anthropology, logical positivism and later the philosophy of 'symbolic forms';[3] the consciousness of the modern cultural crisis, the preoccupation with literature as a way to meet its challenge, and hence the new demands on and expectations about literature; the formulation of theories about the origin and evolution of drama, and the relations between drama, ritual, myth, symbol and archetype.

The advent of new literary and critical values and the way they bore upon significant shifts of viewpoint in Shakespeare criticism can be outlined first. The determination to believe in the integrity of literature, and to approach literature as literature, 'poetry as poetry, and not as another thing', is the basic major develop-

---

[3] Proposed by Ernst Cassirer and elaborated by Susanne Langer. Cassirer, trans. R. Mannheim, *The Philosophy of Symbolic Forms*, vol. I, *Language* (New Haven, 1953); Cassirer, trans. S. Langer, *Language and Myth* (New York, 1946); S. Langer, *Philosophy in a New Key* (Cambridge, Mass., 1942), *Feeling and Form* (New York, 1953) and *Mind: An Essay on Human Feeling* (Baltimore, 1967), for instance.

ment. This underlining of the integrity of the work of literature made it necessary to fix one's attention on the medium of the art, which was taken to be words and language. Indeed giving close attention to the *medium* would seem to be a characteristic modern preoccupation, whether on the part of the writer or the critic. The modern critical attitude may be said to hinge on the view taken of the function of words as elements rather than as materials going to make up the medium.[4] The application of this principle to the study of Shakespeare's plays resulted in their being regarded as poems, not plays, and poems without genre distinction at that. When the plays came to be treated as though they were lyric poems, and moreover with certain typical modern ideas about the nature of poetry, the theatre-language and theatre-context of Shakespearian drama tended to be ignored, or only fitfully recognised.

Certain typically modern concepts of the constitution and function of poetry and a characteristic modern attitude to poetry govern the critics' handling of Shakespeare's text. It starts with the basic presupposition that poetry is a unique mode of discourse, unparaphrasable, especially in rational prose and direct statement. Close analysis of the words on the page, concentrated reading, or verbal analysis, identity features of Shakespeare's poetry hitherto not generally much regarded – such as imagery, qualities of association, suggestiveness; symbolical, mythical, archetypal and ritual significances; thematic patterns; and other oblique modes of communication which are part of poetry.

It is appropriate here to point to the circumstances under which the new poetic of the twentieth century emerged, as a reaction against Romantic, Georgian, and Edwardian poetry; how the

---

[4] Mallarmé's remark to Degas 'Poetry is written with words' is full of implications. The question is how words used in poetry differ from words used in other modes of discourse, whether words are the elements or materials of poetry or both. The question is discussed by W. Y. Tindall, *The Literary Symbol* (Bloomington, 1955), pp. 8–9. That words are materials is repeatedly insisted on by the Chicago critics, this being their chief quarrel with the 'new' critics, especially those of Shakespeare; 'Poetry is not words but verbal; a chair is not wood but wooden.'

Elder Olson, 'An Outline of Poetic Theory', *Critics and Criticism*, edited by R. S. Crane (Chicago, 1952) and also in *Tragedy and the Theory of Drama* (Detroit, 1961), p. 9 and p. 12 respectively.

new cultural situation produced a new relationship between poet, poetry and audience. No extended account is needed of the new concepts of the psychological make-up and functioning of the poet's personality, the impersonal theory of poetry, the awareness of cognitive elements in the composition and appreciation of poetry, the need for the involvement of all the facets of the poet's personality in composition and all the faculties of the reader in appreciation, and hence the implied need for an 'association' of sensibility, and how these new preoccupations resulted in general effects of obscurity in poetry. A primary consequence of the new creative practice and the critical theory underlying it was a recognition of modes of meaning and of communication in poetry other than the traditionally recognised direct, rational ones; and newly-conceived ideas of structure in literary works replaced conventional concepts of linear, logical and rational structure.[5]

This emphasis on 'the sub-rational layers of meaning' and on the oblique suggestion and 'intimations' of 'elliptical' poetry gave new bearings to modern literary criticism and Shakespeare criticism in particular.[6] Critics came to feel that instead of considering narrative sequences in the plays in terms of plot and character, they should consider 'the logic of the imagination' in a single play, or, more significantly, in a sequence of plays, or in the canon as a whole, discarding the older notions and expectations of a discursive progression or logical structure. It may appear paradoxical that this insistence on 'intimations' and indirect suggestions in poetry, and the appeal to faculties other than the conscious should have been made by a movement which set itself against what it took to be the emotionalism and sentimentalism of the Romantics and the Victorians, and the lack of discipline in their intellectual and rational faculties. A movement which strove for 'dryness' (to use T. E. Hulme's expression), for 'fundamental brainwork', to adopt a phrase of D. G. Rossetti, for rational intelligence and critical judgement in control of the making as

[5] C. K. Stead, *The New Poetic* (London, 1964) provides a succinct account of these developments.

[6] Graham Hough, *Image and Experience* (London, 1960) emphasises this aspect of modernist poetry.

well as the reading of poetry, at the same time encouraged the intuitional in interpretation. Given these two seemingly opposed currents in the modern movement, if the intuitional is thought to predominate over the cognitive, it would be logical to see the modern movement in literature and criticism as a continuation of the Romantic movement.[7] As a matter of fact, the ideal hankered after, however difficult in practice, was the co-extensive development, fusion or function in unison of the emotional and the imaginative sensibilities, and of the faculty of reason and judgement.[8] The implied pursuit of this ideal led Eliot to put forward the concept of a unified, or undissociated sensibility. Though his handling of the concept has received a good deal of criticism in recent years,[9] and though he himself might have been surprised to find how this expression (and the phrase 'the objective correlative') had acquired such status, the phrase pinpoints an undeclared ideal of the modern movement. The new poetry of Yeats, Eliot and Pound, and the poetic behind it, brought into being a taste to which the verse in Shakespeare and Elizabethan drama, and a good deal of seventeenth-century verse other than Milton's, especially the Metaphysicals', immediately appealed, and to which other kinds of poetry – Spenser, Milton, the Romantics and the Victorians – did not. Eliot gave much of his critical attention to comparison and analysis of the verse of the Elizabethan and Jacobean dramatists; it is curious, but understandable in the light of his master-strategies, that he did not, as a rule, tackle Shakespearian verse itself.[10]

It was in the twenties, then, a significant period in literary history, that the new approach to Shakespeare was taking root and, on occasion, sending out its shoots; though it was in the early thirties that the approach came to full bloom. The new critical faith was consolidating itself during this period. The inter-

[7] Frank Kermode, *Romantic Image* (1957); G. S. Fraser, *Vision and Rhetoric* (1959); and Hough, *Image and Experience*, take this view of modern poetry.

[8] The idea is well summed up in Yeats's phrase 'blood, intellect and imagination, all running together'. *Essays and Introductions* (London, 1961), p. 10.

[9] In Kermode, *Romantic Image*; Rosemund Tuve, *Elizabethan and Metaphysical Imagery*; and J. E. Duncan, *The Revival of Metaphysical Poetry*, for example. G. D. Klingopulos, 'Historical Fact and Critical Myth', *Universities Quarterly* (1963) defends the concept.

[10] T. S. Eliot, *To Criticize the Critic and Other Essays* (London, 1965), p. 18.

connections between the new movement in creative literature, poetry and fiction especially, and the accompanying new movement in criticism obviously run both ways. In the criticism of Shakespeare, besides a shift of interest from the conventional categories of character and plot, to the qualities of the language and poetry such as rhythm, imagery and their suggestive power, there was a concentration of attention on how the words serve as embodiments of, not mere vehicles for, significances or themes; and, most strikingly of all, of values which could be 'realised'[11] or 'incarnated'. This tendency to see Shakespeare's plays as embodiments and conveyors of value has been noted and criticised by John Holloway.[12] Where works of literature came to be so regarded a new sort of indirect link and active communication between literary values and the cultural condition came to be perceived. The signs at present are that this outlook is going out of fashion.[13] Eliot himself implicitly at first, and more explicitly later, postulated a relationship between the literary qualities of a work of literature, the cultural situation in which it was produced and its common scale of values, but came to feel that, despite the links between religion and culture, literature cannot be a substitute for religion.[14] But this belief in a key relationship between literature, culture and values has been influential. It is small wonder that in the modern search for values, the tendency grew of regarding literature – and the supreme instance of Shake-

---

[11] 'Realised' is used by F. R. Leavis and 'Incarnated' is used by R. P. Blackmur and G. Wilson Knight. The term 'incarnation' was originally employed by Wordsworth with reference to poetic language.

[12] *The Story of the Night* and the article on twentieth-century Shakespeare criticism in *A Shakespeare Encyclopaedia*, edited by O. J. Campbell and E. G. Quinn (London, 1966), pp. 837–41.

[13] Graham Hough, *The Dream and the Task* (London, 1963); Lionel Trilling, *Beyond Culture* (New York, 1965); John Holloway, *The Colours of Clarity* (London, 1964); Stephen Spender, *The Struggle of the Modern* (London, 1964).

[14] 'Religion and Literature', *Selected Essays* (2nd edn), pp. 388–401, p. 388 and also *Notes towards the Definition of Culture* (London, 1948).

   In his 'The Social Function of Poetry', in *On Poetry and Poets* (London, 1957), Eliot made a classical formulation of the relationship between poetry and the cultural condition of the community. He suggests that the function of poetry is not merely to preserve values, but to preserve the capacity to feel at all, 'not merely to express, but even to feel any but the crudest emotions'. In *What is a Classic?* (London, 1945), and 'Virgil and the Christian World' (1951), the relation is implicitly hinted at.

spearian drama – as a treasurehouse of values. It is in the context of this cultural preoccupation of modern literary criticism (which harks back to Arnold and the Romantics) that the poetic-critics' habit of isolating themes of 'moral values'[15] in the plays of Shakespeare must be set.

The new principles of literary criticism, accepting as more or less axiomatic the beliefs of the new poetic, inevitably led to an 'intrinsic' and internalistic sort of commentary on the Shakespearian text where everything is left, as it were, to the commentator and the text with nothing to intervene. It was in Shakespeare criticism, and by the inaugurators of the poetic school, G. Wilson Knight especially, that the principles of 'critical monism' and 'intrinsic' criticism were first applied.

The main implications of the poetic approach are best seen at work, and in overt formulation, in the writings of Leavis and of the *Scrutiny* critics. It is true that writings of Eliot and Richards might have been primary sources of inspiration, and that Richards had played a historically earlier and pioneering role in the establishment of the Cambridge English School. But in Leavis's writings, in his monumental contribution in the form of nearly twenty years of *Scrutiny*, we have the modern critical movement embodied most characteristically. Leavis insisted on the need for the closest and most sensitive attention to the words on the page, to the exploratory–creative use of words, and hence to the realisation, embodiment and enactment of values in words. Literature became an embodiment of the values of life, 'moral' values in the Arnoldian sense.

A sort of groundbass to a good deal of commentary on Shakespearian drama was formulated by Leavis in his 'Tragedy and the "Medium"', *Scrutiny*, 12 (1943–4), 249–60, reprinted in *The Common Pursuit*. Shakespeare in his mature drama makes an

---

[15] A liberal construction is to be put on the term 'moral'. Cf. Arnold's use of the word in the essay 'Wordsworth', and also of the term 'interpretative'. After calling poetry, because of its conscious synthesis of thought and emotion, 'the most adequate and happy' of all the manifestations 'through which the human spirit pours its force', Arnold concluded: 'This is what we feel to be interpretative for us, to satisfy us – thought, but thought invested with beauty, with emotion.' Fraser Neiman, ed., *Essays, Letters and Reviews by Matthew Arnold* (Cambridge, Mass., 1960), p. 238.

exploratory–creative use of words. Instead of trying to express some preconceived tragic philosophy or thought by putting it across in direct statement, he engages in an exploration of the resources of words so that simultaneously ideas and images create and *realise* themselves in terms of one another, in a sense ensuring that the *medium writes itself*. This belief that the great poet handles the medium of words heuristically and constitutively corresponds with the idea, formulated by D. W. Harding in a *Scrutiny* article ('Aspects of the Poetry of Isaac Rosenberg', *Scrutiny*, 3 (1934–5), 358–69, especially p. 365) and developed in 'The Hinterland of Thought', *Metaphor and Symbol*, ed. L. C. Knights and B. Cottle (Glasgow, 1960), reprinted in D. W. Harding, *Experience into Words* (London, 1963), pp. 175–97, that Shakespearian verse captures thoughts and feelings even in the very process of formation. The view provides a sufficient guarantee against 'the intentional fallacy'.

Most influential of all has been Leavis's advocacy of the educative value of the close reading of poetry and the kind of discrimination it fosters. The faculties of reason, emotion and imaginative sensibility are developed harmoniously; the education of the sensibility should produce mature and responsible individuals able to face the challenge of the modern cultural crisis associated with mass communications, industrialisation, technological advance for its own sake, and the challenge of the dichotomy between mass civilisation and minority culture. These concerns and urgencies, this search for values, activate the poetic approach to varying degrees; they serve as basic promptings behind the Shakespeare criticism of L. C. Knights and D. A. Traversi. G. Wilson Knight's basic stand will be found to be in broad general agreement with these concerns, though not without some reservations which he formulated in '*Scrutiny* and Criticism', *EC*, 14 (1964), 32–6.[16]

[16] Among other important demonstrations of how Shakespearian verse enacts and realises significances is Leavis's reading of speeches in *Macbeth* in *Education and the University* (London, 1948, first edn, 1943), 77–83 and 122–5 and his '*Antony and Cleopatra* and *All for Love*: A Critical Exercise', *Scrutiny*, 5 (1936–7), 158–69. A number of Shakespearian essays by L. C. Knights and D. A. Traversi appeared in *Scrutiny*. A harsh judgement of the value of the Shakespeare criticism which appeared in *Scrutiny* is J. M. Newton's '*Scrutiny's* Failure with

The belief in the discipline of close reading by the poetic critics of Shakespeare and the associated principle of 'critical monism' was encouraged by another factor: the reaction against certain by-then rather stale and overworked academic traditions of scholarship. At one level, the serious one, it seemed an uncritical pursuit of sources, influences, analogues and 'background'. In its would-be lighter or livelier moments, it was biographical anecdotage or fantasy, sentimental gush, literary 'yatter' (Ezra Pound's word) or vague panegyric. Some reaction against apparent academic dilettantism, irrelevancy, triviality, and petty criticism was overdue. More directly, the critics who started giving close attention to the poetry of Shakespeare's plays felt an instinctive distrust of the excesses of historical or 'realist' criticism – and its externalist, mechanist, determinist and reductive tendencies. Not that all the poetic critics were strict 'monists', refusing to use the findings of historical scholarship. As has been seen, the historical scholarship of the thirties and forties and subsequently supplied not only part of the foundation, but structural support.

The elements of poetry which claimed the attention of these critics were imagery, the four-fold complex of meaning (in Richards's terms), thematic patterns, realisation of moral values in terms of poetic texture and, in many cases, significant uses of metaphor, symbol, myth and ritual. One reason for this interest is that these were elements not previously given sufficient attention. Another reason is that these elements predominated in the new poetry of the twenties. The new critical interest in these components of contemporary poetry rapidly extended to the poetry of the past, and the drama of the Renaissance, like the poetry of the 'Metaphysicals', became fruitful areas to explore.

One striking result of the modern critical concern with deeper layers of meaning and their subtle expression was a tendency to associate with poetry qualities of irony, ambiguity, or tension between pairs or series of opposed or ambivalent meanings or ideas, and hence effects of unresolved paradox. Such qualities

Shakespeare', *Cambridge Quarterly*, 1 (1965–6), 144–77. One of Leavis's influential essays is 'Diabolic Intellect and the Noble Hero: A Note on *Othello*' in *Scrutiny*, 6 (1937–8), reprinted in *The Common Pursuit* (London, 1952).

marked the poetry of Eliot, Pound and Yeats, and also some
works of experimental fiction. Eliot, in his comments on
Elizabethan and Jacobean dramatists and the verse of some of the
Metaphysicals, and I. A. Richards in his comments on poems in
Practical Criticism had drawn attention to these qualities in poetry.
William Empson applied them systematically to the close study
and analysis of poetry in his *Seven Types of Ambiguity*, at the
suggestion of Richards and following the example of Robert
Graves and Laura Riding. The practice of seeing in the plays a
conflict of themes, of two concepts set against each other, is allied
to this new kind of reading.[17] The basic concept is the postulation
of 'an open form' in great literature, allowing the dramatisation of
ideas in a straight fight, or the exploitation of a tension (the
assumption being that while this may be psychologically undesirable, it is artistically fruitful) between two attitudes by the
author who can represent both in full by keeping his mind open
to them.[18]

The poetic critics' interpretation of the plays' symbolic and
mythic meanings has generally come to be regarded as the most
distinctive practice of this school; and it has provoked a good deal
of disagreement – though not all the exponents of this approach
offer symbolist interpretations to the same degree. The perception of symbolic connotations in Shakespeare has been the result
of the growth of literature and drama consciously ordered in the
symbolist mode; and the habit has been fostered by a number of
extra-literary factors, which I discuss later in this chapter (see
pp. 57–9). Modern thinking in philosophy and other branches of
knowledge has also made use of symbolic modes,[19] and a good
deal of attention has been paid to the nature of metaphor and
myth and allied topics. The power and value of symbol,

[17] As O. J. Campbell, 'Shakespeare and the "New" Critics', *J. Q. Adams Memorial Studies*, edited by James G. McManaway *et al.* (Washington, DC, 1948), sus-pected.
[18] R. M. Adams, *Strains of Discord: Studies in Literary Openness* (Ithaca, New York, 1958); Cleanth Brooks, *The Well-Wrought Urn* (London, 1947).
[19] A. N. Whitehead, *Symbolism* (1958) and *Science and the Modern World* (1926) and D. G. James, *Scepticism and Poetry* (London, 1937), chapter 1 'The Prime Agent', pp. 15–43. Ernst Cassirer, *The Philosophy of Symbolic Forms* (1923; translated into English, 1953), *Language and Myth* (1946), and *An Essay on Man* (1944; translated 1956) emphasise the role played by symbols in the activity of the human mind.

metaphor and myth, and their integral and indispensable function in all imaginative thought and feeling, both as modes of
apprehension and as modes of expression has been fully recognised.[20] Furthermore, they have served as vital links between the
'contextualism' of the 'new critics' and their belief that literature
should serve as an embodiment of values, and this establishes a
relationship with life, man and society.[21]

Analysis of the significances of symbol, myth and ritual, combined with the habit of regarding literature as an institution – the
only one alive, accessible and actively communicating values –
has facilitated the finding of specifically Christian values in the
plays, their interpretation in terms of the central ideas (or
'myths') of Christianity, and even, at times, in terms of the finer
points of theology. Among the poetic critics, Wilson Knight was
the first to use such ideas in Shakespearian commentary, and it is
a question how far he Christianises in his interpretation. As will
be seen in chapter 3, although he was the first major critic to
identify Christian ideas such as the Resurrection in the plays, his
frame of reference is a private one more or less like Yeats's and
embraces more than his rather idiosyncratic Christology. At any
rate, it is too heterodox to accord with any denomination of
Christianity.[22]

A number of commentators read the plays in the light of their
knowledge of particular or specifically denominational theological traditions of the age of Shakespeare.[23] For instance, Ivor

[20] In Middleton Murry, *The Problem of Style* (Oxford, 1922), especially p. 114, and
Owen Barfield, *Poetic Diction: A study in Meaning* (London, 1928), for example.
[21] Murray Krieger, *A Window to Criticism* (Princeton, 1964), outlines the links.
[22] Both Ronald M. Frye in his *Shakespeare and Christian Doctrine*, and Sylvan Barnet
in his 'Some Limitations of a Christian Approach to Shakespeare', *ELH*, 22
(1955), 81–92, reprinted in Norman Rabkin, ed., *Approaches to Shakespeare*
(McGraw-Hill, 1964), pp. 217–30, hold Wilson Knight responsible for Christianising interpretations. Wilson Knight's rejoinder is in 'Shakespeare and
Theology: A Private Protest', *EC*, 15 (1965), 95–104 and 'Symbolism', a special
article in *A Shakespeare Encyclopaedia* (New York, 1966), edited by O. J. Campbell
and E. G. Quinn, pp. 837–41.
[23] An important early essay is K. O. Myrick, 'The Theme of Damnation in Shakespearean Tragedy', *SP*, 38 (1941), 221–45. Other examples are Roy W. Battenhouse, '*Measure for Measure* and the Christian Doctrine of the Atonement',
PMLA, 61 (1946), 1029–59 and *Shakespearean Tragedy: Its Art and Its Christian
Premises* (Bloomington, 1969); and books by M. D. H. Parker, J. A. Bryant, Jr and
Peter Milward.

Morris, *Shakespeare's God* (London, 1972) with a good deal of flexibility and circumspection, applies an Augustinian emphasis on the need to avoid the besetting sin of insidious glorification or exaltation of the self to a reading of the tragedies, especially in relation to the tragic heroes. Other critics like S. L. Bethell and Paul N. Siegel, for example, study poetic components such as imagery, but interpret them in terms of the central beliefs of Christianity. These developments are striking, for at the beginning of the century the prevailing view was that Shakespearian drama, and Elizabethan drama as a whole, was strictly secular, and that Shakespeare deliberately avoided religious issues. It was also thought that Shakespeare and his contemporary dramatists did not incorporate a scheme of moral and social values into their plays or wish to enquire into them.[24] The reading of religious, specifically Christian, significances into Shakespearian drama has been encouraged by the general readiness to relate the plays to the traditions and currents of thought of Shakespeare's time, and also by the religious revival of the twentieth century, the advent of the 'neo-religionists', and the tendency towards the mystical which led Westerners to Oriental religions such as Zen.

The habit of 'Christianising' has come under fire from rationalists and agnostics who consider such a habit reactionary; from professional theologians who consider the critics' dabbling in theology amateurish and ill-informed; and from those who hold that the secular humanism of Shakespearian drama is traduced in such interpretations.[25] Confronted with a 'Christianising' interpretation, a reader of the play in question will probably ask three questions. Do the eschatological judgements pronounced

[24] A. C. Bradley, George Santayana, Macneile Dixon, and a more recent commentator, Clifford Leech, have proposed what may be called an a-religious attitude in Shakespeare; Bradley thought no scheme of moral values could be deduced from the tragedies. But Arthur Sewell, D. G. James, G. Bush, and Irving Ribner have isolated patterns of moral values from the plays. According to these critics, 'What shall we do to be saved?' is a preoccupation in the plays. Moulton and Jusserand, among older critics, were concerned with the moral sense in Shakespeare. See Aron Y. Stavisky, *Shakespeare and the Victorians: The Roots of Modern Criticism* (Oklahoma, 1969), chapter 3, 'The Moral Victorians', pp. 51–108.

[25] R. M. Frye, *Shakespeare and Christian Doctrine*; Helen Gardner, *The Business of Criticism*; 'The Noble Moor', *PBA*, 42 (1956).

on the characters by the critic fall within the limits of relevance? Does the interpretation from an orthodox religious standpoint entail an undue withdrawal of imaginative sympathy from the central character or characters, so reducing the play to the level of mere exemplum? Does the attribution of typological or analogical religious significances to characters and situations violate their straightforward human or literal meanings?

But there is more to the modern critical climate than formulable doctrines and ideas. One of the factors facilitating a proper appreciation of the role of verse in Shakespearian drama was an increasing recognition of the dramatic element in non-dramatic verse of the past and the predominance of the dramatic element in a good deal of significant modern non-dramatic verse, especially that of Yeats and Eliot. One of the distinctive features of the verse of the Metaphysicals is its dramatic quality. The ready reception that verse finds with modern readers is one of the reasons why the Metaphysicals became fashionable in the twentieth century. In Donne's poetry, the dramatic qualities appear especially pronounced.[26]

Another factor was the development in the writing of fiction of what Stephen Spender called the practice of the 'poetic method'.[27] This is seen in the novels of D. H. Lawrence, James Joyce and Virginia Woolf, to mention the three most prominent novelists. Image and theme, the analysis of the texture of human consciousness through the so-called 'stream of consciousness', or the interior monologue, rather than the conventional categories of narrative plot and externally-defined character, became real foci of interest. The ground for these developments had been prepared by Henry James's Prefaces and in his practice in his fiction. He displayed the seriousness and integrity of the novel as an art-form, its ability to embody moral values, and its need to use the techniques of oblique (hence more effective) communication in imagery and thematic emphases[28] in order to

[26] J. B. Leishman, *The Monarch of Wit* (London, 1951), p. 18, 'in almost all Donne's best poetry there is a dramatic element, an element of personal drama, which is no less characteristic than the argumentative, scholastic or dialectical strain'.
[27] Stephen Spender, *The Struggle of the Modern* (London, 1964), p. 115 and pp. 116–18.
[28] In modern commentary Shakespeare has been compared with Henry James,

realise inner states of consciousness. When the novel in the twenties was bidding fair to turn into poem, it was not surprising that the play-as-poem approach began to command a critical following.

A third influence on the modern critics' interest in the poetry of Shakespeare's plays was the revival of modern poetic drama. Under this heading I consider the views and theories about poetic drama expressed by 'practitioners' as well as critics, the plays composed in this form, and also the new techniques of modern dramatists, as they have bearing on developments in dramatic criticism. Before the verse drama of Gordon Bottomley, Stephen Phillips and others in the second decade of the century, there was the drama of Yeats, and his theories.[29] Lascelles Abercrombie's 'The Function of Poetry in the Drama' had appeared as early as 1912 (in *The Poetry Review*, reprinted in *English Critical Essays*, edited by Phyllis M. Jones (Oxford, 1933)). The advent and vogue of the 'realist' drama of Shaw, Galsworthy and Archer, Shaw's habitual uncomplimentary references to verse drama; and Archer's onslaughts on Elizabethan drama, and its use of verse,[30] offered a challenge and provoked a response in some significant critics who sought to show that verse, at least in many Elizabethan plays, could succeed as a medium for drama. Eliot began to outline his views on poetic drama from the start of his critical as well as his creative career, though his plays themselves

the historian of fine consciences, and his theatre to the theatre of consciousness, as P. R. Grover, 'The Ghost of Dr Johnson: L. C. Knights and D. A. Traversi on *Hamlet', Essays in Criticism* (1967) points out. There is a paradox in the influence of James's art of fiction. A great master and theorist of the novel of psychological realism he was also the inspiration behind the new modes of fiction and literature which, with the emphasis on 'aesthetic' formalism and technique, abandoned realistic conventions.

[29] The 'theatre began in ritual, and it cannot come to its greatness again without recalling words to their ancient sovereignty' W. B. Yeats, 'The Theatre' (1899), *Essays and Introductions* (London, 1961), p. 170.

   Yeats in 'The Tragic Theatre' challenges the notion that 'the dramatic moment is always the contrast of character with character. . . . Character is continuously present in comedy alone.' ('The Tragic Theatre', *Essays and Introductions* (London, 1961), p. 241). 'Tragedy is passion alone, and rejecting character, it gets form from motives, from the wandering of passion; while comedy is clash of character' (Yeats, *Estrangement*, p. 286, cited from *Yeats: Selected Prose*, edited by A. N. Jeffares (London, 1964), p. 114).

[30] William Archer, *The Old Drama and the New* (London, 1923).

were to come later. Eliot's objections to realism in drama were stated forcefully in his essays on Elizabethan dramatists.[31] The revival of poetic drama coincided with the revival of interest in Elizabethan drama, which can be traced back to the Romantics' – especially Lamb's – interest in the Elizabethans. Eliot's essays on the Elizabethan dramatists and his views on poetic drama need to be read against this background. (Significantly, Eliot maintained that Elizabethan dramatic verse was to be avoided as a model by the modern writer of poetic drama.) The result of modern thinking on poetic drama was a firm belief in the indissoluble fusion of poetry and drama, so that the drama lies in the poetry, and the poetry in the drama.

The shift of interest from character and plot to theme which was effected mainly through the poetic critics' commentaries on Shakespeare may be attributable partly to the drama of ideas. Attention was, in effect, redirected to the medium of the words in which drama is couched and to the role of ideas in it, by Ibsen, Shaw and Galsworthy in whose 'discussion drama' the centre of interest was ideas rather than character, character itself being an embodiment, or even a mouthpiece, of ideas. This development intensified the poetic-critics' concern with the words and themes of Shakespearian drama. They may not have been directly influenced by these dramatists,[32] since their thinking emphasised the non-naturalistic aspects of Shakespearian drama and was opposed to realistic drama. These critics obviously have closer affinities with the rebirth of poetic drama, which was a reaction against discussion drama. However, paradoxical as it may seem, the seriousness bestowed on drama by Ibsen, Shaw and Galsworthy, as a medium for the communication through debate of important ideas did help to create the right atmosphere for the poetic-critics' work. So the use of new techniques and modes by British, American and European dramatists, and Western acquaintance with the dramatic traditions of the East, especially

---

[31] For instance, 'For Elizabethan Dramatists', *Selected Essays* (2nd edn), pp. 91–99.

[32] An exception is Wilson Knight, deeply influenced by the drama of Ibsen. Schücking, for all his pioneer role in drawing attention to the conventional basis of Elizabethan drama, admired the drama of Ibsen and Shaw.

India, China and Japan,[33] are parallel developments with, if not
influenced on, the new trends in dramatic criticism.

  Another important development at this time was the formation
of new ideas about the origins, early evolution and later
development of drama. These theories resulted from the impact
of newly-explored areas of knowledge such as the study of folklore, of primitive cultures, of social and cultural anthropology.[34]
Even before anthropology acquired the status of an academic
discipline, or the publication of J. G. Frazer's *The Golden Bough*
(1915), the 'Cambridge' school of classical anthropologists, Jane
Harrison, F. M. Cornford and Gilbert Murray[35] (the last from
Oxford) were putting forward their views on the source of Greek
drama in religious ritual, and the close affinities in structure and
spirit between drama and religious ritual. The researches of E. K.
Chambers and Karl Young on the early evolution of English
drama from religion were also being published. The views of the
'Cambridge' school of Greek scholars were later challenged by
other scholars, especially A. W. Pickard-Cambridge;[36] but the
speculations caught on, and in the twenties and thirties assumptions tended to be taken as facts. T. S. Eliot's views were particularly influenced by theories about the ritual origin of drama.[37] The

---

[33] Translations of drama from Sanskrit, and the Noh and Kabuki plays of Japan
    made possible Western acquaintance with dramatic traditions which rely on
    symbolic modes rather than 'character in action'. W. B. Yeats, 'Certain Noble
    Plays of Japan'. *Essays and Introductions* (London, 1961) and H. W. Wells. 'Indian
    Drama and the West', *The Journal of Commonwealth Literature* (No. 1, September
    1965) 86–94.

[34] Edward Tylor, *Primitive Culture* (1871) and Andrew Lang's writings are among
    the earliest examples of such studies.

[35] R. R. Marett, ed., *Anthropology and the Classics* (Oxford, 1908); Jane Harrison,
    Themis (1912) and *Ancient Art and Ritual* (1913); Gilbert Murray, *Euripides and his
    Age* (1913), *The Rise of the Greek Epic* (1907), and 'Hamlet and Orestes', *The
    Classical Tradition in Poetry* (1927); F. M. Cornford, *The Origin of Attic Comedy*
    (1914); Lord Raglan, *The Hero* (1936); and Joseph Campbell, *The Hero with a
    Thousand Faces* (1956).

[36] A. W. Pickard-Cambridge, *The Dramatic Festivals at Athens* (Oxford, 1927) and
    Dithyramb, Ritual and Tragedy (Oxford, 1927). Also Sir William Ridgeway, 'An
    Appendix on the Origin of Greek Comedy', *The Dramas and Dramatic Dances of
    Non-European Races in special reference to the Origin of Greek Comedy* (Cambridge,
    1915) refuted the Cornford hypothesis. So does H. D. F. Kitto, 'Greek Tragedy
    and Dionysus', *TS*, 1 (1960).

[37] As witness his 'The Beating of a Drum' in *The Nation and the Athenaeum*, 34
    (6 October 1923), pp. 11–12, and his 'Dialogue on Dramatic Poetry', *Selected
    Essays* (London, 1932).

poetic critics of Shakespeare cannot all have believed in these theories; but their thinking was influenced to some extent by such assumptions.

The way speculations about the origin and early growth of drama were related to the findings of anthropology illustrates the striking intercommunication between modern literary criticism and the new sciences of the twentieth century.[38] The parallel developments in and the indirect influence of new philosophies like logical positivism, and, latterly, the philosophy of 'symbolic forms', are striking enough to command attention. Modern literary criticism, and modern creative literature as well, show the influence of modern psychology, first of Freud's ideas and psychoanalytic techniques, and then of Jung's. The exploration of the manifold nature of human personality, and the existence of layers of consciousness within it – the unconscious, the subconscious, and the 'collective unconscious' – has had an equivalent impact. Apart from the direct application by professional or amateur psychologist-critics (the second outnumbering the first) of psychoanalytical techniques to literary analysis (which Freud paved the way for, as 'a man of literature' in the Johnsonian sense), the key ideas of psychology passed into the common stock of instruments of literary criticism. One could well suppose that reliance on techniques of obliqueness in modern literature, and the sensitivity to oblique modes of expression in the literature of the past are partly attributable to the findings of psychology becoming part of the modern climate of opinion.[39] Leading literary-critical theorists, such as Yeats, Eliot and Lawrence were, either intuitively or as a result of influence, putting forward ideas which bore a relationship to modern psychological and anthropological findings. Similar discoveries were reflected in their creative work. In his critical theories, I. A. Richards registered perhaps the fullest and most acute response to the new psychology – in its behaviourist and positivist forms at first and, in his later writings, to its less material and more 'mythically' oriented

---

[38] Stanley Edgar Hyman (*The Armed Vision*, p. 3) shows how 'the *organised use* of non-literary techniques and bodies of knowledge to obtain insights into literature' is a unique feature of modern literary criticism.

[39] Graham Hough, *Image and Experience* (London, 1960).

manifestations. Richards's early inclination towards logical positivism, with its semantic rigours and its insistence on the evidence of sense experience, often reduced to neural sensation, yielded place, in his later development, to more general, open philosophies of communication. F. C. Prescott made pioneering use of Freudian and Jungian ideas. His distinction in *The Poetic Mind* (1922) between 'conscious meanings' and 'unconscious meanings' in poetry can be looked upon as a sort of charter, unrecognised, for a good deal of critical commentary which followed later. In Shakespearian criticism, the effect was that the poetic critics could discover a number of 'unconscious meanings' through their characteristic attention to indirect rather than direct suggestion, to associations of speech and to such modes of communication as metaphor and symbol. But more significant than the implications of Freudian findings is the impact of Jungian ideas. Jung's theory of a common 'collective unconscious', a departure from the Freudian idea of the individual unconscious, and his fortunate discovery that the collective unconscious is a rich storehouse of 'myths' usually embodied in 'primordial images' or 'archetypes' which can be found in mythology and literature, have been of great importance to the poetic criticism of Shakespearian drama.

The interest of the poetic critics in metaphor and symbol, in myth and ritual, increasing with the passage of time,[40] has turned out to be a major preoccupation. It has for its frame of reference the new critical absorption in the word and the ramifications of semantic suggestion, and also the anthropological and Jungian accent on symbolic values in language, thought and feeling. Two early attempts to draw upon insights of this kind are the little-known *Poetry and Myth* (1927) by F. C. Prescott, and the influential book by Maud Bodkin, *Archetypal Patterns in Poetry* (1934). The vulgarisation of psychological theories, such as the mindless use of Jungian concepts such as the Persona or the Mask, the anima–animus (the male–female principle) interrelationship, and above all the concept of psychic rebirth and the mechanical application of the rebirth-archetype to literary study, are to be

[40] Robert B. Heilman, 'Historian and Critic: Notes on Attitudes', *SR*, 73 (1965), 426–44, brings out the shift of emphasis towards myth in recent criticism.

deplored. Nonetheless the insights once had freshness, and usefulness and, properly handled, they still have power.

It may be helpful to go into a little more detail about the
relationship of T. S. Eliot's critical theories to trends in the poetic
criticism of Shakespeare.[41] Eliot's critical utterances about
Shakespeare were small in number but great in influence.[42]
Besides his notorious essay on *Hamlet* ('most certainly an artistic
failure'[43]), in which there was already embedded the influential
concept of the 'objective correlative', there are his essays on the
Elizabethan and Jacobean dramatists and on the metaphysical
poets. The essays on the Elizabethan dramatists drew the
reader's attention to the quality, especially the rhythm and
imagery, of Elizabethan dramatic verse; and the essay on the
metaphysical poets put forward the concept of a 'dissociation of
sensibility' which, though recently vigorously challenged was,
historically speaking, the guideline for modern studies of
sixteenth- and seventeenth-century drama and poetry. As one
looks back on it, Eliot's account of the use of 'myth' in literature,
seen in relation to his own practice in *The Waste Land*, in his
review of Joyce's *Ulysses*,[44] especially the remark, 'Instead of
narrative method, we may now use the "mythical" method', is a
prophetic pointing towards the road which Shakespearian criticism was to take. In 'Shakespeare and the Stoicism of Seneca',
Eliot considered the question of the relationship between the
poet-dramatist and the philosophy of life he presents in his
writings. His view was that the poet-dramatist expressed 'the
emotional equivalent of thought rather than thought itself', the

[41] Helen Gardner, 'Shakespeare in the Age of Eliot', *TLS* (23 April 1964), 335–6.
Also C. B. Watson, 'T. S. Eliot and the Interpretation of Shakespeare in our
Time', *Études Anglaises*, 19 (1964), 502–22 and Philip L. Marcus, 'T. S. Eliot and
Shakespeare', *Criticism*, 9 (1967), 63–79.

[42] Apart from 'The Problem of Hamlet' and 'Shakespeare and the Stoicism of
Seneca', there are stray comments in other essays, and an essay on the earlier
Shakespeare critics in *A Companion to Shakespeare Studies*, edited by
H. Granville-Barker and G. B. Harrison (Cambridge, 1934). His lecture on the
last plays has not been printed. But poems like 'Coriolan' and 'Marina' are
inspired by the study of the plays, and Wilson Knight's commentary on them.

[43] 'I was then hand in glove with the critical methods of J. M. Robertson' – Eliot, *To
Criticize the Critic*, p. 19.

[44] 'Ulysses, Order and Myth', first published in *The Dial*, 5 (1923); reprinted in
Forms of Modern Fiction, edited by William O'Connor (Minneapolis, 1948),
p. 123.

first expression of his theory of 'poetic thought'. Significantly, in this essay, Eliot outlined his attitude towards the character of the tragic hero in Shakespearian drama. He did this in his unsympathetic reading of the dying speeches of Hamlet and Othello, seen as an egoistic 'cheering oneself up'. This initial phase in Eliot's thought shows a thorough distrust of personality and its expression in literature. The later, significant revision of his impersonal theory of poetry was made in the Yeats Memorial lecture delivered in 1940; but as early as 1932, in his essay on John Ford,[45] Eliot was insisting on the need to see the body of Shakespeare's work as a totality, and to consider his development – an indirect acknowledgement of the need to relate the plays to 'the poetic personality' of Shakespeare. Of interest too, is Eliot's suggestion that in our reading of past literature, more important than the need to transport ourselves, with the help of our historical sense, into the past age and its climate, is the need to approximate the age and the work to our modern sensibility. This may not be totally unconnected with the partly anti-historical bias of a good deal of 'new' critical commentary on past literature, especially on Shakespeare. Eliot's emphasis on the relationship between literary qualities and the cultural values of the society producing the literary work has also been influential.

Related to the changed, modern attitude to character in Shakespearian drama is the twentieth-century anti-Renaissance, anti-Romantic and anti-humanist rejection of the claims of personality – an askesis and attempt to quell the ego, or efface the personality. With this rejection are associated the names of T. E. Hulme, Pound and the early Eliot. The trend found support in the authoritarianism of the period, in the Anglo-Catholic revival, in the general temperament of the neo-religionists and the neo-mystics, and in the anti-heroic, 'debunking' attitude of modern man, an attitude sometimes touched with cynicism, as in the biographies of Lytton Strachey. The hero – already in eclipse in Victorian fiction – declined into the anti-hero or the unheroic hero in modern fiction and in a good deal of modern drama. It is in a way understandable that, often as a result of unconscious projec-

---

[45] 'John Ford', *Selected Essays* (1932), p. 196.

tion, the stature of the Shakespearian hero is scaled down in modern criticism, though he is seldom reduced to the level of the modern unheroic hero. By the same token, new concepts of character and new modes of character-portrayal, influenced or paralleled by the new psychological ideas employed in modern fiction and drama, point to a rejection of the old, comparatively simple, orderly notions of character in Shakespeare criticism.[46]

[46] D. H. Lawrence announced the disappearence of 'the old stable ego of the character' as early as 1914 (*Letters of D. H. Lawrence*, edited by Aldous Huxley, (London, 1932), pp. 197–8). Though Lawrence did not regard the tragic protagonists in Shakespeare as unheroic, he found fault with what he considered their egoism and thus anticipated a good deal of modern criticism, which is opposed to the narcissistic nature of the tragic hero.

> I can't very much care about the woes and tragedies
> Of Lear and Macbeth and Hamlet and Timon.
> They cared so excessively about themselves.
>
> *Collected Poems*, p. 508

3

The 'spatial' interpretation of Wilson Knight – I

Pre-eminent among the exponents of the new poetic interpretation of Shakespeare is G. Wilson Knight. Besides initiating a new approach,[1] he provided a theoretical framework for it and applied it to the various plays, with interesting variations, in book after book for upwards of three decades. He is, in one sense, a typical representative of major trends in modern criticism and in Shakespeare criticism in particular. Yet, in another sense, he is not only different from, but opposed to, the general run of modern critics; there is a paradoxical relationship between modern criticism and his substantial contribution to it, which remains both within and outside it. The historical importance of his interpretation is obvious, in view of its currency; its intrinsic value, which is no less remarkable, lies in the extreme individuality of his perceptions and insights, the obverse of which is a more-easily noticed and frequently-deplored eccentricity of view. He has been accused of writing non-criticism or metacriticism, and of reading into Shakespeare and other texts ideas belonging to those quasi-esoteric or spiritualist philosophies which are his hobbyhorses. It is a measure of the vitality of

---

[1] John Jones ('Shakespeare and Mr Wilson Knight', *The Listener*, vol. 52, 1954, pp. 1011–12) seems to have been the first to recognise this: the reason why we look at Shakespeare in a new way is that 'in 1930 Mr Wilson Knight published *The Wheel of Fire*' and the book 'marks the greatest advance in the understanding of Shakespeare, since the time Coleridge was lecturing, 140-odd years ago'. Deploring the general lack of recognition of this, he goes on: 'And so the claim is not Wilson Knight was responsible for the modern revolution in critical method; in fact, I am going to argue that he stands outside the movement; it is simply that he had something to say about Shakespeare that was new and of the first importance' (p. 1011).

Wilson Knight's commentaries that they should provoke extremes of approval and disagreement. Whatever our reservations about his subjectivism or his pursuit of extra-literary interests in the name of interpretation, the energy and devotion which inform the commentaries have to be acknowledged. What is more, his intuitions about the plays, requiring as they do the correctives of historical scholarship, at an equal number of points seem to coincide with scholarly findings. Wilson Knight's experience in the staging of Shakespeare, experimental and idiosyncratic as it was, enabled him to write with an eye on how the play is realised in the theatre.

Though the work which had a revolutionary impact on later Shakespeare criticism, *The Wheel of Fire*, came out in 1930 (an *annus mirabilis* in Shakespearian commentary which saw the publication of William Empson's *Seven Types of Ambiguity*, Mgr Kolbë's *Shakespeare's Way* and Caroline Spurgeon's *Leading Motives in Shakespeare's Imagery* among other books), Wilson Knight had been trying out his new theories in the mid and late twenties in essays on Shakespeare which appeared in *The New Adelphi* and *The Shakespeare Review*. His first interpretative work, on the last plays, appeared in 1929 as a monograph entitled *Myth and Miracle*.[2]

From the beginning, Wilson Knight has taken care to state the theory behind his approach to Shakespearian drama. He has always been conscious of breaking new ground in interpretation, at times showing a characteristically modern self-consciousness, and he has been at pains to elucidate and defend his interpretations against objections and misconceptions.[3]

---

[2] Reprinted in *The Crown of Life* (1947). *Thaisa*, on the last plays, written in 1928, was never published.

[3] 'The Principles of Shakespeare Interpretation', his 'manifesto' orginally published in *The Shakespeare Review* (1928); 'The Poet and Immortality' (1929), and 'On the Principles of Shakespearian Interpretation', both in *The Wheel of Fire* (1930); 'Imaginative Interpretation' in *The Imperial Theme* (1931); Introduction to *The Shakespearian Tempest* (1932); 'The Prophetic Imagination', 'Symbolism', 'The Shakespearian Art-Form', 'The Seraphic Intuition', in *The Christian Renaissance* (1933 and 1962); *Tolstoy's Attack on Shakespeare* (1934). 'The Shakespearian Play' and 'Shakespeare and Ritual' in *Principles of Shakespearian Production* (1936); and *Shakespearian Production* (1965); 'The Shakespearian Integrity' in *The Burning Oracle* (1939); the preface to the 1953 edition of *The Shakespearian Tempest*; *The Crown of Life* (1947); 'The New Interpretation' in *Essays in Criticism*

It is more profitable to think of his interpretative venture as inspired by a fruitful interaction between his individual talent and both the tradition and the contemporary practice of Shakespearian studies, rather than as a revolt pure and simple; though one may trace both revolutionary departure from and continuity with certain lines of tradition. Wilson Knight's efforts, doubtless, sprang from a deep dissatisfaction with the contemporary state and traditional branches of Shakespeare study. To the ordinary observer, he is the man who led the revolt against Bradley and against 'character'. Yet, at the start of his career, Wilson Knight acknowledged Bradley as a pioneer, however faintly, of the approach to a play through its 'atmosphere', and claimed that he had only developed certain perceptions of Bradley's.[4]

As a convenient shorthand term for his approach, Wilson Knight called it the 'spatial' interpretation, using a metaphor. The approach entailed a radically new conception of the nature and function of Shakespearian drama in that, instead of attending to the temporal sequence of dramatic incidents and situations, it envisaged a play as a *shape* in space, rather than an event. This conception was at once the cause and effect of attention being directed to certain elements in drama hitherto unregarded – or at least not given primary status. The result was that new and active interconnections came to be perceived among these elements and between them and the more conventionally recognised elements. This concerned the imagistic and thematic suggestions of the verse, or the prose for that matter; the dramatic shapes and colours; the presentation on stage of persons, places and proper-

(1953); 'Symbolic Eternities' in *The Laureate of Peace* (1954); 'Some Notable Fallacies' in *The Sovereign Flower* (1958); 'New Dimensions in Shakespearian Interpretation' (1959), reprinted in *Shakespeare and Religion* (1967); 'Scrutiny and Criticism' in *Essays in Criticism* (1964); 'J. Middleton Murry' in *Of Books and Humankind* (1964); 'Shakespeare and Theology' in *Essays in Criticism* (1965); and 'Symbolism' in *A Shakespeare Encyclopaedia* (1966); besides a number of letters to various journals.

4 Wilson Knight pays tribute to Bradley several times. 'Symbolism' in *A Shakespeare Encyclopaedia*, p. 837 and p. 840; *Shakespeare and Religion*, pp. 200–1; *SF*, p. 287 and p. 291. But in a brief general study of Wilson Knight, Arthur M. Eastman in his *A Short History of Shakespearean Criticism* (New York, 1968) stresses the obvious differences between Knight and Bradley, while taking note of Bradley's influence on, and anticipation of, Knight, by instancing both the critics' interpretations of *Macbeth* (chapter 12, 'G. Wilson Knight', 239–49, especially p. 247).

ties, which Wilson Knight would characterise as symbols; and sound effects, offstage and onstage. Such cross-references could be made easily once the play came to be seen as extending in space, rather like a map or unrolled tapestry; or like a vast picture with certain elements – generally referred to as symbols, images, suggestions, overtones – standing out like features on a relief map. Instead of considering primarily the sequence of plot, (which is the sequence of time) or of character in action in linear fashion, Wilson Knight wants the play to be seen as having new dimensions, as existing in 'a fourth dimension', in a space–time continuum rather than in mere time or space. It is to this kind of reception that Wilson Knight's 'spatialising' of the plays leads. This concept lifts the Shakespeare play to a new level of existence. Another analogy which might help our understanding of Wilson Knight's theory may be drawn from the geometry of distinct planes in space, as in projective geometry; Wilson Knight's technique, as it works in practice, is to project what appear to be surface features or realities of the plays to other different planes of reality or, at times, remote planes of infinity. In other words, what Wilson Knight is able to achieve in his imaginative vision of a play is a Bergsonian interiorising of time as space. This is misunderstood by those who hold Wilson Knight guilty of a neglect of the temporal orientation of drama. Dramatic action does indeed unfold itself in a temporal sequence; but in his interpretative re-experience of it, the critic need not be blinkered by this fact, and surrender the freedom of an imaginative reconstruction of the drama in a space–time continuum. This has the important effect that the whole play is held in the mind as structure, and all the parts referred to each other. Wilson Knight's spatialisation of drama (and poems, as witness his study of Pope, *The Laureate of Peace*, and of the Romantics, *The Starlit Dome*) is analogous, in literary commentary, to the dominance of spatial form in modern creative literature and of the space-orientation of modern culture emphasised by Walter J. Ong and Marshall McLuhan, and described by Joseph Frank.[5] It is also worth noting

---

[5] 'Spatial Form in Modern Literature' (1945), reprinted in *Criticism: The Foundation of Modern Literary Judgment*, edited by Mark Schorer, Josephine Miles and Gordon Mckenzie (New York, 1948).

that Wilson Knight envisages not only the single play or group of
plays but the whole canon as a picture in space, almost in a single
act of mind.

Wilson Knight's insistence on the distinction between criticism
and interpretation, and on his claim that his own work is
interpretation and not criticism may seem obsessive or whimsi-
cal.[6] The validity of the distinction may be questioned.[7] Yet a
similar distinction between what he termed inductive and judi-
cial criticism had been made earlier by R. G. Moulton (some of
whose 'interpretations' in certain respects suggest modern
analysis).[8] In place of the detached, objective intellectual assessment, of the judgements of value and of quality which criticism
requires, interpretation is based upon personal emotional
engagement in the literary work, in the belief that its value or
quality is beyond question. The distinction, as Wilson Knight
puts it, at once calls attention to certain characteristics of his kind
of commentary and gives a defence against charges of omission
and commission brought against him. For one thing, the
interpreter has a licence, 'the liberty of interpreting', which is
denied to the critic. For another, the interpreter is not obliged to
see the work interpreted steadily and to see it whole and to take
into account all the parts and elements in a balanced mode of
apprehension and expression. In matters of emphasis or proportion, the interpreter enjoys a comparative freedom.[9]
Furthermore, he is not obliged to make critical discriminations of
poetic quality. Hence the personal validity of the distinction for

[6] On occasion Knight himself forgets the distinction. 'On the Principles of
Shakespeare Interpretation', *WF* (1949 edn), p. 16.
[7] 'In recent criticism the formal act of judgment tends to be subsumed under
interpretation', Graham Hough, *An Essay on Criticism* (1966), p. 67. 'The concept of adequacy of interpretation leads clearly to the concept of correctness of
judgment' – Wellek, *Concepts of Criticism*, p. 18.
[8] Wilson Knight notes the significance of Moulton's commentary in his preface to
Shakespeare and Religion, p. vi, n., though he does not note that the distinction
was originally made by Moulton, *Shakespeare as a Dramatic Artist* (Oxford, 1892),
pp. 2–5.
[9] E. D. Hirsch, Jr, 'Objective Interpretation', *PMLA*, 75 (1960), elaborates the
distinction between interpretation and criticism, citing the authority of August
Boeckh, *Encyclopädie und Methodologie der philologischen Wissenschaften*, ed. E.
Bratuscheck (Leipzig, 1886), p. 170. Interpretation is concerned with meaning,
while criticism is concerned with the 'relevance' of the text, in a larger context.

Wilson Knight and its central place in the general design and operation of his commentaries.[10]

Such are the objectives of 'spatial' interpretation and its distinction from criticism. The practical principles advocated by Wilson Knight are of two kinds: the rejection of certain conventional frames of reference, speculative instruments or categories of thought; and the adoption of certain new axes of reference and coordinates of interrelationship, the negative or destructive force of his attempt being as important as the positive contribution.

Basically, Wilson Knight's stress is on intrinsic commentary and on the integrity of Shakespearian drama (which had then to be defended against the 'disintegration' vigorously afoot). Insofar as it directs attention to the work itself, his commentary is in line with the characteristic tendency of modern criticism to concentrate on the 'words on the page', but it is so only in a limited sense. Wilson Knight's conception of the reality of Shakespearian drama, of its mode of existence and function, led him to underscore its poetic quality, its poetic essence. This in turn gave him a sense that traditional approaches to Shakespearian drama failed to perceive it as it really was. In contemporary Shakespearian studies, Wilson Knight noted the continuing treatment of the plays as novels and stories, to the neglect of the poetic qualities; and the more recent tendency to consider the plays in terms of their dramatic and theatrical possibilities. The tendency of historical scholars to explain the plays in terms of their sources, and the theatrical scholars' habit of emphasising the intentions of the dramatist as a commercial playwright seem especially to have provoked his disapproval. To counter these tendencies and bring out the nature and function of Shakespearian poetic drama, he enunciated his theory and principles of interpretation in clear, analytic terms, which appear too schematic when compared with his flexible and varied interpretative

[10] Wilson Knight anticipated Northrop Frye (*Anatomy of Criticism*) in his claim for freedom for the literary commentator from the obligation to make qualitative judgements. Wilson Knight outlined a theoretical basis for, and practised, what is known as the 'criticism of consciousness' which is associated with the Geneva school of critics, and with J. Hillis Miller and which involves the critics' spatialisation of, and immersion in, the consciousness of an author as revealed in the whole of his work. Cf. Wellek, *Concepts of Criticism*, p. 216. 'I suspect that Georges Poulet (a critic of the Genevan school) had read Wilson Knight.'

practice. Among the principles he laid down are 'absolute loyalty
to our aesthetic reaction to the poetry', 'truth to our own imaginative reaction', 'a new artistic ethic'; the strictly 'intrinsic' approach; attention to the peculiarities of style in each play, to the
imaginative and intellectual atmosphere of each play, to the
'world' of the play; attention to the 'Shakespeare Progress' as
evidenced in the group of plays from *Julius Caesar* (1599) to *The
Tempest* (1611); and the importance of 'direct poetic symbolism'
and the examination and correlation of Shakespeare's poetic
imagery throughout the whole canon.

A Shakespearian tragedy is set spatially as well as temporally in the
mind. By this I mean that there are throughout the play a set of correspondences which relate to each other independently of the time
sequence which is the story.   (*The Wheel of Fire* (1949 edition), p. 3)

we should regard each play as a visionary whole, close-knit in personifi-
cation, atmospheric suggestion, and direct poetic symbolism: three
modes of transmission, equal in their importance.   (p. 11)

a true philosophic and imaginative interpretation will aim at cutting
below the surface to reveal that burning core of mental or spiritual reality
from which the play derives its nature and meaning.   (p. 14)

in Shakespeare there is this close fusion of the temporal, that is, the
plot-chain of event following event, with the spatial, that is, the omnipresent and mysterious reality brooding motionless over and within the
play's movement.   (pp. 4–5)

We should thus be prepared to recognize what I have called the 'temporal' and the 'spatial' elements: that is, to relate any given incident or
speech either to the time-sequence of story or the peculiar atmosphere,
intellectual or imaginative, which binds the play . . . we should not look
for perfect verisimilitude to life, but rather see each play as an expanded
metaphor, by means of which the original vision has been projected into
forms roughly correspondent with actuality, conforming thereto with
greater or less exactitude according to the demands of its own nature.
                                                          (pp. 14–15)

These and similar utterances have been repeatedly quoted as
setting forth the essential principles of Wilson Knight's commentary. It is interesting that an often-quoted, extreme statement in
the original edition of *The Wheel of Fire* (p. 16), 'The persons,
ultimately, are not human at all, but purely symbols of a poetic

vision', was deleted in the revised and enlarged edition of the book in 1949.

The implications of these hermeneutic principles are significant and varied. They can be divided into three kinds – aesthetic, metaphysical, and ethical or 'religious'.[11] The ontological and epistemological deficiencies of the aesthetic behind Wilson Knight's interpretation have been well brought out by Morris Weitz who, with characteristic scepticism, holds the ontological venture in literary commentary futile.[12] The intuitive, expressionist, roots in Croce of Wilson Knight's conceptions and the affinity with Pater and Longinus in his impressionistic response to the plays are easily noticed. The projective technique of 'spatial' analysis was fundamentally an attempt to invest the primarily temporal art of literature and drama with dimensions of space. The attempt tended to collapse one art into another, to obliterate distinctions of medium, by interchanging characteristic modes of expression, in the way that Croce approximated one art to the other. This aesthetic is juxtaposed, but is in no way linked, to a metaphysic which is a highly individual combination (those not in sympathy would call it a gallimaufrey) of ideas culled from disparate sources.

The approach has led Wilson Knight to see in the plays, 'an omnipresent and mysterious reality brooding motionless over and within the play's movement'.[13] The belief in a set of metaphysical values goes with a tendency, ultimately Hegelian, though with Nietzchean and Bergsonian overtones, to think in terms of a dialectical pattern of antinomies. Everyday ethical standards which are usually applied to the judgement of Shakespeare's characters and to the placing of them as good and evil are rejected as inadequate. The interpenetration of good and evil, good in evil characters and evil in good characters, and their

[11] As will be seen later , the 'religious' frame of reference alters. The early Wilson Knight uses a number of Christian concepts. The later Wilson Knight seems to have left the Anglican communion (the implication of his statement about his brother and T. S. Eliot in 'T. S. Eliot. Some Literary Impressions', *SR* (1966), p. 251). The later Wilson Knight's religion is a private affair, so idiosyncratically mystic and visionary that it could be called a religious 'non-religion'.
[12] *Hamlet and the Philosophy of Literary Criticism* (Chicago and London, 1964), pp. 34 and 314.
[13] Knight, *WF*, pp. 4–5.

attainment to a state beyond good and evil make a new, supra-ethical approach necessary.[14]

In the earliest writings one could easily isolate the immediate and acknowledged influence of the commentaries of John Middleton Murry and John Masefield. In particular, Masefield's Romanes Lecture of 1924, 'Shakespeare and Spiritual Life' (reprinted in *Recent Prose*, 1932), seems to have been a source of inspiration and an abiding influence. So was Colin Still's interpretation of *The Tempest, Shakespeare's Mystery Play* published in 1921.[15] The stage, the theatre, Wilson Knight's own experience of it, are also important influences' especially important for his 'spatial' view of drama was his early impressions of the productions of Henry Beerbohm Tree and Gordon Craig as well as those of William Poel and Granville-Barker.[16] His 'spatial' view of drama and literature is, on Wilson Knight's own admission, influenced by Lessing's *Laocoön*, Nietzsche's *The Birth of*

[14] This concept of categories beyond good and evil is influenced by Nietzsche. Wilson Knight's view that average ethical standards are inapplicable or inadequate to Shakespeare can be contrasted with Alfred Harbage's view and that of Russell A. Fraser. Harbage, *As They Liked It*; Fraser, *Shakespeare's Poetics in relation to 'King Lear'* (London, 1962).
   Eugene M. Waith, *The Herculean Hero in Marlowe, Chapman and Shakespeare* (London, 1962) and also *Ideas of Greatness: Heroic Drama in England* (London, 1971) has used the idea of the superman, not so much in Nietzschean terms as in those of the late medieval and Renaissance interpretation of the Hercules myth. The Hero in a play of this kind is modelled on Hercules. With his excess of heroic virtue, he rises above the common degree of human virtue, and compels admiration.

[15] Wilson Knight says that he read Colin Still's book after he had written *Thaisa* (unpublished) and *Myth and Miracle*; but, surely, he makes references to *The Timeless Theme* (the 1936 version of Colin Still's work) in *The Crown of Life* (1947). However, in *Shakespeare and Religion*, p. 201, Wilson Knight admits Colin Still's 'thesis had apparently been known to me before, since a note on an early review of it turned up later among my papers'.

[16] 'Since my own Shakespearian commentary has been so largely given to exposing, by a mental spatializing or staging, Shakespeare's more elemental, colourful and spiritual properties, its relation to Tree's productions may be assumed' – Wilson Knight, 'Tree and Craig; Poel and Barker', in *Shakespearian Production*, p. 210. Wilson Knight notes the debt his account of Caliban owes to Tree.
   'His interpretations of Shakespeare do not please the academicians for he approaches the plays as an actor, but an exceptional actor who thinks about the work he is interpreting as a vision of life. He therefore interprets them as moral and human works and above all practical in relation to his life, his own life seen in imagination, as though the plays were written for him.' C. B. Purdom in a letter in *The Listener*, vol. 52 (23 December 1954), p. 1120.

Tragedy, and the views of the French aesthetic and dramatic theorist of the last century, François Delsarte.[17] The 'religious' reference of Wilson Knight's approach and findings is difficult to analyse. In gerneral discussions, a 'Christianising' tendency is ascribed to Wilson Knight who is frequently described as the originator of this tendency. As I have already pointed out (see p. 51), Wilson Knight in some of his earlier writings certainly used Christian concepts and specific Christian references. But one could trace in the later writings an attempt to burst the bounds of Christianity and to think in terms of a heterodox compound of visionary religious ideas. The use of such an ideological frame of reference is, ultimately, like the practice of several other significant modern critics.[18]

Wilson Knight's response to the work of the early analysts of Shakespeare's imagery in the twenties was a complex one. Though Caroline Spurgeon published her findings about Shakespeare's imagery in pamphlets as late as 1930, she had earlier been giving lectures in London in which she presented her findings. Wilson Knight may or may not have known about these lectures; it is hardly necessary to postulate the influence of Spurgeon on Wilson Knight's first works of interpretation.[19] Among other literary influences D. H. Lawrence may be noted. Though Wilson Knight found fault with Swinburne's panegyrical commentary, the influence of both Swinburne and Pater is writ large on Wilson Knight's pages. The metaphysical and ideological influences in the early writings and the religious and spiritualist influences in the later are so disparate that one might

---

[17] See *The Laureate of Peace* (London, 1955), pp. 80–90.
[18] 'In other American critics such as R. P. Blackmur and Kenneth Burke or in the English critic G. Wilson Knight the function and claims of criticism are similarly expanded to make criticism something like a total world-view or even a system of philosophy' – Wellek, *Concepts of Criticism*, p. 34.
[19] That Wilson Knight may owe some of his interest in Shakespeare's imagery in his pre-1930 writings (the influence of Spurgeon on *The Imperial Theme* is clear enough) to Caroline Spurgeon's lectures was suggested by Allardyce Nicoll and by Stanley Edgar Hyman. Nicoll, *The Year's Work in English Studies*, 11 (1930), p. 151 and 12 (1931), p. 149, and Hyman, *The Armed Vision*, p. 220. Wilson Knight has discounted the influence. Another study, influenced by the methods of Spurgeon, and which might have influenced Wilson Knight, is Una Ellis-Fermor's book on Marlowe. Wilson Knight acknowledges the influence of her *Christopher Marlowe* (London, 1927), in the preface to *Shakespeare and Religion*, p. vi.

think that Wilson Knight's private religion, his visionary synthesis, is a system which is as much of a medley as Yeats's private
mythology. Indeed, his private religion bears a relationship to
Wilson Knight's commentary very similar to the one which
Yeats's system bears to his poetry. Yet certain preoccupations
recur. Governing ideological emphases are: the Bergsonian concept of *élan vital*, appearing as the theme of life-force; an almost
Kierkegaardian insistence on the paradoxical union of negative
with positive emphases in the idea of death; the Nietzschean
dialectic of the Apollonian and the Dionysian, and later the
Nietzschean concept of the superman and the reconciliation of
paradoxes in the ideal of the superman. These go with a highly
individualised concept of royalism and the visionary notion of
patriotism which accompanies it (and which could become a
vehicle of practical war propaganda in *The Olive and the Sword*,
1944).[20] These convictions are reinforced in turn by Manichean
and Blakean views of the relations between good and evil; the
belief in an ideal of bisexuality, the fusion of masculine and
feminine principles; an actor's interest in the possibilities for
expression of the human body; and, in the later phases, a Yeat-
sian faith in occultism and spiritualist ideas and experiences. That
such disparate ideas culled from sources so unrelated to one
another, should go to make up the general ideological frame of
reference for Wilson Knight's interpretative commentary is not as
surprising as it seems, and is part of the general wide search
for ideological moorings by writer and critic in our age. Small
wonder that S. E. Hyman characterises it as 'oracular and
nebulous'.[21]

Summing up the general outcome of his findings at two different stages of his career, Wilson Knight isolated the following
significant results of his interpretation: (i) the tempest-music
motif, (ii) the last plays as 'myths of immortality', (iii) the 'crown'
idea and (iv) the importance of what he calls 'direct poetic symbolism', especially such as has to do with the supernatural and

[20] Richard C. Clark, 'Shakespeare's Contemporary Relevance', *A Review of
National Literatures: Shakespeare and his England*, edited by J. G. McManaway, 3
(1972), 185–97, considers royalism and patriotism one of the central preoccupations of Wilson Knight's commentary (especially pp. 191–6).
[21] *The Armed Vision*, p. 236.

the occult. The real questions are: which of these are the best fruits of his interpretation; whether it is better to trust the interpretation and never to trust the interpreter and his theory; and whether there is a conflict between his theory and his actual interpretative practice? I will attempt to answer these questions as I demonstrate how Wilson Knight's 'method' actually works, and how, in his manner of proceeding with the plays, his 'method' undergoes shifts and modifications.

Among his contributions, there are his illuminating insights into new aspects of, and new relations in, familiar plays such as the great tragedies; there are what may be called his rehabilitations of the less familiar and generally neglected plays such as *Troilus and Cressida, Measure for Measure, All's Well that Ends Well, Coriolanus* and *Timon of Athens*; there are the new significances which he sees in the last plays; and, finally, there are the patterns and emphases perceived by him throughout the plays as a whole or in groups of plays.

I take up first his treatment of the neglected plays, which are usually considered to be less successful. How a highly idiosyncratic mode of approach to these plays could, at the same time, be representative of the temper of the age is particularly well illustrated in Wilson Knight's 'discovery' of the problem plays, and plays like *Timon of Athens* and *Coriolanus*; their fascination for modern readers, and the great critical interest they have evoked in this century are well reflected in Wilson Knight's commentaries.[22] The way in which these plays yielded results to Wilson Knight's methods of interpretation is a mark of its effectiveness. It may not be extreme to claim that Wilson Knight's handling of these plays discovered them for our age, showed them to be works of art successful in their own way, and pioneered many interpretations of them. *Measure for Measure*, which was refractory to commentary in terms of the conventional categories of

---

[22] As witness some of the remarks of Eliot, Middleton Murry and Bonamy Dobrée, typical of the modern attitude. Eliot called *Coriolanus* the 'most assured artistic success' of Shakespeare; 'Hamlet', *Selected Essays*, p. 144. Bonamy Dobrée (review of WF, *The Criterion*, 11 (1931–2), p. 344), '*Timon*, for Mr Knight, and most of us nowadays will go with him part of the way, is one of the most superb and profound things that Shakespeare ever wrote'. Middleton Murry, 'Coriolanus', *John Clare and Other Studies* (London, 1950), pp. 222–45.

plot and character, and which was called a 'hateful' and 'painful' play by Coleridge,[23] took on a new meaning and a new unity in its interpretation by Wilson Knight. His emphasis on what he takes to be the distinctive 'atmosphere' of the play, and his use of it as a key put the whole play in a fresh light.[24]

Wilson Knight sees the play as pervaded by an ethical atmosphere, the ethics being those of the Gospels, the superior ethics of mercy rather than justice, based on tolerance and the suspension of judgement ('Judge not, lest ye be judged') which transcends the conventional equation of crime and punishment, and of sin and expiation. Against this background, the Duke is seen as Providence incarnate rather than as a man, and all the happenings in the play are seen as ordained and stage-managed by him, his purpose being to test the fallible humans by the standard of the ethics of the Gospel.[25] The 'spatial' approach enables Wilson Knight to see the determining factor in the play as the ethical atmosphere, and to see the characters as two-dimensional. In other words, the conventional expectations of psychological verisimilitude and consistency of character or the cause-and-effect sequence of action had led readers and commentators to feel dissatisfied with the play. Wilson Knight's view of the play, as spread out in space, and of the characters as flattened, tends to allegorise the play; yet does not prevent Wilson Knight's perceiv-

[23] *Coleridge's Shakespearian Criticism*, edited by T. M. Raysor, I, pp. 113–14.
[24] Jones, 'Shakespeare and Mr Wilson Knight' (p. 102) has noted how Wilson Knight won recognition for the play; yet it was slow in coming, both for his insights into this play or his contribution to Shakespeare studies in general. Robert M. Smith in his 'Interpretations of *Measure for Measure*' in *SQ*, 1 (1950) 208–18, does not mention Wilson Knight nor does J. Isaacs, in his account of Shakespeare criticism in *A Companion to Shakespeare Studies*, edited by Granville-Barker and Harrison.
[25] 'True, in 1910, E. K. Chambers had seen "Providence" in *Measure for Measure* (under the searchlight of irony). Yet I think there is no doubt that R. W. Chambers had read Wilson Knight's *Wheel of Fire* (1930) and its essay on "*Measure for Measure* and the Gospels", though he never mentions it (in 1937 T. S. Eliot, who wrote an Introduction for the book, was still a suspicious character)', A. P. Rossiter, *Angel with Horns*, p. 113. The influence of Pater's commentary on the play, *Appreciations* (1889), postulated by Kenneth Muir (*SS*, 4), is a case more of a parallel than of actual influence. Complaints about the general neglect of his work are made by Wilson Knight in *RES*, October 1946; *The Kenyon Review* (Winter, 1949) and *TLS* (21 April 1950, p. 245). In the last Wilson Knight complains about Tillyard's non-acknowledgement of his work on the problem plays.

ing, and fully responding to, the human warmth and significance of the characters. His reading of the characters springs from imaginative sympathy with them. It is worth noting that, as a consequence of his elevating the Duke to the superhuman level of a Providence figure, his treatment of Angelo (and Claudio and Lucio) and of Isabella as victims of a testing process initiated by the Duke shows how the 'spatial' approach entails an altogether new view of the functions of character in poetic drama.[26] The impression of reality made by the characters is never in doubt; their interrelationships, which are perceived in terms of theme and atmosphere, are the new circumstances that alter the case. The penetration of Wilson Knight's analysis of the character of Angelo may be seen as a development in depth when we compare his view of the character in the *Wheel of Fire* essay with that in *Shakespearian Production* (pp. 256–8); and it is significant that the growth in awareness and sympathy is a result of Wilson Knight's experience of playing or watching the role in performance. Similarly, Wilson Knight's later attitude to Isabella is more sympathetic than in the *Wheel of Fire* essay.[27] The range, depth and permanent value of Wilson Knight's reading of *Measure for Measure* lie in the fact that he could win for the play a general recognition of its nature and its kind of excellence by his 'intrinsic' mode of commentary. Some of his intuitive insights have been confirmed by the findings of historical scholars.[28]

Yet the question arises whether, in this play as in the others, the atmosphere is as homogeneous as Wilson Knight would have us believe, and whether the variety (or the indiscriminate mix-

[26] Wilson Knight's sympathetic reading of the Duke and Angelo influenced Leavis's view of the play and the characters, as expressed in his 'The Greatness of *Measure for Measure*' in *Scrutiny*, 10 (1941–2), which was a reply to L. C. Knights's 'The Ambiguity of *Measure for Measure*' in the same volume and number. Wilson Knight's idealisation of the Duke is in direct contrast to the sceptical and unsympathetic view of him taken by commentators such as Empson and Traversi.

[27] The earlier view, though less unsympathetic than Quiller-Couch ('rancid in her chastity'), was critical of the lack of human warmth in Isabella.

[28] The resolution of the paradoxes of the play's relation with its sources is given by Mary Lascelles and M. Doran, *Shakespeare's 'Measure for Measure'* (London, 1953), and appendix II in Doran, *Endeavors of Art*. The relationships with medieval narrative, especially romance, and medieval ethical standards are discussed by W. W. Lawrence, whose *Shakespeare's Problem Comedies* appeared in the same period as Wilson Knight's book.

ture) of moods and tones in the play is accounted for sufficiently
by his description. Wilson Knight's system enables him to resolve
the complexities and ambiguities of the play. It cannot be said
that it fails to take into account the play's ambivalent probings,
yet one wonders whether his way of looking at the general
pattern does not act as a solvent for the ironies and ambivalences
which are there for all to feel? (This is a question separate from
Wilson Knight's refusal, following the first principles of his
method, to note topical allusions, significances, sources and conventions, or the question of the occasion of the play.[29]) Even so, it
has not been sufficiently recognised that Wilson Knight's intuitive findings, complemented by the findings of historical scholarship, paved the way for such approaches as those of R. W.
Chambers, Roy W. Battenhouse, and E. M. Pope.[30] To put it
another way, the difficulties for our understanding of the play,
which modern scholars try to resolve by relating it to contemporary social concerns like the *de praesenti* and the *de futuro* marriage contracts of the Elizabethan age,[31] or to the personality,
habits and writings of James I,[32] are circumvented though not
solved by Wilson Knight's method.

Similarly, some germinal insights and perceptions mark his
account of *Troilus and Cressida*, a play which had previously
provoked general dissatisfaction, remained intractable to com-

[29] Two cool yet forceful expressions of disapproval of modern enthusiasms for the
play are by E. M. W. Tillyard and Alfred Harbage. Tillyard, *Shakespeare's Problem
Plays* (London, 1950); Harbage, *Conceptions of Shakespeare* (Cambridge, Mass.,
1966), pp. 35–6.
[30] Chambers, 'The Jacobean Shakespeare and *Measure for Measure*', British
Academy Lecture, *PBA*, 23 (1938), 135–92. Battenhouse, '*Measure for Measure*
and Christian Doctrine of the Atonement'. Pope, 'The Renaissance Background
of *Measure for Measure*', *SS*, 2 (1949), pp. 66–82.
[31] Chilton L. Powell, *English Domestic Relations (1487–1653)* (1917) and Davis P.
Harding, 'Elizabethan Betrothals and *Measure for Measure*', *Journal of English and
Germanic Philology*, 49 (1950), 139–58; E. Schanzer, 'The Marriage Contracts in
Measure for Measure', *SS*, 13 (1960), 81–9, and also S. Nagarajan, '*Measure for
Measure* and Elizabethan Betrothals', *SQ*, 14 (1963), 141–52, for his scepticism
about arguments from Elizabethan marriage contracts.
[32] J. W. Lever, Introduction to the New Arden edition of *Measure for Measure*
(London, 1965). J. W. Bennett, '*Measure for Measure*' as Royal Entertainment*
(1966). David L. Stevenson, 'The Role of James I in *Measure for Measure*', *ELH*, 25
(1958), 188–208. Herbert Howarth, 'The Puzzle of Flattery', *The Tiger's Heart*,
pp. 120–42.

mentary, and hence was relatively neglected; though it was in 1931 that W. W. Lawrence's study of the problem comedies and their relation to medieval romance conventions appeared. The signal contribution of Wilson Knight is, again, to have seen the play (however schematically and naïvely in terms of a thematic pattern – of an antithesis between intuition and intellect as represented by the Trojans and the Greeks respectively – instead of considering character in relation to plot.[33] This approach through the 'philosophy' of the play leads Wilson Knight to conclude that 'human values are strongly contrasted with human failings', the two primary values vividly present in the play being love and war. According to Wilson Knight, these values are embodied in the Trojans ('the love of Troilus, the heroism of Hector' and also, 'The symbolic romance which burns in the figure of Helen'), who have 'an intuitive faith' in, or 'an intuitive recognition' of them; but they are opposed by the 'scurrilous jests' and lazy pride of Achilles, the stupidity of Ajax and the mockery of Thersites. 'The Trojan party stands for human beauty and worth, the Greek party for the bestial and stupid elements of man, the barren stagnancy of intellect divorced from action, and the criticism which exposes these things with jeers' (*WF*, p. 47). Thus 'rational untrustworthiness' is seen to be 'in conflict with the intuitive validity of romantic insight'. The intellectual and analytic quality of the language of the play is isolated and stressed so that the contribution of this aspect to the theme of the play is made clear. But Wilson Knight's antithesis is much too neat. The simplistic antinomy which he postulates leads him to idealise the Trojans including Pandarus and, to the same extent, to be over-severe in his treatment of Achilles, Ajax and Thersites. A second important

---

[33] As L. C. Knights has it ('Education and the Drama in the Age of Shakespeare', *The Criterion*, 11 (1932), 599–625), 'a moment's consideration of such a play as *Troilus and Cressida*, however, should make it plain that there is a real problem, and that the traditional method of criticism is in need of some re-orientation. It should not be necessary to insist that in *Troilus and Cressida* the real interest centres not in the "characters" such as they are, but in the themes of which the play is composed and the way in which Shakespeare handles the language to obtain an unusually complex emotional response' (p. 624).

Later commentators such as Terence Hawkes in his *Shakespeare and the Reason* (London, 1964) have taken up Wilson Knight's idea of an intellect–intuition opposition in this and other plays.

theme that he identifies is the order-disorder antithesis; and
another is the theme of Time.[34]

Despite a typically romantic over-simplification of the ironies
and complexities of the play, Wilson Knight's account is remarkable for its penetrating commentary on certain aspects of individual passages such as the 'degree' speech of Ulysses, and 'This
is, and is not, Cressid' by Troilus. It is not surprising that Wilson
Knight does not consider sources, or the question of the occasion
and original audience for the play, or the relation of the play to
'comicall satyre', or the probable relationship of the play to the
War of the Theatres, or the textual issues. Rather, apart from
pointing out the opposition of Trojan and Greek, Wilson Knight
emphasises the intellectual and analytical nature of the speeches,
the abstract debate and the element of satire in the play. It is an
instance of the common ground between historical scholarship
and intuitive criticism; how sensitive critical commentary can, in
its intuitions, almost unconsciously capture the fruits of historical
findings; and how scholarship can deepen as well as confirm
critical perceptions. Yet for the student of the play, in this case as
in others, Wilson Knight's perceptions have to be supplemented
or modified by the findings of scholarship.

One might have expected that Wilson Knight would have shed
equal light on the third problem comedy, *All's Well*; but his late
essay (in *The Sovereign Flower*) disappoints. Ideological preoccupations – in this case, spiritualism and the bisexual ideal – have
run away with the interpreter. A glancing reference to the presence of these two themes in *All's Well*, in Wilson Knight's essay,
'The Shakespearian Integrity' (1939), has been developed at
inordinate length in *The Sovereign Flower*. The absence of a
dominant idea or atmosphere in the play makes Wilson Knight
almost give up his usual method of interpretation. Taking the cue
from what he takes to be a 'climate of thought' in the play, he
enlarges upon the themes of 'virginity' (a Parolles-like view of it
at that!); of female and male honour, which merges into the
theme of bisexuality; and of Helena as an embodiment of the
bisexual ideal and as the miracle-worker. For the first and last

[34] A theme which has been widely noticed subsequently in the Sonnets, and in
several other plays, for example, by L. C. Knights and D. A. Traversi.

time in discussing any of the plays, Wilson Knight raises the question of date, and proposes that the play belongs with the group of last plays. In the play's element of the miraculous 'points of contact' with *Hamlet* as well as with the last plays are pointed out. But it hardly helps to say for this reason, as Wilson Knight does, that 'Helena assumes male prerogatives as Diana's "knight" ' (*The Golden Labyrinth*, p. 70) or to call the play 'Shakespeare's most forceful reading of female power' or 'that subtlest of plays' ('Some Notable Fallacies', *The Sovereign Flower*, p. 251).

Scrupulous avoidance of the biographical fallacy in Wilson Knight's interpretation of these 'unpleasant' plays and of the tragedies is a fortunate consequence of his strictly 'intrinsic' commentary. Well before C. J. Sisson's 'The Mythical Sorrows of Shakespeare' and R. W. Chambers' lecture on *Measure for Measure*, Wilson Knight had established implicitly through his commentaries the irrelevance of such speculations. Nor does he postulate a turning-point or crisis in the artistic personality or evolution of Shakespeare, as Charles Williams and Middleton Murry do. No doubt, the characters and situations in these plays which provide dramatic humour are either ignored or misread by Wilson Knight. But what is remarkable is his capacity to see and to stress positive emotions where negative ones are usually seen to predominate, as in plays like *Timon of Athens* and *Coriolanus*.

Timon of Athens has always been a particular favourite of his. It is a play which has remained 'difficult', leading scholars to wonder whether the extant play is unfinished.[35] Through extensive commentary on it, and enthusiastic experimental productions in which he himself played the title role, Wilson Knight has, again, 'discovered' it for our age. The spatial view enables us to visualise the play, 'the most masterfully deliberate of Shakespeare's sombre tragedies', (*WF*, p. 219) as an area spread out in the mind's eye and divided into two clear-cut, contrasted halves. The first half, consisting of the first three acts, deals with Timon's

---

[35] E. K. Chambers saw in the play signs of something like a nervous breakdown on the part of Shakespeare. *William Shakespeare*, 1, 86.

Una Ellis-Fermor is among those who suspect that the play is incomplete in its extant version. '*Timon of Athens*: An Unfinished Play', *RES*, 18 (1942), 270–83.

generosity in the entertainment of his guests and visitors; the second half deals with Timon's withdrawal from Athens after being rendered penniless by his own extravagance – his ungrateful 'friends' and fellow citizens refusing to help – and the magnificence of his rage and hate. The essay in *The Wheel of Fire*, entitled 'The Pilgrimage of Hate', is an elaboration of this pattern of spatial contrast and is remarkable for its close analysis of the speeches and situations and also the characters and actions of the play, and its remarks on the symbolism of gold. The analysis of the imagery of the play in *The Shakespearian Tempest* is in terms of the music–tempest antithesis and the associations of splendour and disorder with these two axes. These essays and the discussion of Timon in *Christ and Nietzsche, The Sovereign Flower, Shakespearian Production* and *The Golden Labyrinth* constitute a full commentary which takes account of every aspect of the play. It is a striking proof that spatial analysis has the greatest value when it is combined with attention to the 'temporal' elements of plot-sequence and character. Understandably, Wilson Knight, immersed in his novel vision of the play, tends to over-rate it and to ignore weaknesses; but among his penetrating insights some deserve special mention. There is, for example, the idea of the relationship between Timon and the atmosphere of the play, a merging of the tragic hero with the atmosphere which Wilson Knight sees in the tragedies in general, so that the change in the condition of Timon and the change in the atmosphere match each other. The relationships between the characters, Timon, Apemantus and Alcibiades are well analysed in terms of the spatial pattern. The gold symbolism which Wilson Knight saw in the play, though it was denied by Caroline Spurgeon, is more a matter of the idea of gold recurring as a key motif, a case of symbolism working in terms of dramatic and ideational rather than verbal imagery. The associational train of this symbolism is shown to be of basic importance in the play. ('The gold in *Timon* is part of the symbolic action, more important than imagery. It is with a stage eye that Shakespeare's symbolism must be read', 'Symbolism', *A Shakespeare Encyclopaedia*, p. 838).

Timon's generosity in his prosperity is conveyed by this train of suggestion, so that when the image of gold is presented in the last two acts, there is a fund of ironical and paradoxical significance attaching to it. Wilson Knight is at his best in his interpretation here. Taking the play as a 'parable or allegory', with 'its rush of power', in the later Timon's nihilism and anarchism, and in his long diatribes of universal hatred, as he steps 'from time into eternity' (*WF*, p. 221), he finds a positive meaning and grandeur. In Timon's speeches to the Bandits and to Alcibiades, outbursts of hatred though they are, something constructive is seen emerging. Wilson Knight's interpetation of Timon anticipates Leavis's interpretation of Swift. Touches of a characteristic extravagant fervour appear in Wilson Knight's idealisation of Timon. 'Timon, in love or hate, bears truly a heart of gold. He is a thing apart, a choice soul crucified . . . when Timon's servants part to wander abroad separated . . . they are as disciples of the Christ meeting after the crucifixion' (*WF*, p. 235), 'this Nirvana-like apprehension of Timon'[36] (*The Golden Labyrinth*, p. 79). Ideas of the superman and royalty are drawn upon to describe and account for his nihilism. Other positive qualities in the play, such as the loyalty of Timon's servants, are given due weight 'Timon himself personifies the one positive of which these others are all negative, and mutually, shadows' (*SF*, p. 56). Timon is like other 'great unmoral and anarchic dramatic persons': 'spurning morality, they nevertheless channel powers from which good, not bad, will spring'. The special setting Wilson Knight prescribes for the last act of the play (*The Golden Labyrinth*, p. 79) is at once an indulgence of subjective taste and an imposition of it on Shakespeare. The same partiality, born of an excess of enthusiasm for the play, is obvious in his claims for the influence of *Timon of Athens* on later writers and dramatists.[37]

Wilson Knight's interpretative findings about 'the great tragedies' have, naturally, attracted the widest notice and pro-

---

[36] Jarold Ramsey, 'Timon's Imitation of Christ', *Shakespeare Studies*, 2 (1966), 162–73 and Roy Battenhouse, *Shakespearean Tragedy: Its Art and Its Christian Premises*, pp 91–2 consider Timon a sort of inverted Christ.

[37] In an article on 'Timon of Athens and its Dramatic Descendants' in *A Review of English Literature*, 2 (1961). Wilson Knight's reading of the play as a 'spatial' diptych of Timon in prosperity and in adversity anticipates M. C. Bradbrook's view that *Timon of Athens* is more a show or pageant than a play (*Shakespeare the Craftsman*).

voked a good deal of comment. These, first put forward in the *Wheel of Fire* essays, have been improved upon and modified in the later writings. The test-case as with most studies of Shakespeare, is the discussion of *Hamlet*. From time to time Wilson Knight has employed the whole apparatus of his interpretative method and of his ideologies in his studies of various aspects of the play. The attention he paid to the death-theme, the hate-theme and the life-theme in the play, and the relationship between these themes and its 'atmosphere', made it possible for him to see the characters as imbued with a new mode of existence and function and as situated in a new pattern of relationships. As R. S. Crane and Morris Weitz have shown, Wilson Knight's reading of the play invested it with a new ontological status, while itself constituting an epistemological innovation in the mode of apprehending the 'reality' of Shakespearian poetic drama.[38]

The emphasis on the key status of the theme of death, and on Hamlet's melancholy, which is almost a merging with the idea of death,[39] as it first appeared in the *Wheel of Fire* essays, was a fresh and profound insight which offered a needed corrective to conventional readings. Again Wilson Knight discovered his favourite dialectical pattern of antinomies. He saw the play as built round the pitting against each other of life themes, represented by Claudius and Laertes, and death themes (and the associated themes of hate and evil) embodied, according to Wilson Knight, in the figures of Hamlet and the Ghost. The views of Hamlet, Claudius, Polonius and the Ghost entailed by this reading turned out to be a scandalous reversal of the received impression, as shocking as Eliot's earlier pronouncement that the play was 'most certainly an artistic failure'. Though Wilson Knight's commentary in the *Wheel of Fire* suggested that there was much else in the play than the Prince of Denmark, it still looked rather as though

---

[38] Crane, *The Languages of Criticism and the Structure of Poetry*, pp. 34–5. Weitz, *Hamlet and the Philosophy of Literary Criticism*, p. 29.

[39] 'When I called at Eliot's office he told me that he found its emphasis on death more illuminating than previous commentaries', Knight, 'T. S. Eliot: Some Literary Impressions', p. 239. While Wilson Knight does arrive at negative conclusions from a perception about the theme of death which might lead to a positive estimate, the fact remains that the emphasis on the theme anticipates, if not inspires, C. S. Lewis's British Academy lecture 'Hamlet: The Prince or the Poem' (1942) (London, 1964).

the 'sweet prince' if not exactly 'an arrant Knave' was almost the villain of the piece, as Turgenev made him out to be in his Hamlet and Don Quixote, translated by Robert Nichols (London, 1930). In the later essays, especially in 'Hamlet Reconsidered' (WF, the 1949 edition), Wilson Knight corrected this impression, coming out in support of Hamlet by seeing him as an example of the Nietzschean superman. Yet even in the early commentary there is nothing approaching disapproval of Hamlet's engagement with death, hate and evil, for Wilson Knight's view of these negatives even at that period was Blakean and Manichaean. There is no doubt in Wilson Knight's mind that Hamlet is one of the 'power-bearers', 'one of the dramatic supermen' (GL, p. 74). Strangely enough, in his later commentary, in place of the conventional idealisation of Hamlet as the Renaissance man, the noble tragic hero, we get a vision still generous and sympathetic, but of a different kind.

Hamlet, according to Wilson Knight, aspires to, and all but achieves, the ideal poise of the superman and also nearly achieves the Renaissance synthesis of action and inaction as well as the reconciliation of the Apollonian and the Dionysian instincts. Hamlet's interest in the arts of drama and fencing are part of his quest for this poise. This more favourable view was developed in the light of Wilson Knight's reading of Nietzsche,[40] and of his own performance of the role. His favourable reading of Claudius is not without parallels, especially his analysis of Claudius's soliloquy.[41] Wilson Knight's likening the state of Hamlet to that of 'the sick soul' described by William James is a perception which is capable of favourable interpretation different from the one which he puts on it. Wilson Knight's insistence on the disjunction between the hero and the atmosphere of the play is a characteristic strategic stroke of his poetic interpretation. Starting from this perception, Wilson Knight is able to isolate an antinomial pattern; the way his thematic analysis comprehends

---

[40] Both the general influence of Nietzsche's ideas, and Nietzsche's specific remarks on Hamlet influence 'Hamlet Reconsidered'.

[41] Such may be seen in J. W. Draper, The 'Hamlet' of Shakespeare's Audience (Durham, NC, 1938), and 'King Claudius as a Diplomatist', Neuphilologische Mitteilungen 66 (1965) 347–54; and Howard Mumford Jones, The King in 'Hamlet' (Austin, Texas, 1918).

strands of imagery is remarkable for its adroitness in shifting
focus rather than for its logical invulnerability. The logical clash of
points of view is perhaps unavoidable when two different essays,
the one dealing with life-themes and the other with death-
themes, treating more or less the same scenes, are put in juxtaposition with each other. Here again, one should not forget that
the atmosphere of the play is complex rather than simple, and
that with a play like *Hamlet*, which has an 'epic' variety of moods
and tones and whose unity is achieved despite this diversity, a
prismatic or kaleidoscopic shifting of points of view is not difficult
to justify.

The old psychological chestnuts about Hamlet's delay and
about his 'madness', cease in Wilson Knight's spatial interpretation to be 'necessary questions of the play', and become incidental questions implicitly answered, once we see Hamlet as an
approximation to the superman. Characteristically, he avoids
questions about the element of stratification in the play, or the
textual problems (with a single exception), or the dramatic conventions of the Revenge tradition,[42] or Elizabethan melancholics
or the malcontent or the probable topical references in the play.[43]
The result of his commentary on the play is to establish its
integrity and wholeness as a work of art. Wilson Knight is not the
first critic to react unfavourably to the character of Hamlet, but in
the study of no other play has the questioning of the traditional
response to the hero been taken up with such vigour[44] and the
perspective offered by Wilson Knight so fully exploited by mod-

---

[42] Though Wilson Knight avoids concerning himself with this favourite preoccu-
pation of historical scholars such as Stoll or Helen Gardner, at one point he
suggests that Hamlet questions the old morality of Revenge. *IT*, p. 124. Cf. John
Lawlor, *The Tragic Sense in Shakespeare* (London, 1960) and F. T. Bowers,
Elizabethan Revenge Tragedy (Princeton, 1940); 'Hamlet as Minister and Scourge',
PMLA, 70 (1955); 'The Death of Hamlet', *Studies in English Renaissance Drama in
Memory of K. J. Holzknecht*, edited by J. W. Bennett, *et al*. (New York, 1959); and
'Death in Victory: Shakespeare's Tragic Reconciliations', *Studies in Honor of
DeWitt T. Starnes*, edited by T. P. Harrison (Austin, Texas, 1967).
[43] Wilson Knight's vigorous disapproval of Dover Wilson's thesis about the Ham-
let–Essex correspondence was expressed in a review of *The Essential Shakespeare*
in *The Criterion*, 12 (1932–3), 122–4, esp. p. 123.
[44] Many (one could say most) modern readings of *Hamlet* are harsh in their verdict
on the hero: L. C. Knights, Rebecca West, S. de Madariaga, Lily B. Campbell,
John Vyvyan, and Eleanor Prosser.

ern commentators.[45] The reading of the play in *The Golden Labyrinth* is as 'the balance of the two furthest Shakespearian quests, those "mighty opposites" of superman and royalty'.

In his eagerness to bring the darker aspects of the character to our attention, no doubt Wilson Knight is over-severe towards Hamlet – his list of charges against him is formidable. But, incidentally, Wilson Knight has drawn our attention to a number of significant features of the play, such as 'the sick soul' of Hamlet, his being hero and clown at once, and the use of the disease motif to suggest the sickness of Hamlet spreading outwards like a contagion.[46] The affinities between *Hamlet* and the problem comedies, and the Jacobean characteristics of the play are also well brought out. The positives he finds in the death of Hamlet are much like those he finds in Cleopatra's death. Such 'imaginative solidities' (*WF*, p. 299), poetic and dramatic, as the Ghost scenes, the Graveyard scene, the final group of dead bodies, Hamlet's attire and his soliloquising stances, and the poetic realisation of death as a living presence in the play are given primary emphasis. The player scenes are interpreted as reflecting the poise of the superman acquired by Hamlet the artist (*WF*, p. 310).

The provocative, indeed unpopular value-judgements about the way leading characters are to be perceived, and which mark Wilson Knight's interpretation of *Hamlet*, are conspicuous by their absence in his studies of the other tragedies, especially *Othello*. What distinguishes Wilson Knight's analysis of *Othello* is the sensitive attention he gives to qualities such as the wording and phrasing of the speeches, together with his attention to the 'spatial dimensions'. In what Wilson Knight himself calls 'an intellectual interpretation', which is nonetheless imaginative, he makes a close analysis of the suggestions and associations of words instead of commencing with atmospheric effects, as is his usual practice. From the speeches of the characters, he apprehends their selves and it is through his ideas of 'the characters of characters' that he isolates themes in this play. His examination

---

[45] Such as Roy Walker and Francis Fergusson. The approach to the play through its atmosphere has been well exploited by H. D. F. Kitto, *Form and Meaning in Drama*, pp. 231–335.
[46] As Wolfgang Clemen, *pace* Spurgeon, shows. *The Development of Shakespeare's Imagery* (London, 1951), 113–18.

of the poetic effect of dramatic utterances is noteworthy for its truth to our experience of the play, as well as for its unusual delicacy and sensitiveness of response and for the subtlety of its discriminations. Indeed, it is an instance of the right balance of subjective impressions and objective truth; an instance remarkable in Wilson Knight's commentary, for subjectivist (not merely subjective) impressions usually outweigh.

At the outset, in the chapter 'The *Othello* Music', Wilson Knight makes it plain that '*Othello* is a story of intrigue rather than a visionary statement' and that the 'persons' (Wilson Knight's scrupulous avoidance of the conventional term 'character' at once strikes us as amusing) tend to appear as warmly human, concrete. Yet, starting from this perception, he wants to consider the characters in their roles as – what Wilson Knight himself calls them elsewhere – 'symbolic personifications', in their interrelationships. The idiosyncrasies of the play, which mark it off from the other plays, are convincingly brought out. Among these are, on the one side, the disjunction between the 'protagonist' and the other persons, and the 'atmosphere' on the other; the modes of speech which are distinctive of the persons of the play; and at the same time the characteristic, general mode of utterance which is called 'the *Othello* music', and which is distinguished from other Shakespearian poetry by the effect it has of isolating image from image, word from word, by the absence of fusion and cohesion, by its 'concrete, visual, detached' quality. Wilson Knight points out how the references to the sun, moon and heavenly bodies are used in *Othello*, in contrast to those in *Macbeth* and *King Lear*, so that the human drama, instead of being brought into a reciprocal relationship with the drama of nature and the universe, is merely contrasted with it. The images of the celestial bodies 'though thrown momentarily into sensible relation with the passions of man, yet remain vast, distant, separate, seen but not apprehended; something against which the dramatic movement may be silhouetted, but with which it cannot be merged' (*WF*, p. 98). He draws attention to the effect of 'grand single words' like 'Propontic', 'Hellespont', with their sharp, clear, consonant sounds, constituting defined aural solids typical of the *Othello* music; and of fine single words, especially proper names like

Anthropophagi, Ottomites, 'the base Indian', Mauretania, the
Sagittary, Mandragora, Olympus, Othello and Desdemona. The
words produce a stately, consonantal music and carry suggestions of an exotic glamour which evokes, or at least adds to, the
romantic personality of the Moor. Wilson Knight's account of
Othello's mode of speech is a classic piece of his commentary;
besides enumerating and illustrating the characteristics of the
Othello music, he shows acumen in noting the shifts of tone in the
later speeches and in his use of those two tools of criticism,
comparison and analysis. Wilson Knight's findings about the
extremes of stateliness and ugliness between which Othello's
speeches can shift, and about the brutal, 'unbeglamouring',
realistic speech of Iago, and the interchange of the two styles, are
the basis on which his symbolical interpretation is founded.
Instead of starting with symbolical preoccupations, as he does in
other plays, Wilson Knight works outwards from his experience
of words and characters, and then goes on to find a symbolic
pattern and to see the characters in its terms. Othello is seen as a
symbol of faith in the human values of love, or war, and of
romance in a wide and sweeping sense. Divinity and warmly
human domestic qualities co-exist in Desdemona; likewise, the
handkerchief is seen both as a domestic symbol and a symbol of
the supernatural. The storm in the play comes in for extended
commentary in *The Shakespearian Tempest*; it does nothing but
good to Othello and Desdemona; but while they are able to
weather this storm, they succumb to the domestic tragedy. The
cynicism of Iago and his lack of belief in Othello's and
Desdemona's continued love, from which his designs spring,
receive particular emphasis. The Iago-Devil associations, as well
as the contrast between the devil references and the *Othello*
music, and the effect of the infernal 'associations' creeping into
Othello's later utterances as well as of the *Othello* music entering
Iago's utterances, are among the most interesting facets of Wilson
Knight's poetic interpretation.[47] The view that Othello loses bal-

---

[47] These original findings were developed and interpreted variously by Leavis,
S. L. Bethell, Paul Siegel, and R. B. Heilman, in 'Diabolic Intellect and the Noble
Hero'; 'Shakespeare's Imagery: the Diabolic Images in Othello', *SS*, 5 (1952);
'The Damnation of Othello', *PMLA*, 68 (1953) and *Magic in the Web; Action and
Language in 'Othello'* (Lexington, 1956) respectively.

ance and dignity and becomes incoherent in the last scenes, expressed in *The Wheel of Fire*, was revised after Wilson Knight had acted Othello's role (*SP* pp. 51–2).

A good example of how Wilson Knight's theoretical principles of interpretation are modified, though not contradicted, in actual application to particular plays, is to be found in his commentaries on *King Lear*. For though the primary object of the two essays on the play in *The Wheel of Fire*, 'King Lear and the comedy of the Grotesque' and 'The *Lear* Universe', is to consider correspondences and interconnections in the imaginative atmosphere and themes of the play, Wilson Knight, while noting these spatial features, manages to link them with the temporal elements of character and plot. What emerges is a comprehensive view of the play, which, while focussing on a number of key themes and qualities of thought and atmosphere for the first time, does not contradict the traditional view of the play and its characters (except for a sympathetic reading of Edmund), but deepens it.

'King Lear and the Comedy of the Grotesque' strikes the reader today as a brilliant anticipation of the insights of the modern 'theatre of the Absurd'; indeed what Jan Kott has to say about the play is included and transcended in what Wilson Knight says. Likening *Macbeth* to Dostoevsky and *King Lear* to Chekhov, Wilson Knight stresses the 'peculiar dualism' in the play. This manifests itself in the intermixture of tragedy and comedy, in the richness of character delineation combined with the working-out of a purgatorial philosophy, and in the commingling of the imaginative and the fantastic. The contrast between the neo-classical critic's bafflement at the intermixture of comedy in tragedy and Wilson Knight's acute perceptions of the counter-pointing and intensifying poetic-dramatic function of the element of comedy and its indissoluble integration with the essential tragedy, is instructive. Despite theoretical riders by Wilson Knight, such as his statement 'I shall notice here the imaginative core of the play, and, excluding much of the logic of the plot from immediate attention, analyse the fantastic comedy of *King Lear*', (*WF* p. 161), the logic of the plot is followed closely enough and there is no distortion of the play. The comic aspect of the opening situation, its 'greatness linked to puerility', is well brought out. He also draws attention to the grotesque reversals and inversions attendant upon the purgatory of mind, the madness which Lear endures. Both these features of Lear's character (Wilson Knight's refusal to use the term involves him in the circumlocution, 'the Lear-theme') are reflected in the upheaval in 'the Lear universe' and in the character of Gloucester. Wilson Knight identifies and discusses certain linked themes, such as the renunciation of family ties, the child–parent relationship, authority and the abdication of authority, and he shows their importance in the play. He shows the imaginative and dramatic way in which the fantastic, grotesque elements and the strain of demonic cruelty and sadistic torture work in the play. The two-fold choric and counterpointing function of the Fool, and his emphasising the potentialities for comedy in Lear's behaviour, are other valuable insights. Wilson Knight's avoidance of sentimentality about the Fool is a mark of his sanity and strength. His comment on the centrality of the mock-trial of Goneril and Regan is 'The core of the play is an absurdity, an indignity, an incongruity. In no tragedy of Shakespeare does incident and dialogue so recklessly and miraculously walk the tight-rope of our pity over the depths of bathos and absurdity' (WF, p. 168). Wilson Knight highlights the confluence of the tragic, the terrible, the fantastic and the absurd in such climaxes of dramatic action as the gouging-out of Gloucester's eyes, grim pilgrimage to Dover Cliff and the mock suicidal fall. His reference to contemporary Elizabethan taste for 'watching both physical torment and the comic ravings of actual lunacy' is, incidentally, an example of the kind of historical knowledge occasionally invoked. When we read Wilson Knight's pages on the integral function of the incongruous and the fantastic in the play ('the very heart of the play' WF, p. 173) and his summing up of his analysis, 'we watch humanity grotesquely tormented, cruelly and with mockery impaled: nearly all the persons suffer some form of crude indignity in the course of the play' (WF, p. 173), we note how his comments complement Caroline Spurgeon's on the play's imagery of pain and torture. His investing Edmund with a tragic dignity (WF, pp. 173–4) is an aspect of the Manichaean tendencies of his commentary.

The essay on 'The *Lear* Universe' is Wilson Knight's overall analysis of the themes and world of the play. Starting with an emphasis on the variety and abundance of forms of life in the play, which he calls (in his idiosyncratic use of the term) the 'naturalism' of *King Lear*, Wilson Knight draws our attention to the sense of unactualised spaces, the vagueness of locality and time, and the inconsistencies and impossibilities which constitute a brooding presence, an atmospheric suggestion which gives the play the universality of a work of philosophic vision, of Purgatory. He divides his analysis of the *Lear* universe into five parts: (i) the naturalism of justice, human and divine; (ii) its 'gods'; (iii) its insistent questioning of justice, human and divine; (iv) the stoic acceptance of purgatorial pain; and (v) the flaming course of the Lear theme. The idea of 'nature' (like that of 'Death' in *Hamlet*, 'fear' in *Macbeth*, and of 'time' in *Troilus and Cressida*) recurs and the animal imagery in the play carries a good deal of symbolic suggestiveness. Characteristically, Wilson Knight brings together almost all the references to nature in the play, without paying any attention to the different meanings and connotations they have in different contexts, though he subsumes them in convenient categories as they relate to characters and situations. The predominance of natural and animal references in the speeches of Edgar in the guise of mad Tom is seen as antiphonal to Lear's experience and speech. The contrast between man in the trappings of civilisation and 'unaccommodated man' is illustrated by Lear in his madness revolting from man and trying to become a thing of elemental, instinctive life. Wilson Knight raises the question of the complex relationship between the morality of human nature and unmoral nature and the inapplicability of nature as a standard in ethical judgement. Though the implications of Edmund's commitment to nature are well explained, Wilson Knight does not pay sufficient heed to the uncertainty and unreliability of the criterion of nature, and the alternating approval and disapproval accorded to it in Elizabethan times (which are, for example, well brought out by Edwin Muir, Danby and Heilman). He goes on to talk of the 'three modes of religion' stressed in the play. These are the references to the 'gods', the thoughts about ethical 'justice' and the moral or spiritual development illustrated by the characters. Gloucester's references to the gods are sensitively analysed, and it is shown how

As flies to wanton boys are we to thy gods –
They kill us for their sport

is not a usual, but an occasional, unusual thought of his. The 'fiends', too, are given their due. The relationship of both the gods and the fiends to the phenomena of nature is suggested. Without directly raising the question whether the play is a Christian one about a pagan world, or a pagan play about a Christian world, Wilson Knight would see in Lear's phrase about 'God's spies' (v. iii. 17), the idea of God slowly and painfully emerging from the *Lear* naturalism, born of disillusionment. As important as the working-out of these themes is Wilson Knight's summary of the ways in which they are intertwined. Involved in the conception of justice in the play are the idea and experience of stoic acceptance and purification through sympathy, and the process of groping after the 'gods'. Wilson Knight's discussion of the theme of justice is a classic exposition of a key preoccupation in the play. The purgatorial concept receives due emphasis, Wilson Knight's commentary at this point being based on A. C. Bradley's. Wilson Knight's enthusiasm for this theme leads him into certain extravagances. Conclusions like the one about Edgar being the high-priest of the play's stoicism are, though true, not true enough, for the reason that they do not spring from an awareness of the total dramatic context but from narrow attention to one idea. Mingling the evolutionary idea with the purgatorial one is neither happy nor helpful. The suggestion that Edmund, Lear and Cordelia correspond to the three periods in man's evolution – the primitive, the civilised and the ideal – is perhaps more usefully developed with reference to Elizabethan and Jacobean thought and the Chain of Being than with reference to nineteenth-century evolutionary thought.[48] Wilson Knight does

---

[48] As is done by J. F. Danby in his *Shakespeare's Doctrine of Nature* (London, 1949). In a controversy with Wilson Knight in *Scrutiny*, Danby denied that his book owed anything to Wilson Knight's essays (16 (1949), p. 327). Findings of the same kind are common to the interpretations of Wilson Knight and Danby, and similar insights are to be found in Edwin Muir, 'The Politics of *King Lear*' and 'The Natural Man and the Political Man', both in *Essays on Literature and Society*, 31–48 and 151–65.

not go so far in his idealisation of Cordelia as to make her a Christ-figure. For all his statement that he has viewed the *Lear* universe objectively in this analysis, what Wilson Knight effectively does is to live within the mind of Lear, as in Lamb's reading of our experience of the play ('We *are* Lear'). It is through such romantic identification of the self with the universe of the play that we have perceptions; for example, seeing the *Lear* universe travail and bring forth its miracle in the good deed which Edmund intends to do in his dying moments. Good thus emerges out of evil, and through a ruthless facing of the ultimate cruelty – through 'a full look at the worst' – positive values are tested and corroborated.

Wilson Knight's reading of the climax of the storm is to be found in *The Shakespearian Tempest*. Storms and music are the two poles of imagery, according to Wilson Knight, on which the whole Shakespeare canon revolves. The storm in *King Lear* is at once symbolic and realistic. An association of animal imagery with the storm imagery is posited. Only in isolating the antithetical group of music images does Wilson Knight have some difficulty, and though his account of the storm is illuminating and serves to reinforce Granville-Barker's interpretation, the invoking of a storm–music opposition is rather strained.

Wilson Knight's experience of acting in and producing the play lies behind the remarks on *Lear* in *Shakespearian Production*. There is, in Wilson Knight's view, a gathering up in the play of the life-themes, the love-theme, and the hate-themes of the other tragedies. Hence the climatic position of *King Lear* in the total scheme of 'the Shakespearian metaphysic'.

'*Macbeth* is Shakespeare's most profound and mature vision of evil.' Wilson Knight begins his essay '*Macbeth* and the Metaphysic of Evil' with this statement, and elaborates it to show how the atmosphere of evil completely enfolds the play and touches even the good characters like Banquo. Wilson Knight assembles and presents and poetic-dramatic details through which this atmosphere is conveyed; emphasises, for instance, the number of questions asked, through which amazement, mystery and doubt are communicated.[49] The reported scenes and rumours (for example, the two accounts of the fighting, by the Sergeant and Ross) contribute to the same effect. Wilson Knight pinpoints the imagery of darkness and the vivid animal and storm disorder-symbolism. The total effect is one of fear;[50] the word itself, apart from the effect, is ubiquitous, so that the impact is analogous to nightmare. The sleep – and blood-references also come in for detailed attention.[51] The life-themes analysed in detail in *The Imperial Theme* essay, 'The Milk of Concord', are touched upon in this essay, too, lest the opposition between life-forces and forces of evil be missed. The evil–grace polarity is emphasised. 'The logic of imaginative correspondence', as Wilson Knight has it, may be 'more significant and more exact than the logic of plot'; yet the manifold correspondences of imaginative quality and atmosphere are meaningful only in relation to story and characters. A tacit admission of this truth is found in Wilson Knight's study of Macbeth's character. After all, discoveries about theme and imagery have to be referred to characters, their situations and the general line of dramatic action. The exclusion of reference to the concept of the will in the delineation of Macbeth is convincingly explained. In his own way Wilson Knight accounts for the paling into insignificance of the minor characters (*WF*, p. 152).[52] A fruitful and original insight into Lady Macbeth is made: Wilson Knight finds it futile to comment on her in terms of 'ambition' and 'will', and shows that 'she is not merely a woman of strong will: she is a woman possessed' (*WF*, p. 152).[53]

---

[49] Such questioning is a fairly obvious dramatic device; its occurrence at the opening of *Hamlet* has been commented on by Maynard Mack, 'The World of Hamlet', reprinted in *Shakespeare: Modern Essays in Criticism*, edited by L. F. Dean (New York, 1961), first edition 1957, especially pp. 239–40.

[50] In the same year that saw the publication of *Wheel of Fire*, 1930, Lily B. Campbell in her *Shakespeare's Tragic Heroes: Slaves of Passion* commented on *Macbeth* as a study of 'fear', and Caroline Spurgeon emphasises the importance of the image of 'fear' in the play.

[51] Wilson Knight in his preface to *Shakespeare and Religion* acknowledges his probable debt to Dowden who noticed these strands of imagery in the play.

[52] A feature considered a drawback by Bradley – *Shakespearian Tragedy* (1957 edn), pp. 326–9.

[53] Again, an intuitive perception of Wilson Knight's later confirmed through historical scholarship and the study of the occult by W. C. Curry in his *Shakespeare's Philosophical Patterns*. Insights into Lady Macbeth's character complementary to Wilson Knight's are in Eugene M. Waith, 'Manhood and Valor in

The analysis of Macbeth's first soliloquy about the crime is the
forerunner of many such analyses. Wilson Knight's perceptions
about the theme of reversal of values in the play are also among
his seminal findings. His insistence on Macbeth's state of exaltation in the last scenes (very similar to Lascelles Abercrombie's in
The Idea of Great Poetry (London, 1925)), and on what he considers
to be the positive drive and upward thrust of the tragic hero, is a
theme of later commentaries, based on Wilson Knight's acting
experience. The contrast between this view of Macbeth and those
of the other 'poetic' interpreters, like L. C. Knights and Traversi,
is striking. In the essay entitled 'the Mild of Concord', Wilson
Knight subsumes the values of life and health, the creative and
positive ideas behind 'the apocalypse of evil' which the play is,
under four categories: (i) warrior honour; (ii) imperial magnificence; (iii) sleep and feasting; and (iv) ideas of creation and
nature's innocence. Granted that there is a rather indiscriminate
lumping together of references, Wilson Knight's practice could
be defended on the score that the use of categories of classification cannot be dispensed with in commentary. Yet closer attention to the dramatic context of, or the historical and linguistic facts
about, the references would have been in place, in his account of
'sleep', 'feasting' and 'nature'. To classify the witches' cauldron
scene as 'feasting' is evidently eccentric. Nature references blend
with human themes, especially as regards procreation and childhood. The analysis of 'the temple-haunting martlet' speech (*IT*,
pp. 141–2) is the first in, and the inspiration of, a series. Child-
references are seen as the most important of all the suggestions of
life-forces.[54] The repetition of 'grace' is shown to be a thematic
undercurrent.[55] In the later commentaries (the appendix in *ST*,
GL and *SF*) the authenticity of the Hecate scenes is asserted, and

Two Shakespearean Tragedies', *ELH*, 17 (1950), 262–73 and especially in D. W.
Harding, 'Women's Fantasy of Manhood: A Shakespearian Theme', *SQ*, 20
(1969), 245–53.
[54] The influence of Wilson Knight's commentary on Leavis's classic analysis, and
Cleanth Brooks' reading of the play is clear enough. Leavis, *Education and the
University* incorporating *How to Teach Reading*, pp. 77–83 and Cleanth Brooks,
The Well-Wrought Urn.
[55] In *IT* (1951 edn, p. 128, n. 1) Wilson Knight cites Mgr Kolbë (*Shakespeare's Way*
(1930)) as computing that 'phrases or words suggestive of a "sin"–"grace"
contrast occur more than four hundred times in *Macbeth*'.

the child apparitions are invested with a key significance as imaginative solidities, as instances of direct poetic symbolism. The storm references are analysed in *The Shakespearian Tempest*. The importance of music and aural effects such as thunder is discussed in *Shakespearian Production*. The idea for a production of a permanent set with the Madonna on one side and a child image on the other is surely too idiosyncratic (pp. 131–44).

4

The 'spatial' interpretation of Wilson Knight – II

Among the traditionally accepted play-groupings, Wilson Knight has also written extended commentaries on the Roman plays. Though not as influential as his readings of the last plays, or the tragedies, or the 'unpleasant' plays, some of his perceptions about the Roman plays are striking; for example, his identification of a certain quality and colourfulness marking their imagery, and his sensuous apprehension of their dramatic shape and poetic atmosphere.[1] Apart from the sensitive and illuminating study of the imaginative correspondences between Brutus and Macbeth in *The Wheel of Fire*, an analysis of *Julius Caesar* is given in two essays in *The Imperial Theme*. In the first, Wilson Knight examines the imaginative colour of the play, as manifested in the imagery. The beast symbolism (later, in *The Shakespearian Tempest*, considered in its curious yet close relationships with the storm symbolism), the metal references, the body references, and the body-spirit dualism and their effects, are noted.[2] The almost fiery colourfulness of the world of the play is contrasted with its bare, 'Roman' style.[3] Wilson Knight lays special emphasis on the images of blood, which are different in nature from those in

[1] Francis Berry, 'G. Wilson Knight: Stage and Study', *The Morality of Art* edited by D. W. Jefferson (London, 1969), pp. 138–9, comments on Wilson Knight's response to the 'colourful abundance' of Shakespeare. Wilson Knight's vision of colours is the mystic's rather than the neurotic's. See the quotation from *Atlantic Crossing* by Wilson Knight in *The Laureate of Peace*, pp. 89–90.
[2] The comments on some of these strains of imagery, especially the metal references by T. S. Dorsch (The New Arden edition of the play), are an instance of the development of Wilson Knight's insights by scholars.
[3] Wilson Knight acknowledges his debt to Masefield's lecture 'Shakespeare and the Spiritual Life' (1924), printed in *Recent Prose* (1932).

Macbeth,[4] and analyses the interlinking of the fire imagery with the blood imagery. This shows well how Wilson Knight at his best can recapture imaginatively the sense-impressions and reverberations evoked by images, so that justice is done to the dramatic and poetic realisation of imagery in the theatre – at least the theatre of the mind. Indeed the interaction of strands of imagery is another key effect with which Wilson Knight is concerned. In the first of *The Imperial Theme* essays, as later in more emphatic terms in *The Shakespearian Tempest*, Wilson Knight discovers and stresses the conspirators' positive identification of order with Cassius, and their perception of Caesar as a symbol of disorder. Thus, the order–disorder antithesis, which may be seen almost everywhere in Shakespeare, is occasionally reversed by Wilson Knight. The vision of 'fierce fiery warriors who fought upon the clouds, / In ranks and squadrons and right form of war, / Which drizzled blood upon the Capitol' (II. ii. 19ff) is given greater attention later as a symbolic solidity. Wilson Knight calls the world of the play one of a brilliant erotic vision. In the second essay on the play, in *The Imperial Theme*, this perception is elaborated at great length and the characters (or the different 'ideas', as Wilson Knight insists on calling them) in the play are described as lovers. In the accounts of the play in *The Sovereign Flower* and *The Golden Labyrinth*, and in the references to it in *The Burning Oracle*, this idea is developed in relation to Shakespeare's postulated theme of bisexuality. To Wilson Knight there are no 'ambiguities'; it is not a 'problem play' at all.

The essay on *Coriolanus* in *The Imperial Theme* (1931) is one of the first and most comprehensive of the few studies of what was then a generally neglected play. A conflict between the two values of love and war is perceived. Wilson Knight finds the theme to be that there is an 'intrinsic fault in any ambition, or indeed any

---

[4] The difference between the ways in which the blood imagery in *Julius Caesar* and in *Macbeth* is interpreted is as instructive as that between the ways in which character in *Macbeth* and *Othello* is interpreted. As John Jones points out, 'Shakespeare and Mr Wilson Knight', p. 1011, it is illustrative of Wilson Knight's sensitive attention to the 'atmosphere' or the world of each play, 'the vision of each play as an independent universe, saying itself, acting itself, presenting its own myth'.

value, which is not a multiple of love'. His identification of the distinctive quality of the style of the play is apt. Yet the charged metaphors of his emotional style dazzle rather than throw light. The major perception is of the dominance of metal imagery in the play. Wilson Knight shows how these images blend with the town setting and the frequent mention of buildings. Even war is referred to in terms which are metallic, 'impactuous'[5] (*IT*, p. 163). The contrast between nature images and metallic images, like the contrast between strong and weak things in nature, corresponds to the antithesis of Coriolanus and the plebeians. In his account of the character of the hero, 'the Coriolanus-idea', Wilson Knight goes to the heart of the matter when he says 'Coriolanus' "pride" and "virtue" are shown not as two distinct attributes, but rather as a single quality twined in the pattern of his "nature". Each is curiously intrinsic to the other' (*IT*, p. 166). The function of the characters of Volumnia and Virgilia is taken into account; and it is clear that the comments on these two women characters derive in part from Murry's studies of the play. This section of Wilson Knight's Shakespeare commentary enjoys the distinction (somewhat like Wilson Knight's comments on *Pericles* and the last plays) of inspiring a poem by Eliot, 'Coriolan', or so we gather from Wilson Knight's essay, 'T. S. Eliot: Some Literary Impressions', 241–2.

Of all the plays Wilson Knight has devoted the most extensive and enthusiastic attention to *Antony and Cleopatra*. Apart from the two 'Notes' on the play (which I discuss below, on p. 101), there are two essays in *The Imperial Theme*, the first mainly concerned with the atmosphere and imagery of the play, and the second with the characters and their relationships. While we find that the 'spatial' approach to *Antony and Cleopatra* is richly fruitful, it can only be completed and supported by an analysis of characters. The two kinds of analysis are interlinked. Again, Wilson Knight's theory undergoes both modification and supplementation in practice.

Starting from his own impression of 'a visionary and idealistic optimism' in 'The Transcendental Humanism of *Antony and*

---

[5] One of Wilson Knight's several coinages in his commentaries.

Cleopatra', Wilson Knight examines 'the effects which contribute to the prevailing optimism' (*IT*, p. 199). What takes place in the play is aptly described as a process and effect of transfiguration. The metaphorically charged account of the poetry of the play ('of the play's style' as he calls it), though it is a sensitive and individual response, does not go far enough as commentary except for occasional insights about the texture of the verse, such as the one about the recurrence of thin or feminine vowels (*IT*, p. 201). Part of the technique of transfiguration which Wilson Knight perceives in *Antony and Cleopatra* is found in the way the sensuous and the material are sublimated in an ascending scale, mainly by means of ' desensualised medium', rising first to the grand and the magnificent and then to the purely spiritual. The imaginative vision of the play as a complex whole is analysed in terms of the themes of imperial magnificence: the imperial power and warrior-honour which Antony sacrifices for love. The magnitude of Antony's sacrifice is forcefully conveyed, according to Wilson Knight. The physical and sensuous love themes and love imagery, predominate in the dialogue, directly and by suggestion. The recurring symbols of nature, the suggestion of the mating of the elements, the whole ascent from material to ethereal, invest the love theme with an overwhelming stature and significance: spiritual and transcendental. The 'sea' and 'land' imagery blends with the 'world' imagery (stressed by Caroline Spurgeon) and the two main themes of War and Love are interwoven; both the Shakespearian values are idealised with the help of the impregnating atmosphere of wealth, power, military strength, and material magnificence. Feasting and drinking images and associations suggest the 'lower' element of animal desire in the love of Antony and Cleopatra. Wilson Knight conveys the twofold suggestion of sensuous pleasure and positive life-force in such imagery. The physical aspects of love, lust and sex, are stressed as much as the ethereal ones, though the poetry avoids direct sensuous appeal; 'it is a chaste vision of unchastity'.

What Wilson Knight calls the eroticism of the play is communicated through its imagery. The images and associations are enumerated in terms of familiar categories, such as physical, especially facial, features; animal references; and the imagery of nature's bounty. Though this mode of classification is one which Wilson Knight uses again, it does not become stale. He points out, for instance, the suggestive power of the frequent mention of 'serpents' and snakes, and aquatic and aerial creatures. The general impressions of fertility, the life-processes of love, constitute a theme. The way the four elements figure in the imagery creates the impression of element dissolving into element in the play. This is a fitting, if inevitably metaphorical, way of pointing to and naming an effect which readers can recognise in their experience of the play. But when Wilson Knight, to bring out the significance of the juxtaposition of 'water' and 'land', says that 'the sea is associated clearly with femininity, softness, and the East as opposed to manly strength' (*IT*, p. 235), one feels inevitably that the schema has been carried too far. While there is something of 'the vast theme of East and West' (p. 235) suggested in the relationship of Cleopatra and Antony, it is not helpful to state that 'Shakespeare's love-imagery often takes him East' (p. 235). The grouping together of 'sun' and 'moon' references and 'the glittering brilliance of gold and other precious metals' are further instances of arbitrary classification. This is probably because Wilson Knight pays insufficient attention to the immediate dramatic context, and may show the influence of Caroline Spurgeon's methods of classifying and analysing imagery. Wilson Knight suggests that some strands of imagery, like those of 'light' and 'music', are associated with the love theme, and that 'crown' references[6] relate to the idea of the world well lost for love as well as to the apotheosis of love. The 'fortune' concept is interpreted in transcendental terms.[7] 'Sportive' imagery is frequently noted. Wilson Knight suggests that there is a remarkable merging of the imaginative 'atmosphere' with the individual protagonist. The tendency to see in certain central passages a microcosm of the play, which is a device Wilson Knight frequently employs,[8] is

---

[6] The centrality of the 'crown' idea here and elsewhere, is one of the major emphases of Wilson Knight's later commentary.

[7] As against Mgr Kolbë's (*Shakespeare's Way*) interpretation or the interpretation by Marilyn Williamson, 'Fortune in Antony and Cleopatra', *JEGP*, 66 (1968), 423–9.

[8] Well exemplified in his 'The Prophetic Soul: A Note on Richard II, v, v, 1–66', *IT* (1965 edn), 351–67. The method might be called the inversion of the tendency

found in his analysis of two passages – Enobarbus' description of Cleopatra's meeting with Antony, and Cleopatra's dream-vision of Antony. Wilson Knight suggests that the important implication of the closing parts of the play is that Antony and Cleopatra find not death but life, the high metaphysic of love melting life and death into a final oneness.

His second long essay on *Antony and Cleopatra* is an elaboration of the theme of loyalty, which takes the form of a simultaneous romantic idealisation of love and a glorifying paean to Cleopatra. The visionary brilliance of the play includes and transcends sordid realism. Wilson Knight isolates as a striking feature distinguishing almost all the characters a wavering between divided loyalties, so that the dualisms in the play can be seen as a dialectical progression towards ultimate unity in the sublimation of loyalty into love. Of these dualisms the most striking is the conflict in Antony between Love and War. Cleopatra's two main qualities are her essential femininity, and her variety of psychic modes. The final act is the crest not only of this play but of the whole Shakespearian progress.

'Macbeth and Antony and Cleopatra' (*IT*, 327–42) points to the imaginative correspondences between the two plays in much the same way as the correspondences between the characters ('persons' or 'ideas' in Wilson Knight's parlance) of Macbeth and Brutus are outlined in *The Wheel of Fire*. It is inevitable that some straining after parallels occurs in such attempts; and while it is not surprising that *Macbeth* should serve as a standard of reference, it seems to me that effects distinctive of one play are read into the other, although similarities in conception and in technique do exist. In 'A Note on *Antony and Cleopatra*' (*IT*, 343–50), Wilson Knight adduces passages from philosophy, journalistic writing and poetry, to illustrate the fusion of engagement in the physical and passionate and the sublimation of these instincts into the spiritual and eternal, in order to bring out the significance of the play – a simultaneous transcendence and inclusion by a sort of immanence. In his comment on the play in *The Golden*

---

of the poetic critics to analyse the texture of individual passages in relation to the structure of feeling and thought of the whole play.

Labyrinth, after noting the warmth with which the play is suf-
fused and the 'generosity' and 'infinite variety' of Cleopatra,
Wilson Knight perceives the bisexual idea as implicit in the relationships of 'these two grand sexual beings'. The transfiguration
of humanity and the telling irony of life being found in death and
'our greatest love drama necessarily dramatising an illicit love'
are stressed.

Wilson Knight's war-time lectures and his monograph on the
conceptions of royalism and national glory in Shakespeare in
general, and the history plays in particular, were the first modern
attempt at a reinterpretation of the history plays, preceding the
studies by Tillyard, Lily B. Campbell, Dover Wilson, Irving
Ribner and M. M. Reese. Though the reader is left wondering
whether Wilson Knight's commentary is dramatic interpretation
or war-time propaganda, characteristically valuable perceptions
abound. The themes of kingship, order, honour, and martial
glory, as well as the horrors of war and the religious associations
of kingship, are commented upon with sensitivity and acuteness.
3 Henry VI is seen to be a microcosm of later plays, carrying hints
of *Richard III* and *Macbeth*. Illuminating remarks on *Richard II* are
made in *Principles of Shakespearian Production* (1936). Wilson
Knight directs our attention to the comparisons in the play between the weak, vacillating king and Christ and the sun.[9] Wilson
Knight has no interest in the order of composition of the history
plays, or their grouping as two tetralogies. He considers them as
a psychological, rather than a chronological, sequence. That is
why *King John*, usually considered to stand outside the scheme of
the two historical tetralogies, is taken to be essential to the evolu-

[9] He points out how Richard II rises in our estimation in the second half of the
play, a finding based on his experience of acting the role; he finds a similar
quality in Romeo. Wilson Knight talks of a Christ-like quality in Richard II's fall:
'He climbs his miniature Calvary' (*SP*, p. 32). Though seeing characters as
Christ-figures, inaugurated in a very different spirit by Wilson Knight, as he
explains in 'Shakespeare and Theology', has been carried to an extreme by later
Christianising critics, Wilson Knight's intuitive use of the comparison has
warrant in historical scholarship. Dover Wilson, in his New Shakespeare edition, points to the late medieval commentators' conception of Richard II as a
Christ-like king–martyr. Drayton refers to the Passion of Edward II in *The
Barons' War*. That the comparison of the king with the sun is a great Elizabethan
commonplace has been shown by Tillyard.

tion of Shakespeare's national idea and of his conception of the kind of personalities that can fulfil it. Wilson Knight traces the gradations through which the ideal conception of royalty in *Henry V* is arrived at. In Wilson Knight's view the self-critical ironist and the realistic sceptic distinguish English heroism, as opposed to its continental counterpart, and are represented in such 'dramatic supermen' or 'dramatic powers' as Falconbridge and Falstaff. These qualities are at once absorbed and surpassed in the figure of Henry V.

Wilson Knight emphasises the religious associations of the crown and kingship, in the history plays, and also the way in which the distinctive identity and superiority of religion is acknowledged; this is part of his analysis of Shakespeare's comprehensive conception of royalty. However, he applies his idea of royalty to too many other plays, almost obsessively. The concept could have certain uses as propaganda; but when it is used as an interpretative category, the danger is that the interpretation lapses into a mere reading *into*.

Wilson Knight's interpretation of the last plays has been the most characteristic – and among the most influential – of his Shakespearian studies, and the strengths *and* weaknesses of his approach are displayed here most clearly. If one can speak of a twentieth-century revival of critical interest in the last plays, and if the plays have come to be regarded as great masterpieces, like the tragedies, and not as mere indulgences or freaks, the pioneering commentary which inaugurated later writings was Wilson Knight's first monograph on the last plays, *Myth and Miracle*, published in 1929 (though one should also remember Granville-Barker's Savoy Theatre production of *The Winter's Tale*). The more elaborate and definitive interpretation of the last plays – including *Henry VIII*, another critical discovery of Wilson Knight – came in 1947, in *The Crown of Life*. Wilson Knight attaches special importance to his study of the last plays:[10] they mark the success-

---

[10] 'I remember well how it happened. One day I was writing to Middleton Murry that it would be probably centuries before our minds could advance beyond the tragedies to a group of these works; and the next, their meaning was absurdly clear. "Absurdly" for this reason: *all you had to do was to take them at their face value*. This was all; and yet it had never been done. Just as we had always read

ful completion of 'the Shakespeare Progress' (see p. 27). Em-
ploying the argument from the Hegelian, dialectical pattern of
juxtaposed antinomies, he sees the last plays as the ultimate
spiritual synthesis reached after the thesis and antithesis of the
love-theme and the hate-theme, the life-theme and the death-theme,
in the 'sombre' tragedies. Wilson Knight's insight into the last
plays as a group is that they are to be seen as 'myths of immortality'.[11]

Without going deeply into the use of the term 'myth' (ubiquitous in modern criticism) we can see how Wilson Knight uses it as
a key to the whole group of plays. In *Myth and Miracle*, *The
Christian Renaissance*, *Principles of Shakespearian Production* and *The
Crown of Life*, he outlines the way in which the suggestion of
rebirth through death recurs in the plays. Scenes such as Thaisa's
recovery, her reunion with Pericles in Diana's temple, Marina's
meeting with Pericles in *Pericles*, the discovery of Imogen in
Cymbeline, the sheep-shearing festival, the coming alive of the
statue of Hermione in *The Winter's Tale*, the survival of Alonso,
Sebastian and their party in *The Tempest*, the vision of Queen
Catherine in *Henry VIII*, which were previously regarded as
romantic indulgences or as instances of *coups de théâtre*, are seen
to be of central significance. Wilson Knight takes the whole of
Pericles to be by Shakespeare (instead of only the last three acts, as
is generally believed on internal evidence).[12] Questions such as

tragedy as a statement of man's tragic destiny, so we had now to read these
reunions and resurrections as statements of immortality', Wilson Knight, 'The
New Interpretation', *Essays in Criticism*, p. 382 (my italics).

[11] Though *The Crown of Life* came only in 1947, *Myth and Miracle* and the occasional
and incidental commentaries of Wilson Knight on the last plays started appearing from 1929 onwards. (The earliest study of the theme of immortality in the
last plays, entitled *Thaisa* and written in 1927, was never published.) These
writings can be said to have inspired interpretations such as those of D. G.
James, *Scepticism and Poetry*, E. M. W. Tillyard *Shakespeare's Last Plays* (1938),
S. L. Bethell, *The Winter's Tale – A Study* (1947), and D. A. Traversi *Shakespeare –
The Last Phase* (1954). T. S. Eliot seems to have been particularly impressed by
Wilson Knight's *Myth and Miracle*. It inspired his poem 'Marina', and was
behind Eliot's lectures (unpublished) on the last plays. In his review of Middleton Murry's book on Shakespeare in *The Criterion*, 15 (1935–6), Eliot says; 'on
the last plays I have received more help from the writings of Mr Wilson Knight'
(p. 710).

[12] But Wilson Knight has said more recently: 'I have never urged the complete
authenticity of *Pericles*, though I have regarded it as throughout dominated by
Shakespeare's mind' – 'New Dimensions in Shakespearian Interpretation',
Shakespeare and Religion, n. on p. 199.

the relationship of the play to its sources, its date, its kinship with Fletcherian tragicomedy, and its antedating the King's men starting to play at the Blackfriars Theatre, are, characteristically not raised at all.

Wilson Knight's Christological (as distinct from Christian) preoccupations, his royalist and nationalist sympathies, and his ideal of the superman who combines the apparently irreconcilable antinomies of the secular and the religious; these enable him to identify in *Cymbeline* a theme of national regeneration through the union of Rome and Albion, with the Nativity theme in the background of the play.

Wilson Knight's fresh grasp of general themes has been exploited to the full by later commentators; and certainly his insight into the last plays helps us to account for the elements of the marvellous and the supernatural in them. Even those who are usually suspicious of any attempt to allegorise the plays must grant that these plays do admit of an allegorical interpretation. The uncomfortable fact remains that Wilson Knight all too readily finds in the plays grist for the mill of his interest in the 'myth of immortality', in the supernatural, in the miracles of spiritualism and magic, in the royalist or bisexual ideal, and in the ideal of the superman. Nonetheless he is able to take account, in a synoptic view, of most of the characteristic features of the plays, such as the storm imagery, the themes of music, of nature versus nurture and also some of the comic elements, such as Autolycus in *The Winter's Tale*. Wilson Knight's emphasis is on the *creation* of a vision of immortality and, at the same time, on 'dramatic incarnation in close contact with human experience' (*GL*, p. 82) in this drama 'beyond tragedy' which we find in the last plays. In his 'Great Creating Nature: An Essay on *The Winter's Tale* (*GL*, pp. 98–128), Wilson Knight explicates the idea of 'great creating nature' which he sees as the informing principle of the 'myth of immortality' that is the play. He identifies a theme of the creativeness and resurrective and eternalising power of youth and nature (the two being interrelated), and this enables him to offer a unified solution to all three major interpretative cruces in the play – the jealousy of Leontes, the discussion between Perdita and Polixenes on art versus nature, and the statue scene in which

Hermione comes alive. Wilson Knight sees a dramatic opposition between Leontes in the grip of his jealousy and his tyrannical impulses on the one side, and Mamillius, the new-born Perdita, the matronly protectress Paulina and the Oracle on the other. There is also a cumulative effect in the references to childhood, fertility and innocence as forces of natural creativity and grace. Wilson Knight well identifies the impact on the audience of the development of Leontes' jealousy, as well as of the tragic action bred by it. But his apprehension of Leontes as a picture of evil self-born and unmotivated is reductionist. He sees the ironies of the dramatic context of the debate over art and nature in IV. iii. of the play, but he also finds dimensions of eternity and transcendence in the hidden 'royalty' of the prince and princess in two different kinds of disguise, and postulates an association between them. This dimension of eternity links the apparent opposites of art and nature. The 'miracles' of the reunion of father and daughter, of friend and friend, and, supremely, of Leontes and Hermione, when her statue comes alive, all of which immediately follow the wedding in Sicilia of Perdita and Florizel, are presented as a transfiguration of nature and human nurture into the realm of the eternal and immortal. Hence the 'hierophany' of the statue scene is given particular emphasis in this essay and elsewhere. Wilson Knight has a keen perception of the active communication in the play world between the apparent opposites of nature and grace (at once transcendental and immanent) and also of the mediation between nature and art effected by grace. Thanks to this perception, he responds also to the realistic elements in the play, such as the Autolycus scenes, and to the earthiness of many of its situations and utterances.

Prospero in *The Tempest* is the Shakespearian Superman who combines in himself 'religion, art, wisdom and goodness assuming secular authority'; 'the opacity between nature and supernature is dissolved in him'; and 'like Christ, he can control the elements' (*GL*, p.85). He typifies the superhuman phase of evolution. All the elements and grades of life are represented in *The Tempest* as a chain of being, ranging from Caliban to Prospero. Wilson Knight sees the play as gathering up in itself the motifs as well as the character-and-plot patterns of all the earlier plays. He demonstrates how almost all that was in the earlier plays at the level only of verbal reference, image, and suggestion finds in the last plays in general, and *The Tempest* in particular, embodiment on stage. *The Tempest* garners and epitomises all the earlier plays. Yet it is not Shakespeare's farewell to the stage, according to Wilson Knight: just as Prospero returned to his Milan, so Shakespeare returned to the stage with *Henry VIII*, which Wilson Knight takes to be wholly authentic Shakespeare. This view seems to have found favour with a number of scholars.[13] Here, as elsewhere, we have what Wilson Knight would regard as an instance of scholarship catching up with the insights of interpretation. He sees more in the play than mere pageantry and masque elements added to a version of the medieval 'Fall', or *de casibus* tragedy, in the threefold fall of Buckingham, Wolsey and Catherine. He finds the play yields a great deal to the 'spiritual' approach. It is 'a massive, ceremonial piece, in which kingship and religion are co-present and interaffective' (*GL*, p. 85). In this, 'Shakespeare's final and royal statement' (p. 88), the farewell and dying speeches of Buckingham, Wolsey and Catherine, the prophecy of Cranmer, and the vision in which Queen Catherine before her death is visited by angels are significant focal points. The three tragic characters, though king-opposers touched with evil, rise to tragic stature in their last moments. The theophanic scene of the vision of the angels is full of poetic symbolism. Cranmer's prophecy is taken by Wilson Knight as the final, authoritative statement of Shakespeare's royalist and nationalist ideal.

Wilson Knight did not apply his new interpretation of Shakespeare as extensively to the comedies or not with the same degree of illumination. Yet some of his comments are worth attention; they occur in *The Shakespearian Tempest*, *Shakespearian Production* and *The Golden Labyrinth*. In *The Shakespearian Tempest*, the tempest–music opposition is seen in almost all the plays, with its

---

[13] See Peter Alexander, 'Conjectural History, or Shakespeare's Henry VIII', *E & S* 16 (1931); and the convincing arguments of R. A. Foakes in favour of the Shakespearian authorship of the entire play in his new Arden edition. Also Wilson Knight, *Shakespeare and Religion*, p. 5.

associations of disorder, its images of animals, the sea, riches and jewellery, and the association of order with music. *A Midsummer Night's Dream* lends itself to this approach, and the symbolic dimensions of the love-theme in this and other comedies are brought out in for example, the associations of riches, jewellery and adventurous, exploratory voyaging in love.[14] The remarks on *The Merchant of Venice* are stimulating: they include the 'spatial' suggestion of a contrast between Venice and Belmont, analyses of the imagery of storm and riches and gold (the visual values of the casket scene), of the 'dramatic superman' Shylock, and his growth in stature, and the association of divinity and grace with Portia.

Wilson Knight attempted in the 1953 edition of *The Shakespearian Tempest* to reduce his spatial reading of the Shakespearian canon to a diagrammatic sketch, in terms of what he isolates as dominant values. Though he makes no more claims for it than as a convenient guide-map, his diagram is an instance of the schematism which he resorts to in his apprehension of the Shakespearian universe.

Wilson Knight has always stressed the need to pay attention to certain visual and aural elements in the plays, which he calls imaginative solidities or direct poetic symbolisms. This is partly a result of his seeing the plays with a producer's and an actor's stage-eye, and partly a result of his interest in the supernatural and in theophany which is, in turn, part of his enthusiasm for spiritualism. These aural and visual elements are focal points and concentrations of dramatic and imaginative energy. This is not to say that he does not concern himself with imagery: we have seen that he does; and it is understandable that conventionally he is classified as an analyst of imagery.[15] But we need to remember that both in his theory and in his practice Wilson Knight concerns himself with elements other than imagery, which is only one

[14] The development of part of this association by John Russell Brown in his account of the comedies in his *Shakespeare and His Comedies* (London, 1957) is interesting, and is one more instance of the fertilising quality of some of Wilson Knight's insights. Characteristically, he does not note the relation of these strands of imagery to the established love-conventions.

[15] As was done by his reviewers, and also by Una Ellis-Fermor in her pamphlet, *Some Recent Research in Shakespeare's Imagery* (Oxford, 1937).

of the features which he identifies as clues to Shakespeare's art.

The aspects of Wilson Knight's Shakespearian commentary which have caused controversy are his alleged 'Christianising' of Shakespeare, his supposed indifference or hostility to historical scholarship, and his refusal (or, as sometimes construed, incapacity) to make qualitative discriminations – or at another level, the violent disagreements provoked by his principles of interpretation, his 'crotchets', his ideological affiliations, his temperamental manifestations of taste and, above all, his style both in the sense of his mode of feeling and thought, and its expression.

Recent reaction against 'Christianising' interpretations of the plays (see p. 51, n. 22), uses Wilson Knight as a whipping boy. He himself denies that he even countenances the 'theologising' of Shakespeare. By way of reply to Roland M. Frye who, in *Shakespeare and Christian Doctrine*, argued against the trend of 'Christianising' interpretation and called Wilson Knight its inaugurator, Wilson Knight tried to make clear, in 'Shakespeare and Theology' and elsewhere,[16] that he only uses certain Christian categories and terms; and that the concepts of rebirth, martyrdom, and death in the aspect of ritual sacrifice which he uses in his interpretation have a more than Christian significance. One would almost think that in place of clarification Wilson Knight has offered refutation. He implies that the frame of reference of his interpretation is a scheme of values and ideas which includes some, but not all, aspects of Christianity,[17] and which, more importantly,

---

[16] 'Shakespeare and Theology: A Private Protest', pp. 95–104 and the Introduction to *Shakespeare and Religion*, pp. 1–25; 'Symbolism', *A Shakespeare Encyclopaedia*, edited by O. J. Campbell and E. G. Quinn (London, 1966), p. 840. 'While making Shakespearian drama a series of Christian moralities, with "order", which can mean anything or nothing, as a deceptive guide, the commentators have remained blind to the major symbolic powers, none of which – except for the examples that we have noted in *Measure for Measure* and *Henry VIII*, (the Angels) – are Christian' – Preface to *Shakespeare and Religion*, p. v; also, pp. 12, 20–1, 103, 311–12, 318.

[17] 'we can align Shakespeare with Christianity in respect to what might be called his earthly, humanly warm approach to the spiritualistic truths. Christianity, like Shakespeare, while *including* all the spiritualities and among them what we today call "spiritualism", puts a primary emphasis on *incarnation* . . . I have been criticised for suggesting that Shakespeare's tragic heroes may be regarded as "miniature Christs". The remark must be read in its context, where some necessary reservations are made . . . we must moreover distinguish

reaches beyond Christianity to a highly eclectic collection of beliefs and myths. Whatever his personal religious beliefs, his commentary has reference to an unorthodox and certainly heterogenous cluster of ideas, including Faustian, Manichaean and occult ones. Yet it cannot be denied that certain explicitly Christian terms, without the qualifications which Wilson Knight makes in his later writings such as *The Golden Labyrinth* and *The Shakespeare Encyclopaedia* article on 'Symbolism', are employed in the early writings, particularly in *Myth and Miracle*, *The Christian Renaissance* and *Principles of Shakespearian Production*, especially in the chapter 'Shakespeare and Ritual'. Bonamy Dobrée said in his 'On (Not) Enjoying Shakespeare', 'there is admittedly . . . a considerable aura of Christian – I won't call it doctrine exactly, but feeling – about the later plays, as Wilson Knight was, I think, the first of many to point out with any firmness'.[18] Yet Wilson Knight's way of comparing Richard II, Theseus, Duke Vincentio and Prospero to Christ makes it clear that his identification of Christ figures is quite unlike that of other commentators finding analogues of Christ in the plays.

If it is facile to distinguish between a 'good' early Wilson Knight, the critic with stimulating insights, and a 'bad' late Wilson Knight who uses the Shakespearian text as a peg for his own visions, ideals and prejudices, it is only an exaggeration of a truth. For, as we have seen in the previous chapter (p. 72), even in his early interpretations Wilson Knight was using an apparatus of ideas and philosophies, most of which are anything but literary, as a means of opening up new significances in Shakespearian drama. Perhaps almost every major critical advance or interpretative manoeuvre arises because the commentator has some extra-literary axe to grind.[19] The more extensive and vigorous insis-

between "Christ" and "Christianity". In doctrine there are vivid divergencies . . . Christ was a romantic, the Church is realistic' – Introduction, *Shakespeare and Religion*, pp. 11 and 12.

[18] Page 45. Nevill Coghill says in a review of Virgil K. Whitaker, *The Mirror up to Nature: A Study of Shakespeare's Tragedies* (1965): 'A Christian construction, or Christian insights have been seen, of recent years, in many of his plays, whether tragedies or comedies . . . Professor Wilson Knight led the way to such a concept as early as in 1930' – *RES*, n.s. 18 (1967), p. 327.

[19] There is an interesting discussion of this question with reference to modern Milton criticism in Miriam K. Hartman, 'The Militant Miltonist or the Retreat

tence on a complex of ideas and ideals in Wilson Knight's later commentaries brings out assumptions and interests implicit in his early commentary, and now assuming larger proportions. The evolution of Wilson Knight's career has affinities with that of several major modern critics. The intrusion of ideology into his commentary reminds us of T. S. Eliot, Allen Tate and R. P. Blackmur in their later careers. The difference is that while Eliot and Allen Tate embraced orthodox religion, Wilson Knight uses a medley of myth and belief as a framework of interpretation.

One of the primary problems with Wilson Knight's interpretation of Shakespeare is to determine how far his methodological techniques are valid. Naturally, his methods have been denied general validity; he has been credited with some kind of *pre-critical* innocence; and his 'unprincipled eclecticism' is said to lead him into the fallacy of always translating poetry into what it 'stands for'.[20] His concept of placing Shakespearian drama in a space–time totality brought us new insights. But his preoccupation with the imaginative solidities which the words only hint at, at the expense of their literal meaning, can violate the age-old principle of allegorical interpretation that the allegorical does not supersede the literal meaning, and the basic need to respond to the immediate poetic impact of the words. Wilson Knight has maintained that 'poetic interpretation itself far from opposing scholarship of the right kind, applies the methods of scholarship to that spiritual content of great literature hitherto left to the purely personal appreciation and judgements of literary criticism'.[21] But the trouble is that the methods of Wilson Knight are not subject to the scholarly virtues of caution and circumspection and the indispensable criterion of relevance, even though there is frequently a point of contact between the results of Wilson

from Humanism', *ELH*, 26 (1959), 209–28. As Hyman pointed out in *The Armed Vision*, p. 3, the modern critical enterprise is marked by a systematic application of extra-literary knowledge to the study of literature.

[20] F. W. Bateson (*EC*, 4 (1954), p. 223): 'Mr Wilson Knight's most engaging characteristic is his uncorrupted, incorruptible innocence . . . But a method as subjective as this cannot possibly be taught. There can be no school of "interpretation" '. A. E. Rodway and Gāmini Salgādo, 'The School of Knight', *EC*, 4 (1954), pp. 212–21, formulate the second charge. (Response to Wilson Knight's, 'The New Interpretation', pp. 382–95.)

[21] Wilson Knight, 'The New Interpretation', p. 390.

Knight's interpretation and the investigations of scholars. Wilson Knight's insights, or perceptions made by others along lines suggested by him, have been fruitful in Shakespearian commentary. Indeed, the complaint that many a Shakespearian critic has filched his methods and findings without acknowledgement recurs in Wilson Knight's writings. For one thing, his principles and perceptions have been so penetrating and widespread in their influence that, like all deep influences, they have been too fully and unconsciously assimilated into the general critical consciousness to retain their specific identity. For all his individuality as a person, Wilson Knight was, in the thirties and forties, the great *representative* critic, embodying the *Zeitgeist*. Then again, other critics assimilating Wilson Knight's perceptions, have also tempered, modified and developed them.

The prime achievement of Wilson Knight is to have used the spatial mode of approach to show how the 'latent' content of drama, comprising imagery, symbols, and thematic suggestions, reinforces or modifies the 'manifest' content of plot, character and situation. As well as stressing such distinguishing features of his approach, Wilson Knight has summed up the results of his interpretation, especially in 'The New Interpretation' and 'Symbolism'. This summing up, unfortunately, is biased in the direction of his increasing interest in spiritualism, in the spirit-world, in the 'other dimensions' and orders of life and being. Though he mentions here again the tempest–music opposition and the crown references, both occurring throughout Shakespeare, as essential clues discovered and interpreted by him, the stress on direct poetic solidities rather than on imagery is characteristic of Wilson Knight's extra-literary preoccupation and the orientation of his commentary. This is one of the grounds on which Wilson Knight can be said paradoxically both to stand outside the 'new criticism' and at the same time to inspire and to pioneer it. If the *Scrutiny* reviewers of Wilson Knight's books all deplore the fact that he fails to exercise literary-critical rigour and disciplined discrimination, or a sense of relevance, Wilson Knight merely points to his deliberate disavowal of any *critical* aim and practice, and finds in turn that the *Scrutiny* critics have failed in availing themselves only partially of his interpretative insights and not carrying his modes of interpretation as far as he did.[22] Wilson Knight is concerned with more than 'the words on the page', as he makes plain himself, and as his critics do too.

For one thing, its main concentration is not verbal at all, but, as I have regularly called it, 'spatial'. Its first interest is the structure, the pattern, the body of the work in question, almost irrespective of the exact language used; and also the semivisualization, as of a space-reality, of images, symbols, stage-actions, such as Hermione's resurrection, in all their visible impact and depth of meaning.

In the act of interpretation the new forms begin to appear from *within* the word-wrappings, like Aphrodite from the foam, or a liner from fog. The wrappings, or word-sequences, are relegated to a subsidiary status. True, it is they that have helped us to focus the structure, poised it into imaginative being; but there is always a danger of mistaking the telescope for the view. . . It is quite fallacious to say that since they are expressed *through* words it is impossible to receive the riches in question except by an especial concentration *on* words; and if your concentration on the words be mainly an insistence that the words should be themselves unassertive or transparent, we only have paradox added to falacy. (Wilson Knight, 'The New Interpretation', pp. 384–5.)

Wilson Knight abstracts . . . his attention not only from the characters considered as separately real but from the verbal art considered as locally vivid, thinks of the plays as complex patterns of symbolic imagery, and even sometimes picks out for special praise passages which other critics have thought of either as not by Shakespeare, or as showing Shakespeare at his worst. ('Shakespeare's Craft in Verse', *TLS* (2 July 1954), 424.)

One could say that the evolution of his criticism, from literary perceptions to extra-literary perceptions and 'myths', is anticipatory and representative of the evolution of modern criticism from close analysis to myth-hunting – an evolution which, as Murray Krieger, Walter Sutton and Robert B. Heilman have pointed out, is more or less inevitable as a means of reconciling 'contextualism' and value-oriented theories of literature and criticism. The irony is that there are grounds for the charge of an uncritical approach, and this despite the sensitive response to, and appreciation of, poetry scattered throughout the commentaries, and several instances of close reading. In addition to the

---

[22] Wilson Knight, '*Scrutiny* and Criticism', pp. 32–3.

charge that Wilson Knight fails to make necessary discriminations of literary quality, there are charges of extreme impres-
sionism, emotionalism, solemnity and the misuse of sources and
systems.[23]

Wilson Knight himself seems to believe that his analysis is
anything but subjective. In fact, he distinguishes his approach
from most modern critical analysis, or 'practical criticism' which,
according to him, consists of a subjective account of the impact of
the work of literature on oneself.[24] As for the accusation about his
emotionally charged attitude and expression ('a poet among
critics'),[25] Wilson Knight would declare such enthusiasm of
response and of utterance both legitimate and necessary. This
sense of commitment and feeling of gusto in interpretation, suggesting self-engrossment as well as engrossment in Shakespearian drama and in a number of fixed ideas, do lend a tone of
solemnity to Wilson Knight's utterances. But the lack of a sense of
humour is a charge that could be brought against many of the
classic documents of modern literary criticism, products of a
generation which has always taken itself very seriously. One may
ask whether Wilson Knight, in addition to borrowing a mish-
mash of ideas from a variety of sources and systems, has in
mixing them together, also misused them. Though he has
brought these ideas liberally to bear upon his interpretation, he
maintains, at least in theory (one more instance of the hiatus
between his practice and his theory), that he is strictly 'intrinsic'

---

[23] 'Febrile' (John Holloway), 'idiosyncratic style' (D. J. Palmer), and in a 'frankly
evocative way' (John Jones) – such are the remarks of commentators in general.
The charge of an impressionistic lack of a sense of relevance was made by Leavis
in his review of Wilson Knight's *The Christian Renaissance*, in *Scrutiny*, 2
(1933–4), 208–11, especially p. 209 and also by Dobrée in his otherwise sympathetic reviews of Wilson Knight in *The Criterion* (vol. x, 342–7 and vol. xiii,
326–9). René Wellek's summing-up lists most of the charges: 'We all have
learned from Wilson Knight . . . His spatial approach, the way of seeing "a
poem or a play at once in a single view, like a patterned carpet" has become the
model of many later readings. But most of us have become increasingly dissatisfied with the arbitrariness of his association, the intrusion of a crude
psychoanalysis and of a strangely misused Nietzsche' – in 'Romanticism Re-
examined', *Concepts of Criticism*, p. 216.

[24] 'The New Interpretation', p. 386.

[25] Hardin Craig in his review of a reprint of *The Imperial Theme* in *Shakespeare
Quarterly*, 3 (1952), 267–71, esp. p. 271.

in his interpretation;[26] according to him, only interpretation can be completely intrinsic; critics, on the contrary, have to import standards from the outside. His highly individualistic manipulation of psychoanalytic ideas and Nietzschean philosophy is characteristic; and when such a variety of systems and beliefs is drawn upon, their modification or transformation is inevitable.

The student cannot but be struck by the richness, complexity and unity of Wilson Knight's contributions to Shakespeare studies and staging. Whatever the qualitative discriminations we might have to make about the later commentaries, however much we prefer the earlier ones, a certain wholeness of the temper, habits and interests link the two. Wilson Knight is a critic individualistic to the point of eccentricity. His critical endeavour was a sharp reaction against the orientation and preoccupations of contemporary Shakespeare scholarship. Yet it is remarkable that a good many of his intuitive findings are confirmed by historical scholars and fellow-critics; although it remains true that some of his intuitions need modifying or revising and, at times, rejection. Confirmation of his views by other interpreters has often led Wilson Knight to claim priority in this discovery or that, and also to accuse them at times, of using his work without acknowledgment. (For instance, RES, October 1946; Kenyon Review, Winter 1969; Scrutiny, December 1949; TLS, 21 April 1950, p. 245; TLS, 26 October 1946, p. 521.)

One may take, as a specific example of his influence, Wilson Knight's symbolist interpretation of the last plays of Shakespeare. The reading of the plays by Tillyard (Shakespeare's Last Plays), as marking the completion of the tragic pattern with their emphasis on regeneration and renewal, and that by D. G. James (Scepticism and Poetry), as concerned with the theme of recovery and restoration after loss and after breakdown of relations, both lend support to Wilson Knight's view of them as 'myths of immortality', though James thinks that the myths fail in their cognitive endeavour. The influence of Wilson Knight is also evident in Traversi's interpretation of the last plays.

---

[26] 'The New Interpretation', p. 385. Similarly, he would maintain that his symbolist readings are only 'literal' (despite their tracing of 'supraverbal mythemes').

More striking is the indirect corroboration of Wilson Knight's basic findings (though not for his indulgence in elaborating them), by discoveries of scholar-critics such as Arthur C. Kirsch (*Jacobean Dramatic Perspectives*, Charlottesville, 1972) and Jackson I. Cope (*The Theatre and the Dream: From Metaphor to Form in Renaissance Drama*, Baltimore, 1973), about the name and nature of the genre of tragi-comedy. These two critics, using the theoretical defence by Guarini of his pastoral tragi-comedy, *Il Pastor Fido*, have underscored the importance of the ideas of the Fortunate Fall and of miraculous rebirth for the structure of tragi-comedy and Shakespeare's tragi-comedies in particular.

The scholars who have shown the influence of the masque tradition on the last plays, and those who have interpreted Jonson's masques, the 'court hieroglyphics' (in Jonson's phrase), in terms of neo-platonic or transcendental frames of reference (D. J. Gordon and Angus Fletcher), have indirectly sanctioned Wilson Knight's transcendental reading of the last plays, however much it may be governed by a private system of values and myth.

In his study of the influence of Shakespeare on his immediate successors, *The School of Shakespeare* (Cambridge, 1968), David Frost examines the Jacobean habit of planting deeper significances in romance in drama, and in non-dramatic literature (pp. 218–24). According to him, 'both the tradition represented by Spenser and contemporary allegorizing in the court masque (which certainly influenced external features of the romances) would have conditioned Shakespeare's audience to look for this kind of meaning' (p. 223). D. C. Allen, in *Mysteriously Meant: The Rediscovery of Pagan Mythology and Allegorical Interpretation in the Renaissance* (Baltimore, 1970), iconologists like Erwin Panofsky and Edgar Wind[27] have established that allegorisation flourished in the Renaissance period. A. D. Nuttall and Edward

---

[27] Panofsky, *Studies in Iconology* (Harper Torchbooks edn, 1962, original edn, New York, 1939); Wind, *Pagan Mysteries in the Renaissance* (London, 1958) and *Symbolic Images* (London, 1972); also, Jean Seznec, trans. Barbara F. Sessions, *The Survival of the Pagan Gods* (New York, 1953); E. H. Gombrich, 'Icones Symbolicae: The Visual Image in Neo-Platonic Thought', *Journal of the Warburg and Courtauld Institutes*, 11 (1948), 163–92.

Honig[28] in their studies of allegory have shown that in the Elizabethan era allegorical images were apprehended by the Elizabethans as moral or metaphysical realities. This evidence about the assumptions of the age lends support to Wilson Knight's symbolist reading of the plays.

If one takes Wilson Knight's identification and analysis of the recurring tempest–music image theme in Shakespeare, one finds a similarly interesting point of contact and an equally striking disjunction between his intuitions and the facts of medieval and Renaissance literary symbolism brought forward by scholars. Wilson Knight associates images of the storm, the sea, the flood, water and even animal imagery, and subsumes them under the general category of tempest imagery; this latitude is in itself not objectionable, if only because it has warrant in the use and import of such imagery. But when he invokes the storm image in connection with the ducking of Falstaff in a buck basket, or with Pandarus's description of Cressida to Troilus, clearly his schema is running away with him. We may wonder whether his linking, or at times, lumping together of images of the storm, the sea, flood, water, and beasts would not have stopped short of its excesses, if he had taken note of the traditional Elizabethan significances of the sea and music symbolisms. As D. C. Allen, *The Legend of Noah: Renaissance Rationalism in Art, Science and Letters* (Urbana, 1949, 113–38) and Howard R. Patch, *The Goddess Fortuna in Medieval Literature* (Cambridge, Mass., 1927, pp. 101–7 esp. 105–7) point out, the sea and the flood were traditional images for the ubiquitous themes of Fortune, of Time and of Love in Renaissance literature. Nor does Wilson Knight sufficiently consider such archetypal significances of the sea image as have been pointed by Maud Bodkin in *Archetypal Patterns in Poetry*, 1934, and developed by W. H. Auden *The Enchafed Flood or the Romantic Iconography of the Sea* (1967, chapter 1).

As for the music in the tempest–music opposition in Shakespeare, Wilson Knight's findings, anticipating the idea of musical harmony in the 'Elizabethan World Picture' as drawn not only by

---

[28] Nuttall, *Two Concepts of Allegory: A Study of Shakespeare's 'Tempest' and the Logic of Allegorical Expression* (London, 1967); Honig, *Dark Conceit: The Making of Allegory* (London, 1960).

Tillyard but by others, seem inadequate when considered in the light of Leo Spitzer's account in *Classical and Christian Ideas of World Harmony: Prolegomena to the Interpretation of the Word 'Stimmung'* (Baltimore, 1963). Yet Wilson Knight's tempest–music antithesis is supported by the opposition between the type of the *templum* and the antitype of the tempest, which Spitzer notes. It is pointless to regret that Wilson Knight could not relate his account of music imagery to the theory of music and music symbolism in Shakespeare's time later outlined by John Hollander in *The Untuning of the Sky: Ideas of Music in English Poetry 1500–1700* (Princeton, 1961). But the possibility that Shakespeare was acquainted with 'speculative music' or *musica theorica* as distinct from *musica poetica* and *musica practica* cannot be ruled out (cf. Lawrence J. Ross, 'Shakespeare's "Dull Clown" and Symbolic Music', *SQ*, 17 (1966), 107–28).

'We have consciously or unconsciously, assimilated the wisdom and the illumination of his interpretations', says George A. Panichas in a sympathetic estimate of Wilson Knight's interpretation ('G. Wilson Knight: Interpreter of Genius', *English Miscellany*, 20 (1969), 291–312), which he concludes by calling Wilson Knight a Longinian interpreter, who undergoes a transport of ecstasy in the presence of the work and communicates it to the reader. This is not the opinion of Roger Sale ('G. Wilson Knight', *MLQ*, 29 (1968), 77–83), to whom 'Knight is not a good writer on literature simply because his interest in literature is so tangential' (p. 82). Calling *The Chariot of Wrath* (mostly on Milton, written as part of Wilson Knight's war-time propaganda and 'non-criticism') his best book (p. 82), Roger Sale holds that Wilson Knight in general offers no literary criticism, but only occasional shrewd critical asides. While one may have radical reservations about Wilson Knight, not many would take this extreme view; nor would they endorse Sale's still more extreme statement 'Knight is really enjoyed by those as unliterary as he himself' (p. 82). We are brought back to the question whether the intrusion of pet ideological beliefs and prejudices into Wilson Knight's commentary, especially his later commentaries, does not result in irrelevance and a distortion of the text. Nonetheless, the Shakespearian experience behind Wilson Knight's interpretation of the plays is no less authentic for being idiosyncratic. That is, there is no denying the genuine encounter between the critic and the text.

This long process of encounter between the critic and the drama has gone on both in the theatre and in the study, for Wilson Knight has been, from the early thirties, an actor and a producer as well as a constant play-goer. Visionary as his perceptions may be, his interpretations, especially of *Timon*, *Othello*, *Macbeth*, *Romeo and Juliet*, *Twelfth Night*, *Antony and Cleopatra*, *A Midsummer Night's Dream* and *The Merchant of Venice* have been presented by himself on the stage (*Shakespearian Production*). In his stage embodiment of his 'spatial' perceptions, Wilson Knight has conveyed what he calls 'imaginative solidities', by offering visual effects of the symbolic. He has aimed at a colourfulness in the typical Shakespearian scene which derives from verbal imagery and, literally gives a display of colours on the stage, as an equivalent for the metaphorical diction through which the critic tries to convey the colourfulness of scenes and situations in the play (cf. Knight on *Hamlet*, I, ii). Wilson Knight has also tried to give expression on the stage to his theories about key Shakespearian speeches; for instance the rise-and-fall in the rhythms and tempo of a speech; his belief that a speech is an epitome of the movement of the whole play; his notion that a speech like Richard II's 'I have been studying how I may compare' (v, v, 1–41) is a prophetic anticipation of Shakespeare's evolution or the Shakespeare progress; and the allied belief that plays like *The Merchant of Venice* or *The Tempest* embody in plot, situation, character and theme the verbal image-motifs of all the plays which go before them. But, most remarkably, Wilson Knight's stage interpretation of the Shakespeare hero has always been a striking exercise in what one must call 'character-acting'. In his commentaries, even in the earliest, Wilson Knight does offer character-criticism with a difference, for all his scrupulous avoidance of the term 'character'. His stage experience of the plays, deepened and gave new dimensions to his sense of Shakespeare's characters. Francis Berry, 'G. Wilson Knight: Stage and Study', pp. 135–43, maintains that there is no discordance between Wilson Knight's critical interpretations and practice on the stage, and points out that in both Wilson Knight stressed the nobility and the growth in stature and impressiveness of tragic heroes like Romeo, Timon, Othello or Macbeth. There is an emphasis in his productions of Shakespeare as well as in his commentaries on the visually effective stage situation and occurrence, on scenes such as the child apparitions in *Macbeth*, the Vision in which Jupiter appears in *Cymbeline*, the resurrection of Hermione in *The Winter's Tale*, and the death-reversal in *Pericles*. Insofar as Wilson Knight's production and commentary draw attention to the visual meaning of these scenes and their stage-effectiveness, they contribute to our response to the processes of dramatic communication. But Wilson Knight insists that such dramatic phenomena as the child apparitions in *Macbeth* ('New Dimensions in Shakespearian Interpretation', *Shakespeare and Religion*, p. 304) be taken as symbols in themselves, to be understood in their own right and out of their context. This interest in dramatic visions and apparitions is prompted and fed by his preoccupation with spiritualism, as well as by his symbolist reading of Shakespearian drama.

Wilson Knight's approach to these conventional visions and apparitions fails to show sufficient awareness of them as theatrical sensations, and shows no awareness that Shakespeare may have used them in response to prevailing dramatic modes and practices. His use of the apparitions in *Macbeth*, for instance, may have had something to do with the fact that Shakespeare conceived the play as a 'nocturnal' tragedy.[29] But Wilson Knight excludes links between Shakespeare and his contemporaries, because, as an interpreter, he will not invoke the aid of scholarship and its findings. Whatever his prejudices about the

---

[29] W. J. Lawrence, 'The Elizabethan Nocturnal', *Pre-Restoration Stage Studies* (New York, 1927), 122–44. A description of 'nocturnals' as 'nocturnalls of unexpressable figures; Visions, and Apparitions figuring deepe Melancholly and unusuall Representations' is to be found in the 1620 'Proposals for Building an Amphitheatre in London' printed in *Notes and Queries*, 11th Series, vol. 10, 481–2, p. 482. Madeleine Doran in her brief discussion of the 'nocturnal' as a genre, *Endeavors of Art* pp. 412–13, n. 1, concludes that it is a kind of tragedy and cites Marston's *Sophonisba* or *The Wonder of Women* (1606) as a striking example. Geoffrey Bullough believes it likely that Shakespeare had Marston's play in mind when he wrote *Macbeth* (*Narrative and Dramatic Sources of Shakespeare*, VII, pp. 426–7). Chapman's *Bussy D'Ambois* has elements of the 'nocturnal' in it. G. K. Hunter in the New Penguin edition of *Macbeth* refers to the play as a 'nocturnal' (p. 29).

meddling intellect of the critic and the dry-as-dust garnering of facts by the scholar, and however deep his individual emotional engagement with Shakespeare's plays, one cannot but regret that his interpretation, because it is interpretation in contra-distinction to criticism, all too often abandons critical standards, that it leaves the realities of the play behind in its pursuit of ideological red herrings, and that he has practised too austere a self-denial in refusing to take note of the relevant findings of scholarship and to draw on them in his interpretation.

5

The 'thematics' of L. C. Knights: drama as 'moral experiment'

L. C. Knights has been by far the most persuasive and reasonable of the poetic interpreters of Shakespeare. Unlike Wilson Knight, Knights is anything but apocalyptic in tone; yet his commentaries, for all their equability, are as effective and forceful, and have the ring of felt experience and deep engagement, as well as the humane virtues of modesty and courtesy towards the reader.

The sensation created by L. C. Knights's Shakespeare Association lecture (1932), 'How Many Children Had Lady Macbeth?', on its publication as a pamphlet, is well-known.[1] This pamphlet was

---

[1] *How Many Children Had Lady Macbeth?* was published immediately after the lecture, as one of Gordon Fraser's Minority pamphlets, in the same series as F. R. Leavis's *For Continuity*. It came at a time when character-criticism, worked to death by then, had provoked a general reaction. J. W. Mackail, the acme of orthodoxy, was saying in 1930: 'We have no right to invent a life-history of Autolycus's aunts' *The Approach to Shakespeare* (Oxford, 1933), p. 25. Dickens made a telling dig at this trend in his account of Curdle in *Nicholas Nickleby* (chapter 24), who composed a treatise on the life of the deceased husband of the Nurse in *Romeo and Juliet*. The dramatic critic A. B. Walkley had this to say, in a review of Bradley, about what he called the 'wrong-headed methods of criticism' of the Morgann–Bradley tradition: 'The strange habit was acquired of considering the personages of Shakespeare's plays as "historic" beings, as actual flesh-and-blood people instead of fictitious inventions. Thus was the distinction ignored between nature and art, realities and appearances' – 'Professor Bradley's *Hamlet*', *Drama and Life* (London, 1907), p. 148. Edgar Allan Poe in a review in 1845 of Hazlitt's *Characters of Shakespeare's Plays*, complained that: 'In all commenting upon Shakespeare, there has been a radical error, never yet mentioned. It is the error of attempting to expound his characters – to account for their actions – to reconcile his inconsistencies – not as if they were the coinage of a human brain, but as if they had been actual existences on earth. We talk of Hamlet the man, instead of Hamlet the *dramatis persona*.' (*Complete Works*, ed. James A. Harrison (New York, 1902), in 17 vols, vol. XII, p. 225, cited from Norman Holland, *Psychoanalysis and Shakespeare*, p. 300). The expression 'thematics' is used by Murray Krieger, *The Tragic Vision* (New York, 1960), esp. p. 241.

one of several characteristically new studies of Shakespeare, the others appearing in *The Criterion* and *Scrutiny* in the early 1930s. Whatever 'period' touches these essays may carry they have a lasting value, and in their time they brought about a radical reorientation of Shakespearian criticism and a redirection of attention from plot and character to poetry. Their negative function was as a revolt against the tradition of Bradleyan character-criticism, and of laughing its excesses out of court by the parody implicit in the question: 'How Many Children Had Lady Macbeth?'. The historical impact was strong, but is not now as important as the possibilities of a positive enlargement of our understanding realised in the later studies.

Knights assimilated the insights of pioneers such as Middleton Murry and Wilson Knight and used them as a point of departure.[2] In the early essays as in the late, the influence of F. R. Leavis is deep and pervasive, and L. C. Knights's habit of making keen literary-critical discriminations and of proceeding from such literary response to moral diagnoses or to socio-cultural ones is a legacy of Leavis and the Cambridge of the 1930s. It is the sense of critical relevance and literary quality, and of moral values acting conjointly with them, which mark L. C. Knights off from Wilson Knight and Murry, whose preoccupations and orientations could generally be called epistemological and metaphysical, while L. C. Knights's are moral and psychological.

It has been said[3] that a commentator on L. C. Knights's criti-

---

[2] L. C. Knights frequently acknowledges the pioneering lead given by Wilson Knight. Like others of the Cambridge group, Knights had serious reservations about the later evolution of Wilson Knight's interpretation, especially his ideological enthusiasms and his lack of critical discrimination. Probably because of a distrust of the romanticising and transcendentalising tendencies of Middleton Murry's critical writings, L. C. Knights found himself out of tune with them. Though there is no open acknowledgement made to Murry, like the other critics of those times, L. C. Knights did assimilate the fruits of Murry's early work like *The Problem of Style* and the essay on 'Metaphor' (1927), reprinted in Murry, *John Clare and Other Studies*, pp. 85–97.

[3] The complaint that modern approaches to Shakespeare betray a theoretical thinness has been made by Lawrence J. Ross in a review of Norman Rabkin, ed., *Approaches to Shakespeare* (1964) in *SQ*, 16 (1965), p. 359. A. D. Nuttall in 'The Argument about Shakespeare's Characters', complains that L. C. Knights does not make clear the rational basis of his interpretations. But Knights has in his latter commentaries several times stated his credo. See the Introduction to *Some Shakespearean Themes* (London 1959). 'The Question of Character in Shake-

cism faces embarrassment because Knights does not sufficiently expose the grounds of his judgement. But, though no elaborate *a priori* theoretical framework supports Knights's criticism, there are sufficient theoretical assumptions and presuppositions. Knights has from time to time made clear his 'idea of a Shakespeare play', as well as his aims and methods, though in undoctrinaire and pragmatic terms. His 'speculative instruments' are so flexible, however, that one cannot without injustice to him pin him down to one category or mode of interpretation.

In the lecture 'How Many Children Had Lady Macbeth?', after placing the age-long preoccupation with character in Shakespeare commentary in historical perspective Knights goes on to expound his theory of Shakespearian drama and the way in which a play demands a total response from the reader. Applying the ideas and words of Edgell Rickword[4] about fiction and the criticism of the novel to Shakespearian drama, Knights uses the poetry as the point of entry and the goal:

A Shakespeare play is a dramatic poem. It uses action, gesture, formal grouping and symbols, and it relies upon the general conventions governing Elizabethan plays. But, we cannot too often remind ourselves, its end is to communicate a rich and controlled experience by means of words.   (*Explorations*, p.4)

the only profitable approach to Shakespeare is a consideration of his plays as dramatic poems, his use of language to obtain a total complex emotional response.   (p. 6)

the total response to a Shakespeare play can only be obtained by an exact and sensitive study of the quality of the verse, of the rhythm and imagery, of the controlled associations of the words and their emotional

speare'; 'Historical Scholarship and the Interpretation of Shakespeare'; 'Theology and Poetry', *Theology and the University* edited by John Coulson; and an article on 'The Teaching of Shakespeare', *The Use of English*, 19 (1967), 3–16.
[4] Edgell Rickword's 'A Note on Fiction' which appeared in *The Calendar of Modern Letters* (Oct., 1926), (*The Calendar of Modern Letters* (new impression, London, 1966), II, 226–33), and was reprinted in Leavis (ed.), *Towards Standards of Criticism*, has been cited in chapter 2 as a manifesto of the revolt against character-criticism. W. J. Harvey, acknowledging this, points out that in fiction criticism the shift of attention from character to theme, imagery and language followed in the wake of the new development in Shakespeare criticism (*Character and the Novel* (London, 1965), p. 200).

and intellectual force, in short by an exact and sensitive study of Shakespeare's handling of language. (p. 10)

Deploring the 'process of splitting up the indivisible unity of a Shakespeare play into various elements abstracted from the whole' and the 'false assumption about the category "drama"', Knights asserted: '*Macbeth* is a statement of evil . . . it has greater affinity with *The Waste Land* than with *The Doll's House*' (*Explorations*, p. 5).

Some of these statements, particularly the last, might appear radical, especially given Knights's tendency in his criticism to write as though there was no distinction between dramatic and non-dramatic poetry, as though there were no theatrical context for drama. But his engagement with the traditions and schools of commentary of the time called for some such over-emphatic utterance. Quite unlike Wilson Knight, L. C. Knights does not deny himself the findings of historical scholarship about the Elizabethan stage, theatre and dramaturgy, the Elizabethan ideological climate, and the Elizabethan social and economic setting. One can distinguish in Knights's criticism an attempt at an individual synthesis of scholarship and criticism. But his use of the historical sense and the fund of knowledge about the Elizabethan era is a highly qualified, and somewhat partial application of scholarship to criticism.[5] The result is an intermingling of the historical and the unhistorical; now it is the Elizabethan Shakespeare that we see, now Shakespeare modernised, either made our contemporary or refashioned in terms of Knights's outlook on life. It is in Knights's later commentaries that this intermixture is most prominent; but even in the pioneer essays it may be traced.

The parodic title, 'How Many Children Had Lady Macbeth?' (suggested by Leavis), was at once a crystallisation of a growing dissatisfaction with too exclusive concentration on the characters of the plays and an exposure of the irrelevance of misdirected critical enquiries. Knights, particularly chary then of dwelling at

[5] L. C. Knights's view of the use of historical scholarship is set out in 'Historical Scholarship and the Interpretation of Shakespeare', *SR*, 63 (1955), reprinted in *Further Explorations*. It is worth remembering that Knights's later interpretations of *King Lear* and *Macbeth* followed after this essay.

any length on the theoretical foundations of his critical opinions, contented himself with citing Rickword and his pragmatic insistence on the need for apprehending a work of literature as a whole and responding to the total impression it made, and so did not find it necessary to expose the fallacy of excursions into the past and future lives of characters by detailed analysis. Though Knights's main objection might seem to be against the common
— fallacy of abstracting characters from the play, or in principle
— against abstracting from the total effect of the play, the real target
— is irrelevant speculation by drawing wrong inferences, which is
— at once the cause and effect of the critic's failing to stay true to the
— experience of the play. But the limits of the relevance of such speculation are not easily decided. To take the question parodied in Knights's title, it may be flatly stated that Bradley, who raised a number of similar questions and discussed them in appendices in his book, did not ask this question in this form, though he did consider a related question in his discussion of Macduff's remark about Macbeth 'He has no children'.[6] That the question is not altogether irrelevant should be clear when we bring to mind the views on Macbeth's and Lady Macbeth's 'dream children' and their relevance to the play, expressed by Freud, Empson, H. S. Wilson and Cleanth Brooks. Writing a few years after 'How Many Children Had Lady Macbeth?', T. S. Eliot, the inspiration behind the critical revolution inaugurated by Knights, pointed out that to abstract a figure 'is a perfectly legitimate form of criticism though liable to abuses; at its best it can add very much to our enjoyment of the moments of the characters' life which are given in the scene, if we feel this richness of reality in them' (*A Companion to Shakespeare Studies*, edited by Harley Granville-Barker and G. B. Harrison, p. 297).

It is one of the ironies of modern Shakespeare criticism that Bradley, Knights's target, should have, in an unpublished paper

[6] Several commentators have pointed out that Bradley did not ask precisely this question. D. J. Palmer, 'A. C. Bradley', *Critical Survey*, 2 (1964), draws attention to Bradley's words about the question: 'It is immaterial. It does not concern the play'; John Britton, 'A. C. Bradley and those Children of Lady Macbeth', *SQ*, 12 (1961), 349–51, has exposed the all-too-common 'error of confusing Knights's title-phrase with a supposed actual note in Bradley' (p. 351). Roy Battenhouse, *Shakespearean Tragedy: Its Art and Its Christian Premises*, also reminds us that Bradley did not ask the question (p. 70).

extant in manuscript form, written as an address to the teachers
of Liverpool and entitled 'The Teaching of English Literature',
called a Shakespeare play 'a dramatic poem' (the very phrase
used by Knights as his rubric) and gone on to analyse the opening
scene of *Macbeth*. The irony has been brought to light and commented on by Katherine Cooke, *A. C. Bradley and His Influence in
Twentieth-Century Shakespeare Criticism* (pp. 127–8), who points
out that Knights is unlikely to have known the paper.

Some developments in modern Shakespeare scholarship created a climate favourable to the emergence of the poetic approach
to Shakespeare, as I suggested in chapter 1, and Knights was able
to draw upon them. The accumulation and availability of this
knowledge prepared the soil for the growth of Knights's kind
of criticism. As a corrective to 'psychologising' or realistic
character-criticism, which assumed Shakespearian drama to be
no different from the naturalistic novel, L. C. Knights insisted in a
salutary and important way on the foundations of Elizabethan
drama in convention and tradition. Knights's deployment of
knowledge available about the taste, training and education of
the Elizabethan audience, or the stage and theatrical conditions
which made Shakespeare's theatre a theatre of words, is an
illustration of a fine critical grasp and an exploitation of the
essence of theatrical scholarship. In his classic *Drama and Society
in the Age of Jonson* (1937) and subsequent commentary, Knights
makes use of the findings of economic and social historians such
as R. H. Tawney about the shift in the early seventeenth century
in social and economic conditions, and the resultant change of
values – so much so that Knights can be called a pioneer in
socio-cultural criticism.[7] But in his essays, early as well as late, we
almost always reach a point at which Knights seems either to
dissociate himself from the historical standpoint or to adapt his
historical sense to suit the needs of his aesthetic-moral bias.

I consider, as an example, Knights's use of the historical finding that Elizabethan drama is governed by convention. Knights
started with the perception that character was understood and
responded to by spectator then or reader now as one of the

[7] The term is used by Sheldon Norman Grebstein, ed. *Perspectives in Contemporary Criticism* (New York, 1968), p. 161.

conventions in Elizabethan drama, one through which Shakespeare communicates his meanings, which are the themes of the plays and which are exploration of the values of life. The implications of this perception, which are far-reaching, were not fully followed through by Knights; but initially it enabled him to expose the fallacies of the wrong sort of speculation and irrelevant inference-drawing about Shakespearian characters, and also to develop new and profitable responses to the plays. While nobody would want to take the findings of Stoll and Schücking to their logical extreme and talk as though Shakespeare were an inert follower of convention, one should remember that the Shakespearian character, as itself a convention, is shaped and expressed through a series of other conventions – those of rhetoric, poetry and stage-practice. Failure to give due weight to these conventional modes of character-portrayal and presentation adversely affects Knights's response to Shakespeare's characters. The same inhibition, preventing the critic from fully developing the operative force of conventions is found in Leavis too, a revealing exception being his remarkable essay on *Measure for Measure*. This was a rejoinder to Knights's essay on the play, and it supplies exactly Knights's deficiences of awareness concerning the role of convention in the characterisation of Claudio, Angelo, Isabella and the Duke.[8]

This unwillingness to make due allowance for conventions employed in the portrayal of character may be explained by an initial assumption which has weighed heavily with Knights throughout – namely the idea that the tendency of the common reader of popular fiction to identify with hero or heroine more or less uncritically has invaded the ordinary reader's or even the critic's reading of drama. This idea resulted in Knights's deliberate alienation, his withholding of sympathy from the characters, especially the heroes of the plays, and his attitude of severe moral disapproval towards many of them; and this in turn, led to unhistorical readings of characters and plays.

The constructive service performed by Knights in 'How Many Children Had Lady Macbeth?' in demonstrating the right way to

[8] Knights, 'The Ambiguity of *Measure for Measure*', 222–33 and F. R. Leavis, 'The Greatness of *Measure for Measure*', 234–47.

'read' characters in Shakespeare in terms of their poetic constituents and in the total context of poetic drama, is best appreciated in his exposition of the function of characters like Duncan, Banquo, Malcolm, Macduff and other so-called minor figures in the play, and the scenes of the witches and the 'holy supernatural', hitherto neglected or understimated by commentators. Knights acknowledged his debt to Wilson Knight. But his close response to the quality as well as the *feel* of dramatic utterances enabled Knights to expand and to refine upon the perceptions of Wilson Knight. The three interdependent themes that Knights isolated in the play – the theme of a reversal of values, that of unnatural disorder and that of confusion of appearance with reality – were shown emerging through the verse and the imagery. These are among the recurrent themes in Shakespeare discussed by Knights in his later writings, often with reference to historical findings about the world of Elizabethan thought. In the first discussion of these themes,[9] Knights did not invoke historical scholarship, probably for strategic reasons, given the programmatic stance of the essay. But he had historical interests and actively brought them to bear on his study of Shakespeare and Elizabethan drama, particularly around this time; it is an object-lesson in the collaboration of scholarship with critical discoveries. If critical convictions and assumptions at times curbed the play of the historical sense, to the same extent Knights's sensitivity to quality in literature helped him to keep clear of the irrelevancies,

---

[9] In 'How Many Children Had Lady Macbeth?' Knights's treatment of the theme of evil in the play reached conclusions which are corroborated by the study of those medieval theological notions of evil, especially of its illusoriness, inherited by Shakespeare's age, made by W. C. Curry, *Shakespeare's Philosophical Patterns*. Cf. also the insistence on the consummation of Shakespeare's ethical awareness in *Macbeth* which Virgil K. Whitaker makes in *Shakespeare's Use of Learning*, and which he holds due to the influence of Hooker. Knights's studies of Ben Jonson and other dramatists approach the borders where the socio-historical and the literary-critical shade into each other. Inevitably they cover much the same ground as Louis B. Wright, *Middle Class Culture in Elizabethan England*, and C. R. Baskervill, *The English Elements in Ben Jonson's Comedies* (Austin, Texas, 1911). The extreme point of view argued by Wilbur Sanders ('Macbeth and the Theology of Evil', *The Dramatist and the Received Idea*), that Shakespeare attains to a truer insight than Aquinas, whom Curry cites as the source of Elizabethan notions of good and evil, reckons without the axiom that tragedy does not tell the 'whole truth', and that the tragic artist deliberately draws his circle small, making it one within which relations *seem* to end, to adopt Henry James's expression.

excrescences and tangential pursuits of scholarship. He was not given to the reductive and mechanistic fallacies of Marxist and sociological studies or the inadequacies of a positivist approach which could not recognise that a work of literature was a value, and not a mere fact of the physical or sensory experience of the reader. Knights's application of his historical sense to the study of Elizabethan drama brought him the perception that what was involved in the great social and economic flux of the early seventeenth century was a change of ethical values and not a mere shift in habits of calculation or patterns of human relationships.

The techniques of thematic analysis employed by Knights show interesting variations in the evolution of his criticism through the years, and these variations reflect the changing relations between his individual insights and historical knowledge, the two being now convergent, now divergent. In the analysis of the play in 'How Many Children Had Lady Macbeth?' which inaugurated a flourishing school of theme-hunters, Knights, without specifically invoking the Elizabethan background of religious or ethical thought, demonstrated how the problem of evil is explored in the poetic constituents of the play. The idea of grace, though identified as a presence in the play and as in harmony with the idea of nature, is not in that analysis given any particular religious significance.

Historically- and theologically-inclined critics have quarrelled with Knights's analysis,[10] because its apparent historical and theological 'innocence' makes it an easy target. They argue, for example, that we have a Bradleyan, secular, humanist picture of the play at the end of the discussion, for all its anti-Bradleyanism. After all, Bradley, and Dowden before him, noted the images of darkness but would not put primary emphasis on them; and the appearance–reality contrast was noted earlier, though then called dramatic irony. But we, in turn, have to recognise that Knights's

[10] For instance, Paul Siegel, 'In Defence of Bradley', *College English* 9 (1948), 250–6, and Herbert Weisinger, 'The Study of Shakespearian Tragedy since Bradley', 387–96. But Roy Battenhouse, *Shakespearean Tragedy: Its Art and Its Christian Premises*, seems to think that 'How Many Children Had Lady Macbeth?' is 'an attack chiefly on Bradley's philosophy of nature, which obscures, L. C. Knights argues, "those passages in the play in which the positive good is presented by means of religious symbols", by various images of grace and of the holy supernatural' (p. 71).

discussion took place 'outside the Bradleyan frame of reference', that his reading is based on, and leads to, a fresh experience of the play, hitherto unavailable. The irony is that Knights's treatment of concepts in *Macbeth* in this first essay on the play, though not buttressed by explicit reference to historical ideas, is historically impeccable, whereas the extended essay in *Some Shakespearean Themes*, although laced with references to the history of ideas and scholarly work on the Elizabethan ideological world, has an essentially unhistorical nature. When Knights invoked the idea of nature as a key concept in *Macbeth* in his first essay, and showed how nature serves as a carrier of meanings suggesting an alliance of the forces of life, goodness, gentleness, beneficent exercise of power and divine grace, he was making critical capital out of a significant idea full of possibilities. The immediate precedents of the application of the idea to Shakespeare would seem to have been Wilson Knight and F. R. Leavis. As two recent critical followers of L. C. Knights, T. B. Tomlinson and Wilbur Sanders, have pointed out, the most original and valuable among the findings of Leavis and Knights are the insights that Shakespearian verse could occasionally, by virtue of its being a convention of drama, speak 'directly' and 'out of character' to the reader and communicate moral significances; and that one prime emphasis conveyed by Shakespeare is a celebration of nature and life in the generalised connotations of energy, vitality and possibilities of creation and growth.

To a certain extent this idea of nature as a dominant idea in Shakespearian drama provided a means of entering into an experience of the plays. Beyond those limits, though, the insistent use of the idea has verged on mere vitalism and a sort of 'biolatry', if one may coin an expression; and it oversimplifies or bypasses the late sixteenth- and seventeenth-century debate about the concept of nature. It would be wrong to suggest that Knights is guilty of an extreme or mechanical application of the idea of nature, nor does he ignore historical considerations. But there are occasions when Knights's fascination with the vitalist suggestions of the idea of nature seems to get the better of his scruples in handling historical ideas.

In the essay on *Macbeth* in *Some Shakespearean Themes*, Knights employs the notion of the double aspect of nature ('Nature and human values are felt as intimately related, and at the same time as antagonistic') as a key to the play. But, despite the attention paid to the ambivalent relation of man and nature, and although Knights comes to apply the idea after developing it in relation to *King Lear*, the central emphasis runs like this:

There is a similar assurance in the use of 'nature', in that aspect of the play's imaginative structure that impels us to say not merely that Macbeth's crime is unnatural (i.e. inhuman) but that the values against which evil is defined are in some sense grounded in nature.

. . . there is no doubt that whenever Shakespeare envisages a fully human way of life he thinks of it as closely related to the wider setting of organic growth, as indeed, in a concrete and practical way, directly based on man's dealings with the earth that nourishes him.

(*Some Shakespearean Themes*, pp. 123–4)

In short, he ignores the fact, or rather the problem of the transcendence of nature in the plays. There are penetrating analyses of passages which link the theme of nature with the illusoriness, the unreality of evil, and with the theme of time as communicated through the consciousness and human experience of Macbeth. But Knights's preoccupation with the idea of nature, carried over from his analysis of *King Lear*, and also, of course, from the first 1932 study of *Macbeth*, leads to a slight warping of the play – exemplified in his lack of attention to the links between nature and grace, so well brought out in the earlier study. His interpretation of *King Lear* through the idea of nature, illuminating as it is, is marred by weaknesses of method: evidenced in an inadequate application and, at times, a misapplication of the historical context.

Starting with the assumption that in *King Lear* 'some of the most fundamental questions concerning the nature of man are posed in a way that precludes all ready-made answers, that, in fact, so emphasizes the difficulty of the questions as to make any kind of answer seem all but impossible', Knights sees a three-fold significance in the play: 'it is timeless and universal, it has a crucial place in its author's inner biography, and it marks a moment of great importance in the changing consciousness of the civilization to which it belongs'. This is 'a stage in the emergence of the modern European consciousness', and Knights writes that it is an exploration of nothing less than the question *what man is* and of a particular quality of being, through King Lear as 'the centre of consciousness'. After an examination of key situations and passages, he sums it up thus: 'The imaginative discovery that is the play's essence has thus involved the sharpest possible juxtaposition of rival conceptions of "Nature"' (*Some Shakespearean Themes and An Approach to 'Hamlet'*, p. 100). Understandably, he found John F. Danby's interpretation of the play as a Morality-debate on the rival meanings of 'Nature' congenial. (Knights was, in his early criticism, responsible for the tendency in recent commentary to see the Morality-pattern in many Elizabethan plays.)[11] He acknowledges as his sources of inspiration and points of departure for his application of the divided Renaissance concept of nature to the play, Danby, Theodore Spencer, H. B. Parkes, Robert Heilman, R. C. Bald, Louis Bredvold, Wilson Knight, and elsewhere Edwin Muir. That Knights should employ the history of ideas as his frame of reference and provide an explicit historical background and good documentation for his interpretation, marks an interesting departure from his earlier practice of implicitly assuming the historical context and adopting the idiom of the 'new critic'. It points to a healthy alliance between the reading of the 'words on the page', and the gathering and application of historical knowledge. While the principle is sound, the methods evoke certain reservations. First, Knights does not pay enough attention to the complexity of Renaissance thought about nature; nor, for that matter, can Danby, Heilman, Theodore Spencer or Wilson Knight before him be said to have done justice to it. Second, he does not take into account the contexts to which this thought has to be referred. Third, despite his customary caution he occasionally reads into nature-references in the play meanings which are historically improbable because post-evolutionist. Fourth, seeing the play as an imaginative exploration of the two-fold Renaissance philosophy of nature, Knights, despite his scrupulous attempts to stay

---

[11] 'the full force of the morality tradition remains to be investigated' L. C. Knights, *Explorations*, p. 5.

close to the experience of the play, only succeeds in presenting us with a schema whose neatness does violence to the complexity with which the idea is woven into the texture of the play.

Even a reader who has access only to secondary sources can perceive how tangled are Renaissance ideas about nature.[12] A congeries of notions came down to the Elizabethans as a legacy from ancient and medieval periods, from the pagans and the Judaeo-Christian tradition. Questions were discussed such as whether the book of nature was all in all or whether it was to be complemented by the book of God; whether the *lex eterna* and the *lex natura* were identical; what relationship the *lex talionis* bore to the *lex natura*. There were also the questions whether nature was essentially good or corrupted after the Fall of Man, and whether nature was subject to or free from progressive decay and degenerative flux. There was the problem how far nature could serve as an ethical norm. This problem was closely bound up with the questions mentioned earlier, as well as with the question of the relationship of the concept of nature to other concepts such as those of reason, grace, fortune, time and justice.[13] Besides the correspondences and differences among human nature, vegetable nature, animal nature and cosmic nature, in the

[12] See, for example, C. A. Patrides, 'The Book of Knowledge Fair: The nature of Nature', *Milton and the Christian Tradition* (Oxford, 1966), pp. 54–90 and also, pp. 214–16; Robert Speaight, *Nature in Shakespearean Tragedy* (London, 1955); Paul Reyher, *Essai sur les idees l'oeuvre de Shakespeare* (Paris, 1947); A. P. d'Entrèves, *Natural Law* (London, 1952), Ernest Sirluck, Introduction to *Complete Prose Works of Milton*, vol. II (New Haven, 1959), pp. 12–52, besides the sources cited by L. C. Knights.
[13] On the relations of nature and reason in Renaissance thought, see R. Hoopes, *Right Reason in the Renaissance* (Cambridge, Mass., 1962); and S. L. Bethell, *The Cultural Revolution of the Seventeenth Century* (London, 1951). On nature and grace, see Richard Hooker's *The Laws of Ecclesiastical Polity*, Book I (1593); A. S. P. Woodhouse, 'The Argument of Milton's *Comus*', *University of Toronto Quarterly*, 11 (1941); and 'Nature and Grace in *The Faerie Queene*', *ELH*, 16 (1949). The controversy between Woodhouse and T. M. Gang *ELH*, 26 (1959) and 27 (1960), or Woodhouse and A. E. Dyson, *Essays and Studies*, 1955, over the nature/grace antithesis is ultimately a manifestation of the multiple significance of the Renaissance concept of nature. On nature and fortune, see Boethius's *The Consolations of Philosophy*, I, Pr. v (Centaur Classics edition, edited by William Anderson, translated by 'I. T.' (1609)), and Howard R. Patch, *The Goddess Fortuna in Medieval Literature*, pp. 75–76. A more recent study of the Renaissance discussion of 'nature' as well as of certain other currents of thought of the period in relation to the play is William R. Elton, *King Lear and the Gods* (San Marino, California, 1966).

'Elizabethan world picture',[14] there was the important distinction often made between *natura naturans* and *natura naturata*. Furthermore, the rival claims of nature and nurture, of nature and art, were often weighed against one another. Many, if not all, the ideas in this complex have their bearing on *King Lear*,[15] and some on *Macbeth*. Knights must have been familiar with the history of the idea of nature in the eighteenth and nineteenth centuries, as charted by A. O. Lovejoy.[16] A momentary awareness, that the idea underwent radical changes during that period leads Knights to remind his readers, after quoting from Mill's essay on *Nature*, that such things could not have been said in the sixteenth century. But the tendency unduly to modernise Shakespeare and to tear him out of his context of thought is seen when Knights applies evolutionary ideas to the play.

Knights's use of the concept of nature in his reading of the play may be compared with a brief analysis contained in E. C. Knowlton's 'Nature and Shakespeare', *PMLA*, 51 (1936). The scale of Knowlton's analysis is, of course, much smaller. But the various significances with which Shakespeare invests the word 'nature' and some of their ideological contexts are neatly, though rather mechanically, established by Knowlton. He outlines the conflicting attitudes to nature which underlie *King Lear*, and directs attention to the contrast between Lear's invocation of the medieval, traditional idea of nature as the nurse of values and Edmund's faith in nature as animal passion. Knowlton also makes the point that Shakespeare forces Lear to use nature instead of the divine as the ultimate frame of reference, because of his wish to keep the play pagan in atmosphere. The essay serves its purpose of outlining the place of the idea of nature in this play and in Shakespeare in general. Knights's analysis is

---

[14] George W. Williams, 'The Poetry of the Storm in *King Lear*', *SQ* 2 (1951).
[15] Henry Medwall's Morality play, *Nature* (c. 1500) debated the question whether clothing is a necessity or a luxury.
[16] In two essays, 'Nature as Aesthetic Norm', *Modern Language Notes*, 42 (1927), 444–50 and 'The Gothic Revival and Return to Nature' *MLN*, 47 (1932), 419–46, Lovejoy distinguished more than twenty different, often contradictory meanings of 'nature' in aesthetics, and about sixty-six normative uses of 'nature' in ethical, political and metaphysical thought. He showed that the appeal to Nature for standards has been a process of Man's projecting on to nature his own wishes, and reading these into it.

more ambitious, and is an articulation of his response to the poetic communication of the play as a whole. But his commitment to the two-fold concept of nature, though it does throw light on one essential aspect of the play, leads him to neglect or to ignore the multiple connotations and the varied uses of the concept as, for instance, the 'unnaturalness of nature', the relation between the clothing motif and nature, and the attributes of state such as retinue. Similarly, some attention to the separateness and the interconnection between the realm of nature and the realm of grace[17] would have provided a corrective against the elevation of nature to the status of grace and the divine in the later study of *Macbeth*.

Knights might dismiss such objections to his procedure as springing from a debilitating historicism. His views on the role of our knowledge of the intellectual background of the Elizabethans in our experience of Shakespeare, are set out in 'Historical Scholarship and the Interpretation of Shakespeare'. He repeats that what we start from and return to is the individual play or the whole of Shakespeare's work as '*one* poem – . . . united by one significant, consistent, and developing personality' (Knights quotes the phrase used by Eliot, 'John Ford', *Selected Essays*, 1932, p. 196), and so he would use the ideas of the Elizabethans, as reconstructed by modern scholars, only to make his experience of Shakespeare 'deeper and more vivid', so far as these ideas may 'illuminate the relation between living art and the civilization behind it, and so give us a firmer grasp of the nature of a living tradition'. His objection to the ways of historical scholars is two-fold. They apply a framework of ideas mechanically to Shakespeare and so fail to attain to a direct personal responsiveness to

---

[17] The antithesis of Nature and Grace, emphasising both the distinction and interrelation between the two, was used by A. S. P. Woodhouse as an interpretative category with reference to Spenser's *The Faerie Queene* and Milton's *Comus*. 'Nature and Grace in *The Faerie Queene*', pp. 194–228 and 'The Argument of Milton's *Comus*', pp. 46–71. As Knights himself points out in a more recent lecture, printed in *SR*, 84 (1976), 595–613, 'Integration' in *The Winter's Tale*, between Nature and Grace, 'there is no divorce . . . Grace . . . is a consummation of that naturalness and spontaneity that were so beautifully evoked in the pastoral scene. It can only enter when nature has been, not disowned but enlisted in the cause of "honesty" and "honour", love and trust – human values and commitments *of which nature by itself* knows nothing' (p. 612, my italics).

the experience of the plays. Also, they by implication deny 'the liberty of interpreting' and, because of their convictions of historical determinism, do not allow the individual reader to apprehend the meanings of Shakespeare in the context of his own reading and experience of life. The trouble with such anti-historicist formulations is that, while Knights may insist on the need for responsible attention to the work 'as in itself it really is', the historians' viewpoint raises questions about the mode of existence and availability of a work of literature belonging to the past. Is not our experience of the Shakespeare play, the ultimate *experience* that is beyond critical interpretation, to be subtly and sensitively controlled and thus enriched by our knowledge of Elizabethan ideas? Knights reminds us that a masterpiece of literature like *King Lear* may offer different meanings to different generations at the start of his *'King Lear* as Metaphor'. Our knowledge of Elizabethan ideas serves at least as a criterion of relevance, saving us from the 'ego-centric predicament' in interpretation.

Knights explores the senses of 'justice' as at once a key-word and a key-theme in the play in his *'King Lear* as Metaphor' and also in an essay in *The Use of English*, 19 (1967). He explains the new sense in which he uses the term 'metaphor'. After Martin Foss and Philip Wheelwright, he dissociates the word from the notion of analogy, and means by it something like 'an articulation of experience', a particular experience to which Shakespeare is stirred when seized with a theme like justice while handling his dramatic story. The whole play thus becomes a reverberation or resonance of the idea. The exposition of the occurrence of the theme of justice in the play certainly provides an illuminating perspective and leads to a true participation in its experience.

Four other major Shakespearian themes discussed by Knights are those of time; of appearance and reality; of the question of political power and action in the 'public' world, viewed from a 'personalist' angle; and of the status of the individual consciousness in its encounter with the realities of the world outside. In an early essay on Shakespeare's sonnets, Knights developed the idea that the poet has a keenly-felt awareness of what time does to man, to human life and human love, fully realised in the greater sonnets, written out of a poetic compulsion and deep engagement. It is characteristic of Knights that he declines to link Shakespeare's handling of the theme with the great medieval *topos* of 'mutabilitie', and talks entirely in terms of Shakespeare's individual grappling with the issue. The links that Knights forges between this and other Shakespearian themes tell us what 'figure in the carpet' he sees in Shakespeare's work as a whole. When he recognises the theme of time and of death in a history play like 2 *Henry IV*, and gives it great weight, an aspect of the play, previously hardly noticed, is brought to our attention. But Knights does seem to over-emphasise the theme, and aspects of the play as a history, and as the second part of a Morality, which are probably of more central relevance, are as a result obscured.[18]

An instructive contrast is to be found in Knights's essay on appearance and reality in *Troilus and Cressida*, which shows that certain kinds of play respond more fruitfully to thematic analysis than others: the problem plays, in particular, more than the histories and romantic comedies. In the exordium of this essay, Knights makes certain qualification about the nature and purpose of his thematic analysis, as a warning against probable misunderstanding: 'Shakespeare does not deal with his themes in the manner of one embarking on a dispassionate enquiry into the sources of self-deceit and the domination of men by appearances' (*Some Shakespearian Themes and An Approach to 'Hamlet'*, p. 58). Three key speeches in the play are commented on with insight so that the dramatic experience of the play as a whole is recreated for the reader; the speeches are examined with 'a lively sense of the dramatic context' and with a sense of the way the poetry covertly modifies and colours the overt statement, and with an awareness of the mythical and legendary roles assumed by the characters. Given that the play does deal with the ironies of ideas and perceptions and the validity of values, Knights's 'thematics' does justice to the complexity of Shakespeare's poetry in the play. There is no idealisation of Troilus and the Trojans as in Wilson Knight's analysis; the sheer subjectivism of Troilus's outlook on love and life is well brought out, and the play is shown by Knights

[18] Brian Vickers, *The Artistry of Shakespeare's Prose*, p. 2, makes this criticism.

as by others before him (notably by Charles Williams)[19] as a forerunner of the tragedies in 'bringing to consciousness the "irrational" forces that underlie choice and will'.

One valuable contribution of Knights to Shakespeare studies lies in his expositions of the political theme in Shakespeare.[20] Though the original concept that the history plays are actually political plays is not attributable to Knights, he more than others has explored the political theme – Shakespeare's idea of the Monarch, the Governor, the public figure – and the motives and impulses behind political or public action.[21] In this exploration, Knights has combined his capacity for delicate response to subtleties of poetic communication with knowledge of the historical sources of the medieval and Renaissance tradition of political and ethical thought, and the writings of modern historians. All this is associated with what may be described as his 'personalist' philosophy. Knights holds that the political themes, while they dominate the history plays and the Roman plays, occur also in tragedies like *King Lear* and Macbeth. He shows that Shakespeare, true to tradition, believes in the inseparability of politics, ethics and psychology, in the correspondence between the health of the body politic and the body private of the Governor, and in the mutualities of corporate national life. With a characteristic inwardness of vision, sympathy and judgement, Shakespeare, alive to the human realities behind the pursuit of political abstractions and formulas, lays bare the self-delusion and self-

---

[19] *The English Poetic Mind*.

[20] Especially chapter 2 of 'The Public World', *SST; William Shakespeare: The Histories* (London, 1962); 'Shakespeare's Politics' and 'Poetry, Politics and the English Tradition', both in *Further Explorations*.

[21] H. B. Charlton was probably the first modern critic to read the 'histories' as political plays – *Shakespeare, Politics and Politicians*, English Association Pamphlet no. 72 (Oxford, 1929). Lily B. Campbell, *Shakespeare's Histories*; Una Ellis-Fermor, 'Shakespeare's Political Plays', *The Frontiers of Drama* (London, 1945), E. M. W. Tillyard and F. P. Wilson followed suit. A number of Tudor Moralities and Interludes as well as pre-Shakespearian plays, 'histories' and tragedies were 'political' in motivation and theme, not to speak of the 'political' tragedies of the early seventeenth century, such as those of Ben Jonson, Chapman and Middleton. There is evidence that some Elizabethans treated 'histories' as 'moral' plays (A. P. Rossiter, introduction to his edition of *Woodstock, A Moral History* (London, 1946)) and read history for its moral and philosophical implications. We have the ancient historian Livy's statement that history is philosophy teaching by examples, and Richard Harvey's that 'the most morals (is) the best Historie' (cited from *ELH*, 26 (1959), p. 171).

division in which the political characters involve themselves. The questions arise whether Knights, with his personalist bias (the nature of which is outlined below),[22] is not reading into Shakespeare political ideas of a personalist cast, or whether he is not making Shakespeare a paragon of political wisdom, as he elsewhere makes him a fount of perfect moral and metaphysical insights. Yet Knights never forgets that the realm of the plays is that of experience, inner and outer, and not the realm of abstract ideals. As a matter of fact, it is Shakespeare's political and moral 'realism' (not in the Machiavellian or 'permissive' sense) which is emphasised, and it is 'life' rather than morals or ideals which is the criterion. The cautious way in which he uses the overworked order-degree hypothesis, with its assumption of an implicit taboo against rebellion, and allied ideas of Tudor kingship is an example of the freshness of his critical response. While giving due weight to the pervasive presence of these ideas in the Elizabethan ideological climate, Knights is able to establish through the evidence of poetic tone and the undercurrents of suggestion in specific passages that Shakespeare could not have accepted the doctrine wholesale. Shakespeare's first observations of the 'public world' are seen in most of the plays; 'their protagonists are, ostensibly, figures from history, in actuality representative figures from the world of great affairs' (*SST&AH*,

---

[22] A handy account of 'personalism' as a movement in modern thought is J. B. Coates, *The Crisis of the Human Person: Some Personalist Interpretations* (London, 1949). Personalism is 'the name given to a number of philosophies which correlate the conceptions of personality and value, which conceive of personality as a unique entity in every human being which has a movement towards value and is the source of our knowledge of value' (p. 9).

Nicholas Berdyaev and Jacques Maritain, for instance, make an important distinction between the person and the individual. Man has an inalienable right to the freedom of his *personal*, but not his individual life. To quote from Mounier's *Personalist Manifesto* (1936), 'Personalism is the complete antithesis of individualism. . . Man cannot be summed up in abstract concepts "but must be seized existentially as a being incessantly recreating himself by 'meeting', decision and 'engagement' " ' (pp. 21 and 22). Cf. Buber. They stress, like Kierkegaard, the concreteness of personal experience as against the formal and conceptual system which a man may adopt.

Cf. Martin Buber, *I and Thou* (Edinburgh, 1937), pp. 60, 161 and 162 and his well-known distinction between the 'I and It' relationship, and the 'I and Thou' relationship. Among the personalist sources cited by L. C. Knights are Buber, Berdyaev and Paul Tillich; in L. C. Knights's case, personalist thought is refined by psychological insights obtained from sources such as D. W. Harding and Ian Suttie. Personalism may be viewed as a refinement of humanism.

p. 26). The radical criticism of the amoral Machiavellian politician in *Richard III* shows that Shakespeare's political realism and agnosticism are more real than Machiavellian 'realism', in the sense that Shakespeare has a penetrating vision of human realities behind politics. It is only natural that Knights sees Shakespeare's point of view in the 'commodity' speech of the Bastard:

the Bastard represents something fundamental in Shakespeare's outlook on the world; he represents the habit of looking at things directly, of cutting through pretence and getting behind the words that disguise reality. In the greater plays on social and political themes, Shakespeare takes a situation, an attitude, an idea, and asks, *What does this mean?* in terms of specific human causes and consequences. (*SST&AH*, p. 34)

The 'inwardness' with which the King and the rebels are portrayed in *1 Henry IV* takes the form of 'an insistent questioning of the values by which its great men live – with a consequent ironic contrast between public profession and the actuality' (p. 36). The play turns out to be a dramatisation in several modes of the profession and practice of 'honour', in which Falstaff with his ironic inversion of the idea of honour fulfils an essential function. Knights offered this insight into the role of Falstaff as a 'choric commentator' in one of his early essays ('Notes on Comedy', *Scrutiny*, 1 (1932–3), 356–67). One of the instances of Knights's practice of gliding from aesthetic-literary perceptions to moral and metaphysical judgements is to be found in his treatment of *Richard II*. Richard's dramatic posturings and lack of contact with the realities around him point to a radical deficiency in the man and the king. This probing of the moral and psychological make-up of the Governor is brought to completion in *Henry V*. Rather than dismissing Shakespeare's Henry V as an ironical exposure of the popular ideal of kingship, Knights considers it a serious attempt by the dramatist to get inside the mind and heart of a responsible ruler whose claims to kingship may be in doubt.

It is in the Roman plays and the late tragedies that Knights finds Shakespeare probing with the maturest 'inwardness' the processes of thought and feeling, of will and motivation, behind the utterances and actions of the characters who are in some sense public figures. He highlights effectively the irony by which

Brutus and the other conspirators in *Julius Caesar* act by abstract formulas and illusory ideals and ignore reality and basic human values. This technique of analysis and personalist evaluation of characters is particularly effective in Knights's commentary on *Coriolanus*, the 'consummation of political wisdom'. His diagnosis of the central flaw in Coriolanus is shrewd. Using the third act as the point of entry into the play, L. C. Knights shows that it is a city-play, the protagonist being Rome, a city divided against itself, between the plebeians and the patricians. The imagery of disease and surgery used of the city and its present state is an indication that the humanity of the central figure is deeply flawed. As the anecdote about the young Marcius's 'mammocking' and the spirit of his utterances in the play prove, his courage and 'honour' spring from 'hardness and insensitiveness in the face of life'. Hence his 'personal failure to achieve integration and relationship' (*SST*, p. 152 and p. 154).

Knights's commentaries on the political themes of the plays, based on personalist conviction, are supplemented with forays into history and into traditions of political thought and also with references to the typical Leavisite concepts of an 'organic community' of Elizabethan England. Insofar as this idea carries elements of a nostalgic, pastoral myth, for all its core of authenticity, and insofar as a personalist reading of character does violence to the recognised distinction, if not dichotomy, between the public and the private personality, Knights's historical and philosophical framework often leads to application of criteria which are not altogether objective. Some ideological framework is necessary – and a certain bias is inevitable – to construct critical judgements of value; and awareness of the nature of the critic's bias should enable readers to make due allowance for it whenever necessary.

These personalist convictions, and a highly moralistic outlook, govern Knights's estimate of *Hamlet*, *Othello* and *Timon of Athens*. Crucial questions about our general response to character in Shakespeare are raised by Knights's strictures on the central characters of these plays. In line with the partial rehabilitation of 'character-criticism' in Shakespeare which Knights hinted at in his early essay, 'Prince Hamlet', and for which he provided some fairly detailed theoretical sanction in 'The Question of Character in Shakespeare', he examines these characters in terms of the tone and substrata of suggestions, of the poetic dramatic impressions of their speeches. The characters, according to him, exhibit particular 'states of consciousness'. Shakespeare is assumed to be a historian of fine consciences like Henry James. Knights brings to his task of sounding the depths of the ethical consciousness of characters a sophisticated psychological awareness. In his view, Shakespeare, in these three plays in particular, is concerned to depict the individual consciousness's encounter with the realities of the objective world, and its failure, owing to inward flaws, to achieve true integrity within itself and a 'true relatedness' with people and the outside world. The basic questions relate not so much to the admissibility of extended character-interpretation as to the degree of imaginative sympathy evoked by the tragic hero, as to whether a systematic 'debunking' and moral indictment are either warranted or aesthetically viable, and the relevance or appropriateness of the standards of judgements that Knights invokes, in his preoccupation with the themes of ethical and metaphysical states of consciousness.[23]

In his interpretation of the play and the character, Hamlet is a figure of evil, with an unhealthy fascination with death and a consequent recoil from life and its responsibilities for true human relationships. He is full of malice, and given to certain kinds of monkey-tricks; his disastrous psychological flaws are worsened because of his all-too-eager yielding to the influence of the Ghost – an embodiment of evil and death. With his self-righteousness and his self-regarding tendencies, Hamlet, in the cause of cleansing the evil of Denmark, allows the evil in himself to master him

---

[23] P. R. Grover, 'The Ghost of Dr. Johnson: L. C. Knights and D. A. Traversi on *Hamlet'*, *EC*, 17 (1967), 143–57, shows how L. C. Knights forges Shakespeare in the image of a Jamesian analyst of fine consciences. He also draws parallels between Johnson's disapproval of the character of Hamlet and L. C. Knights's and Traversi's, and underlines the common preoccupation of these critics with morality. But an attitude of strong disapproval towards Hamlet is a part of the tradition of *Hamlet* criticism. A want of imaginative sympathy towards Hamlet, is to be found not only in L. C. Knights, Traversi, the early Wilson Knight, John Vyvyan, S. de Madariaga, Lily Campbell, Rebecca West and Eleanor Prosser (this last with certain qualifications), but in Johnson, Steevens, and William Richardson in the eighteenth century, not to speak of Partridge as dramatic critic in *Tom Jones*.

completely, makes 'a pretty bad mess of things' by the deaths and killings he performs or brings about, ending up as little better than a murderer.[24] Similarly, Othello is also an egoist, a self-dramatiser, given to attitudinising, with an incapacity for unselfish feeling, so that his 'love' for Desdemona is no better than crude animal possessiveness. The Iago element of mistrust, negation and denial of values is something which is also inherent in him, hence his easy surrender and his adoption of the Iago idiom in place of the 'Othello music'. The 'Othello music' itself is evidence for Othello's romanticising attitude and his lack of touch with the realities around him. Knights's hostile criticism of Hamlet in part derives from Wilson Knight's early essays on the play, and in part from T. S. Eliot's comments. His disapproval of Othello derives from Leavis's demolition-piece, which in turn follows on from Eliot's remarks.

Timon of Athens, which Knights, flouting generally accepted chronology, takes as a preliminary sketch for *King Lear*, is a satirical portrait of a deeply flawed human being. His phenomenal generosity when rich is motivated by an inordinate desire for self-glorification, and his invective when destitute and in exile, for all its poetic energy, points to a psychopathological condition, with a specific sexual preoccupation.

Faced with such interpretations, one need not simply use Occam's razor and rule out straightaway any attempt at a critical stance towards the character of a tragic hero when he is not a villain-hero. The essential dignity of the Renaissance hero of tragedy is a factor to reckon with. First of all, the ordinary reader or spectator has a spontaneous impression of *Hamlet* or *Othello*. His reaction is one of active sympathy with the hero, often identification with him. While we should not sentimentalise the hero

---

[24] Knights in his more recent 'Shakespeare's Tragedies and the Question of Moral Judgment', *Explorations 3* (London, 1976), modifies the harshness of his earlier verdict. But despite qualifying statements like '(Hamlet) is subject to judgement . . . by criteria that the play itself provides, that Hamlet provides, in terms of vitality, freemoving life and a capacity for relationships' (p. 106), and despite the critic's acknowledgement of 'the finer qualities that go to make "the other Hamlet" ' (p. 107), on balance, the insistence continues to be on Hamlet's flaws, 'his imprisoning state of mind' (p. 106), his 'increasing entanglement in a self-consuming preoccupation with the very evil he is required to set himself against' (p. 107), and his 'trapped and death-directed consciousness' (p. 107).

and accept that his inner nature and deep-laid weaknesses and inadequacies are exposed by the play we cannot at the same time allow our imaginative sympathy to be utterly alienated, to sit merely in cold judgement over the characters, or to consider them as case-studies of basic human flaws, with no emotional involvement of our own in their lot. The right kind of balance or tension between sympathy and judgement, between participation and detachment, which is the secret of true poetic-dramatic response, is then lost. It is a curious irony that at a time when the old Aristotelian idea of *hamartia* or the 'tragic flaw' has undergone a radical reinterpretation, and is supposed to be very restricted in its application, commentators like Knights make it seem as though we have to search hard to find a single redeeming virtue in the tragic protagonist.

When Knights isolates the tendency to self-dramatisation, attitudinising, posing and histrionics in Othello and Hamlet, and proceeds from a psychological to a moral diagnosis, his procedure makes at least three questionable assumptions relating to aesthetic response and moral judgement. It is an irony that modern Shakespeare critics, who laid bare the supposed absurdity of Bradley and the older critics in calling characters such as Richard II, Hamlet, Macbeth and Antony poets, pointing out that the poetry is Shakespeare's, not the characters' and that characters in poetic drama cannot but be poetic, should themselves forget that characters in drama have to be dramatic, even at times stagey in their utterance and behaviour. Furthermore, the dramatist's presentation of a character has to be in terms of a series of conventions which cannot help being rhetorical. Knights does not allow for this inevitable rhetorical dramatic exaggeration, and again, more or less unhistorically, modernises his response without taking account of the fact that in the Elizabethan world a certain theatricality and a certain primitive sort of 'direct self-explanation' were accepted as norms of behaviour. Are we to deny a dramatist of Shakespeare's stature the right to indicate, when he wants, that a particular character is of a poetic temper or given to exaggerated gestures of theatricality? The dramatist on these occasions accomplishes his intentions by deliberately overcoming the barriers imposed by his medium – when, for instance, he shows how theatrical and poetical Richard II is. We can respond to these subtle emphases of the playwright only if we pay heed to the conventions of character portrayal.

There is, next, the fundamental question whether Knights's presupposition about the moral world of a Shakespeare play is admissible at all. Apart from the question whether it is feasible to make Shakespeare a moralist or metaphysician and his drama the last word or the Holy Writ in such matters, there is the immediate problem of deciding whether the plays or a group of them can be taken as constituting a moral 'heterocosm', thus making the universe of discourse about the play a moral universe. Knights's habit of making the play-world appear as though it is little different from the moral world as we apprehend it in real life does violence to drama as fiction and make-believe. It is ultimately based on a fallacy different in degree, but not in kind from the habit of mistaking fictional characters for historical or living personages. The fictional mode of existence of the moral world of the plays and the fact that it is constituted and manipulated by the dramatist should make us aware of the limited operativeness of the characters' free will. Moreover, Knights's own moral convictions are, in effect, attributed by him to Shakespeare. For instance, Knights sees a certain variety of pacifism behind Shakespeare's supposedly unfavourable presentation of Hamlet the revenger. Similarly, Shakespeare is considered to be implicitly expressing disapproval of the love-relationship of Antony and Cleopatra because their love is shown as dependent on the physical stimulus of feasting, drinking and luxury.

Making allowances for the particular nuances of L. C. Knights's moral interpretations, the reader can see that his conclusions about the moral imagination of Shakespeare are more or less the same as those arrived at by other students of the subject such as Alfred Harbage, Donald A. Stauffer and Russell A. Fraser – or for that matter R. G. Moulton.[25] That Shakespeare's morals are universal, not relativist, 'not of an age, but for all time' was

[25] Harbage, *As They Liked It* (1961 edn); Stauffer, *Shakespeare's World of Images: The Development of his Moral Ideas* (New York, 1949); Fraser, *Shakespeare's Poetics in Relation to 'King Lear'*; and R. G. Moulton, *The Moral System of Shakespeare* (New York, 1903).

Harbage's view corroborated by the others. Historical studies only serve to show how Shakespeare's morals have a non-historical frame of reference.

But the main urge behind Knights's consistent efforts to keep his universe of moral discourse inviolate is his belief in the '*cognitive* functions of art'. His insistence that Shakespearian drama, which represents art at its best, 'offers a form of knowledge' and that 'the imagination is not a special faculty but life coming to consciousness', an effective formulation of his credo, has a two-fold significance. First, Knights, like I. A. Richards himself, has come a long way from Richardsian positivism, though it is undoubtedly his point of departure. Second, this belief in literature, especially Shakespearian drama, as a form of knowledge, has strongly entrenched itself in some of the best Shakespearian interpretation of recent times. No wonder that Knights considers a 'formalist' apprehension of the artistry of dramatic structure and organisation totally inadequate, when the 'meanings' of the plays are not experientially grasped. 'These meanings, of course, are not definable units in common currency (as when we speak of "the dictionary meaning of a word"); they are thoughts, perceptions, feelings, evaluations that only exist for us' in the context of the play.[26]

This assumption, shared by D. G. James, who would call *Hamlet* and *King Lear* 'a great labour of knowing', and by Geoffrey Bush, who declares that drama is 'a form of knowledge', has been brought seriously into question as part of the more recent reaction against the 'school of Knight and Knights'.

As a part of the general reaction against the concentration of attention on the themes and images, the poetic tone and movement of the plays, a good deal of criticism has been specially directed against Knights's work in more recent times. How the 'language' of his Shakespeare criticism, based as it is on an apprehension of the poetic and imaginative structure of the play in question, because of its more or less blinkered viewpoint refuses to take note of the genre of a play like *Macbeth*, and its implications for interpretation, was forcefully pointed out by

[26] 'Theology and Poetry', *Theology and the University*, pp. 213–14.

R. S. Crane.[27] He also showed that the semantic orientation of critics such as Knights would naturally lead them to critically monistic and moralistic analysis of the 'meaning' of a play in terms of dualities like appearance and reality, justice and mercy and so forth, without regard to the structural patterns fixed for the play by its 'kind' or genre. It can at once be seen that Knights's analysis is not allowed to lapse into mechanical, rule-of-thumb moral strait-jacketing and that his idea of the Shakespearian play envisages a unity between the texture of key passages and the play's total structure, which he apprehends as a complex of linked impressions.

A series of articles and at least one important review in *Critical Quarterly* have addressed themselves to a scrutiny of Knights's Shakespeare commentaries. Some of these raise relevant critical and interpretative issues, while others exhibit a certain intemperateness of expression. Barbara Everett, in her review of *Some Shakespearian Themes*,[28] holds Knights guilty of a total obliviousness to Henry James's irony in his use of the term the 'figure in the carpet', the tag used by Eliot in the passage which Knights quotes as an epigraph to his book; guilty also, of course, of an abstraction from the Shakespearian experience in his theme-hunting, the figure he sees being more or less a phenomenological illusion. Knights's free improvisations on Shakespearian themes have no relevance to the plays, in Everett's opinion and at the end of it all we come out with 'stale pietisms', where the plays bespeak the humility and reverence of Shakespeare before life-experience, which remains a 'mystery'. The frequency of mixed or buried metaphors in Knights's discourse, according to Barbara Everett, is only one example of the cant, the 'magical' counters, with which he hypnotises the reader, to delude him into the belief that something is being communicated while nothing actually is. '*Hamlet* is treated as though it were Langland's *Harrowing of Hell*' (p. 172).

In her article entitled 'The New *King Lear*', *CQ*, 2 (1960), the same critic has argued that interpretations of the play similar to Knights's have proliferated in recent times, and their prime error

[27] *The Languages of Criticism and the Structure of Poetry*, pp. 178–9.
[28] Barbara Everett, 'The Figure in Professor Knights' Carpet', *CQ*, 2 (1960), 171–2.

is to ignore the essential difference between religion and tragedy and to confuse at the same time the realms of poetry and morality. Pointing out that all tragedies are about 'love' of some kind or other, she deplores Knights's failure to respond to the play as a tragedy. In her view, 'what tragedy is is the sense of an intensity of life that compensates for, yet makes more mysterious and dreadful the evil and loss to which it is inseparably connected' (p. 175).[29] True, Knights at times does not keep the categories of religion, tragedy and morality clear. But he never loses sight of the fact that Shakespearian drama is the product of a rich and complex moral and cultural tradition. His interest in, and insistence on, what he calls the 'life-enhancing possibilities' of Shakespearian drama are sufficient evidence that he would be the last to deny that the spirit of Shakespearian drama is summed up in the lines.

Two more articles in *Critical Quarterly*, 'The Characters of Drama' by Nicholas Brooke and 'The Argument about Shakespeare's Characters' by A. D. Nuttall are striking manifestations of the rehabilitation of character-criticism. Of the two, the second concerns itself more closely with Knights. Nuttall starts by outlining what he calls the prerational historical reaction behind Knights's *irruption* in 'How Many Children Had Lady Macbeth?'; and makes the point that, just as Maurice Morgann inaugurated character-criticism in part as a result of his dissatisfaction with the presentation of Shakespeare's plays and characters on the stage of his time, so also in recoil from the personality movement in the theatre, against which there was a revolt in the Shakespearian theatre of Harley Granville-Barker, for instance, Knights formulated his classic devaluation of character in Shakespeare criticism. Nuttall establishes the legitimacy and the inevitability of drawing inferences about characters, praises Morgann's useful distinction between 'open' and 'closed' characters, and thus defends the tradition of character-criticism. His article was followed by a

[29] In 'Theology and Poetry', *Theology and the University*, pp. 207–19, L. C. Knights answers Barbara Everett: 'Whether we attend to the play's organisation as a work of art – whether to such devices as the parallel plots and the juxtaposition of scenes or the power and complexity of spoken poetry – we find, inevitably, that we are dealing with, *meanings* related to one another in a continually widening, context' (pp. 213–14).

correspondence in which Empson among others, took part, and declared his faith in character-criticism. The grievous omission in Nuttall's essay was his ignoring Knights's own 'The Question of Character in Shakespeare',[30] which had appeared years earlier, and ignoring that Knights has himself of late practised inferential character-criticism.

The reaction against Knights is matched by a repetition and extension of his critical principles and methods by several critics deeply influenced by him. Three of these may be mentioned – T. B. Tomlinson, Wilbur Sanders and Walter Stein.[31] Tomlinson pays Knights the tribute that he of all modern writers on tragedy, save Leavis, has contributed most to the understanding of Shakespearian tragedy. Tomlinson does indeed carry to extremes what I earlier called a sort of 'vitalist' tendency in Knights; he examines various Elizabethan and Jacobean dramatists, using the criterion of the quality of their insights, and finds most of them, except Middleton, wanting. Tomlinson's one dissatisfaction arises over Knights's habit of finding a pattern of consistent development in Shakespeare' in his handling of almost every theme. Sanders judges Marlowe by the criteria evolved by Knights, and finds that Marlowe contrasts unfavourably with Shakespeare. Sanders tries to establish that Shakespeare's political and moral insights about good and evil, and about man and nature, are superior to those of philosophers, political, moral and religious. In fact, Sanders thinks Shakespeare a greater teacher, and a more original thinker, than Aquinas, Hooker and of course, Machiavelli and the lesser fry, in a more literal sense than intended by Milton in his phrase about Spenser. Any reader would endorse Sanders's emphasis on the mutual collaboration between artist and ethos. But one would suppose that Knights, given his implicit acceptance of Shakespeare's debt to moral and cultural traditions, would not consent to the hostility which Sanders exhibits towards historicism. Stein defends Knights and his 'New *King Lear*' against the champions

[30] First published in J. Garrett, ed., *More Talking of Shakespeare* (London, 1959), pp. 55–69.
[31] T. B. Tomlinson, *A Study of Elizabethan and Jacobean Tragedy* (Cambridge, 1964); Wilbur Sanders, *The Dramatist and the Received Idea*, and Walter Stein, *Criticism as Dialogue* (Cambridge, 1969).

of the newer *King Lear*; but he seeks to complement Knights's moral concerns with religious ones, establishing that the next step from Knights's insistence on the hard-earned moral positives that emerge in *King Lear* or *Macbeth* is to explicit religious affirmation. Leavis and Knights, after all, stop short of the religious frontiers.

It is, I hope, fairly clear from what I have said that Knights's more or less divided response to historical scholarship makes for a certain partiality of perspective. This problematic relationship between critical interpretation and scholarship is paradigmatic of the general relationship between the poetic interpretation of Shakespeare (or any classic of the past) and the research of historical scholars. As I have pointed out earlier in this chapter, Knights's critical approach in particular, and the poetic approach to Shakespeare in general, grounds itself, albeit unconsciously, on perceptions and insights about the Elizabethan theatre and drama given currency by historically-oriented commentators. Moreover, Knights's assimilation of the essentials of historical knowledge about the social and cultural milieu of drama enables him in his early and influential essays – 'How Many Children Had Lady Macbeth?' not excepted – and pre-eminently in his *Drama and Society in the Age of Jonson* (1937), to reap a rich harvest of the critical fruits of historical scholarship. The capacity to grasp the critical consequences of historical information and to make unlaboured application of historical fact with an alert sense of relevance – in short, to take scholarship in his interpretative stride – also marks his later writings. The real significance of historical knowledge is brought home to the reader through Knights's flexible relation of historical ideas to the plays. His emphasis, in the political and history plays, on the idea of mutuality between king and subjects, between class and class, and between individual and individual – the old Aristotelian metaphor of the body-politic for the commonwealth, based on the ideal of partnership between the ruler and the ruled – is one of several instances where Knights breathes life into a concept which, in the hands of other commentators, remains for the most part an abstraction.

There is, no doubt, a fruitful dialogue between the critic and the scholar in Knights; at the same time there is a running debate, for the most part more verbal than real, occasionally amounting to a refusal to make full enough use of scholarly research. As John Lawlor has pointed out, after an illustrative argument of considerable length, Knights in his essay 'Historical Scholarship and the Interpretation of Shakespeare' (originally published in the *Sewanee Review*, and reprinted in *Further Explorations*) draws an artificial and hard-and-fast line of demarcation between historical scholarship and the 'Shakespeare experience'. This seeming prejudice against historical scholarship, explicit here but implicit in all of Knights's writing, is not so curious when one remembers the new Cambridge critical school of the late twenties and thirties. Insofar as Knights puts us on our guard against the irrelevances of scholarly burrowing or structure-building, and warns the student off the pursuit of red herrings, he helps to keep clear the line of communication between scholarly research and its critical application. But when he theorises as though Shakespearian drama can speak to us directly, without any intervention or readjustment of the historical imagination based on historical knowledge, and when he in consequence unduly modernises his reaction to Shakespeare, his readings suffer distortion.

The case for proper recognition of the role of historical consciousness of past and present and the interaction between the two, has been well argued by John Lawlor in his rejoinder to Knights's article ('On Historical Scholarship', *Sewanee Review*) and there is no need to rehearse the arguments here. I would point out that it does not smack of the poverty of historicism to say that one's 'intrinsic' modern response to Shakespeare is historically governed in countless ways, for the present is as much subject to history as the past. Awareness of the circumstances of intellectual and cultural history that shape our so-called modern approach to a classic of the past, a sort of historical self-awareness, will help us to have a real encounter with that classic; and that paradoxical combination of self-consciousness and self-effacement can be achieved only with the aid of a keen historical sense. Lawlor makes it clear that appreciation of the need for a historical sense does not mean that we have to take refuge in some sort of antiquarian Elizabethanism and lapse into the merely archaeological. The right kind of semantic sensitivity, an appropriate sense of values, and the reorientation of attitudes and sympathies can only be brought about through a historical consciousness. The function of that consciousness is not the merely negative one of excluding intrusive, invalid modern impulses and meanings. To use historical information as no more than a check on the meanings we put on the literary text of the past is to underestimate the primary role played by our historical sense in entering into the experience of the classic.

It is ironic that a scholar-critic like L. C. Knights should express a distrust of historical findings and at times decline to avail himself of scholarly findings, as in his interpretation of *King Lear*. It is this blunting of the historical sense and his consequent failure to make allowance for historical factors in evolving criteria for judging characters and situations that seems to lead Knights into an almost moralistic indictment of characters, and to treat them as exempla of contemporaneous ethical and sociocultural beliefs. L. C. Knights equates the heroic with the all-too-human image, forgetting that the heroic is all the more heroic for being human.

The dimming of historical perceptions also causes Knights to ignore the working of dramatic conventions and modes of utterance, the intricate mixture of non-naturalistic, 'primitive' devices of characterisation, and the naturalistic presentation of characters which is inevitable in the mixed mode of Elizabethan drama. Knights approaches the Roman political plays and also the history plays from what he himself has called the personalist point of view. But the presentation of a character as a person on the stage, the theatrical revelation of his selfhood by the character, must give the impression of egoism to the observer not attuned to the idiom of dramatic communication. An instance of how the integration of personalism with a certain kind of historical understanding can help to attune our response to character is to be found in an essay of Elias Schwartz's, 'The Idea of the Person in Shakespearian Tragedy', *SQ*, 16 (1965), 39–47, which provides a striking contrast with Knights's unsympathetic attitude to the tragic heroes.

It is possible that Knights, in one of his latest writings,[32] has himself accepted the need to attend to the idiom and mode of dramatic communication, and to understand Shakespeare's thought in dramatic terms. If Knights's commentaries have seemed to other critics such as Norman Rabkin[33] to be guilty of abstracting moral ideas and ethical themes from the plays it is mainly because Knights has not kept track of the dramatic lines of communication in the plays, and so has appeared to pursue his intellectual and moral concerns as embodied in the poetry rather than what transpires from the drama of the interplay of character and situation. But Knights offers a corrective when he suggests in his recent essay that a redefinition of the nature and function of thought in drama is called for, in terms of attitudes governing the response of character to character, elusive factors such as emotional overtones, and also the oblique commentary of action and imagery on statement. One is reminded of Una Ellis-Fermor's call for attention to the distinctive nature of thought in drama, of her emphasis on the distinction between the logic of thought and poetic logic, and between dramatic logic and poetic logic ('Thought in Drama', *Shakespeare the Dramatist and other Papers*). This, doubtless, points in the direction of *true* dramatic criticism of Shakespeare's poetic plays.

John Newton ('*Scrutiny's* Failure with Shakespeare'), in an adverse assessment of Knights's criticism brings the charge that the commentary, insisting on the reader's constant alertness in his experience of the play, lulls him into a false sense that all that reading the play requires is application and thus unintentionally belittles Shakespeare (p. 165). In this respect, according to Newton, the Shakespeare criticism of Bradley and Wilson Knight gives greater understanding and enjoyment of the play. This is one version of the occasional general charge that extended close reading of a work has the effect of superseding it, putting the reader off rather than sending him back to the work itself. But the truth, after all, is that the reader's sensitivity, openness and

---

[32] 'Thought in Shakespeare', *The Hidden Harmony: Essays in Honor of Philip Wheelwright*, edited by Oliver Johnson (New York, 1967) (reprinted in L. C. Knights, *Explorations 3* (London, 1976), pp. 115–28).

[33] *Shakespeare and the Common Understanding* (New York and London, 1967), p. 55.

authenticity of response and his scholarly acumen are not mutually exclusive. Knights's criticism cannot be said to come between the reader and the play. When he sums up the outcome of Shakespeare's poetic-dramatic endeavour as composed of complementary effects of stripping illusions and celebrating all that makes for life, scholarly objectors may point out the need to relate the stripping of illusions to Renaissance platonism or to the 'existential' reality of illusions, or complain about the vitalism underlying the preoccupation with the celebration of life. Yet important negative and positive truths about Shakespearian poetry are well conveyed in the generalisation. Similarly, when Knights speaks of Shakespearian poetry releasing the latent energies of our minds and expanding the boundaries of our consciousness, or of metaphor in Shakespeare embodying and bringing home to the reader realities otherwise not apprehensible at all, or of a whole play like *King Lear* being a metaphor for man's search for meaning in life, or of the Shakespearian image being a new point in the growth of consciousness, such generalities are not made at the level of platitude, but become truths demonstrated on the pulses of his own experience of the plays, which we do not merely share in but make our own, thanks to the effective transmission of the experience through his commentaries.

6

The study of
Shakespeare's imagery:
Spurgeon and after

Images and image patterns can be regarded as *the* literary-critical discovery of the twentieth century; they have certainly provided the basis of several analytic approaches.[1]

One of the more remarkable developments in image analysis is the increasingly broad sense in which the term 'image' is interpreted. Strikingly different answers are returned to the question 'What is an image?', and two broad patterns seem to emerge. An image, which was one regarded as the verbal suggestion of a visual picture, or at least as some kind of an analogy or comparison, may now be no more than a casual reference or the invocation of an idea, object or person.[2] This widening of the term's significance has caused scepticism about its ambiguity and has led to the suspicion that both word and concept have outlived their usefulness. It is a far cry from the eighteenth-century notion of the image as some sort of pictorialisation, to Middleton Murry's liberalisation of the term in his pioneer classic

---

[1] Though Thomas Gray thought that every word in Shakespeare was a picture, none of the eighteenth- or nineteenth-century commentators (with the exception of Walter Whiter), made Shakespeare's imagery a subject of investigation. Some have seen anticipations of imagistic analysis in Coleridge, though. M. M. Badawi, 'Coleridge's Formal Criticism of Shakespeare's Plays', *EC* 10 (1960), 148–62 and Barbara Hardy, '"I Have a Smack of Hamlet"': Coleridge and Shakespeare's Characters', *EC*, 8 (1958), 238–55. Also, Badawi, *Coleridge: Critic of Shakespeare* (Cambridge, 1973), 163–7.

[2] This shift in the sense of the word has been analysed and documented by Norman Friedman, 'Imagery: From Sensation to Symbol', *Journal of Aesthetics and Art Criticism*, 12 (1953), 25–37. Ray Frazer, 'The Origin of the Term "Image"', *ELH*, 27 (1960), 149–61, investigates the history of the expression, and suggests that 'as a critical term, image . . . is thus partly a product of the new (i.e. Romantic and pre-Romantic) way of looking at poetry, the new aesthetics of sensationalism' (p. 155).

'Metaphor' (1927; reprinted in *John Clare and Other Studies*, London, 1950 and Anne Ridler, ed., *Shakespeare Criticism: 1919–1935* (London, 1936)). No less remarkable is the shift from acceptance of the term by Middleton Murry and I. A. Richards, through the criticism of assumptions about its nature and functions in Shakespearian drama by O. J. Campbell and E. E. Stoll, and distrust about the validity of the concept by the aesthetician Harold Osborne, to a plea for its rejection by P. N. Furbank.[3]

Allowing for the fluidity of the term classification scheme for images, we might usefully distinguish three kinds of images isolated and commented on by critics – sensuous, ideational and analogical.[4] The more profitable and successful discussions of imagery in Shakespearian and Elizabethan drama are tolerant in their definition of 'image' and demonstrate a freedom from classificatory rigidity. Caroline Spurgeon clearly shows an awareness of the problems of identity, nomenclature and classification. Not the least of the virtues of her book, *Shakespeare's Imagery and What It Tells Us*, which has been indicted on a number of scores many of them valid, is that in her isolation of images, in her counts at least, if not in commentaries, by way of interpretation she very rightly forgets her narrow definition of an image as a word-picture involving a comparison.[5] On the other hand, Spurgeon's failure to translate the words and suggestions of the play imaginatively into stage-realities stood in the way of her realising the importance of the idea of gold in *Timon of Athens*[6] and

---

[3] O. J. Campbell, 'Shakespeare and the New Critics'; E. E. Stoll, 'Symbolism in Shakespeare', *MLR*, 42 (1947) 9–23; Harold Osborne, *Aesthetics and Criticism* (London, 1955), pp. 181–8; P. N. Furbank, 'Do We Need the Terms *Image* and *Imagery*?', *CQ*, 9 (1967), 335–45, and *Reflections on the Word 'Image'* (London, 1970); Pierre Legouis, 'Some Remarks on Seventeenth Century Imagery', *Seventeenth Century Imagery*, edited by E. Miner (Los Angeles and London, 1970), pp. 187–97.

[4] Something like this three-fold classification is employed by I. A. Richards, *Coleridge on Imagination*, pp. 32–3; Edward Partridge, *The Broken Compass: A Study of the Major Comedies of Ben Jonson* (London, 1958), pp. 22–3; and Frazer 'The Origin of the Term "Image"', p. 149. R. A. Foakes employs a two-fold classification of images in non-dramatic poetry into those of impression and of thought – *The Romantic Assertion* (New Haven, 1958), p. 32.

[5] First published Cambridge, 1935; 1965 edn., pp. 5, 8–9; but especially p. 345.

[6] 'there is only one image from gold throughout the play' (p. 345); 'But gold, however much it may be emphasized was not the *picture* which was constantly before Shakespeare's eyes' (p. 345).

led her to join issue with Wilson Knight on this. It is exactly
Wilson Knight's habit of considering imagery as a matter of more
than words on the page that leads him to the perception of
imaginative realities (and sometimes unrealities) in the plays.
Thus, alongside the tendency among commentators to go beyond considerations of metaphor to take count of direct reference
and evocation arising from the verbal dimensions of images,
imagery has increasingly been recognised as embracing the
non-verbal, presentational aspects of drama.[7] The timely call by
R. A. Foakes ('Suggestions for a New Approach to Shakespeare's
Imagery', *SS*, 5 (1952), 81–92) to recognise the need to consider
imagery in Shakespeare 'in a context of not words alone, but of
words, dramatic situation, the interplay of characters, stage-
effects and the place of the image in a time-sequence' has been
well heeded in later commentary. But, as Maurice Charney's
shift of emphasis from *Shakespeare's Roman Plays* to *Style in
'Hamlet'* reveals – from stress on the stage-realisation of imagic
suggestion to equal emphasis on the dictional, rhetorical and
theatrical – aspects of imagery cannot be considered in isolation from general characteristics as well as details of words and
language, diction and style. Explorations of Shakespeare's
vocabulary and usage and explorations of his imagery have,
nevertheless, run parallel to each other.[8] However arbitrary the
distinction, and despite the inevitable overlap, it is convenient to
keep the two strands separate.

[7] Ronald Peacock, *The Art of the Drama* (London, 1957), is one of the earliest
studies to emphasise non-verbal, presentational imagery in drama. Maurice
Charney's study of the presentational imagery of the Roman plays is an
example of this approach (*Shakespeare's Roman Plays*, Cambridge, Mass., 1961).

[8] E. E. Kellett, 'Some Notes on a Feature of Shakespeare's Style', *Suggestions*
(Cambridge, 1923), besides its rediscovery of 'image clusters' in Shakespeare, is
an example of a pioneer study of imagery together with style and rhetoric.
G. H. W. Rylands, *Words and Poetry* (London, 1928) and 'Shakespeare's Poetic
Energy', *PBA*, 37 (1951); F. C. Kolbë, *Shakespeare's Way*; R. W. David, *The Janus of
Poets* (1935); William Empson, *The Structure of Complex Words* and, of course,
Seven Types of Ambiguity; M. M. Mahood, *Shakespeare's Wordplay* (1957); P. A.
Jorgensen, *Redeeming Shakespeare's Words* (1962) and H. M. Hulme, *Explorations
in Shakespeare's Language* (1962) are important studies of Shakespeare's words
and images. Christine Brooke-Rose, *A Grammar of Metaphor* (1958) thought that
imagistic analysis such as Clemen's should pay greater attention to matters of
rhetoric (p. 20). Brian Vickers, *The Artistry of Shakespeare's Prose* takes imagery
and rhetoric together.

By far the most striking changes in approaches to Shakespearian imagery are the redirection of attention to the dramatic and theatrical: that is, the function of images, and away from the autobiographical or merely 'poetic' aspects of imagery. Wolfgang Clemen's work has been instrumental in bringing about this reorientation; he has concentrated on the dramatic mode of existence of imagery; whereas the studies by Maurice Charney, Alan S. Downer and Clifford P. Lyons, as well as the experiments in Shakespearian production by Wilson Knight, have emphasised the theatrical viability and significance of the plays' imagery.

Before examining the assumptions, techniques and procedures of some leading analysts, I would like generally to chart the problems of interpreting imagery: this may help us to determine whether the commentators recognise them, and how efficiently they deal with them. First, there is the bewildering variety of functions attributed to imagery in drama. Second, there is the distinction between imagery in non-dramatic literature, especially in lyric or symbolist poetry, and imagery in drama; a distinction which is upheld by some students of Shakespearian imagery and ignored by others. Third, is the question whether images should be studied in terms of their subject-matter or their object-matter.[9] Which implications of the imagery's subject-matter are relevant, whether the interaction between the subject-matter and object-matter of the image is not more important than either are issues raised by discussions of Shakespearian imagery. Fourth, there is the problem of the relative weight to be given to interrelations between image and its 'multiform' contexts, especially in drama. Fifth, the findings of Rosemond Tuve about the influence of Ramist logical and rhetorical traditions on the Renaissance writer suggest that choice and function of images were dictated by 'decorum'. This reorientation of outlook on

---

[9] The terms are used by Spurgeon and Foakes; H. W. Wells called the two halves of an image 'major and minor terms', and S. L. Bethell 'oblique and direct' terms. I. A. Richards used the terms 'tenor' and 'vehicle'. Elder Olson uses 'analogue' and 'referent' and calls the meeting ground of the two 'continuum'. Reuben Brower has the terms 'subject' and 'icon' for the two aspects of an image or metaphor.

imagery, has diverted attention from the personality of the creator of the literary work, to the work itself; from the psychological to the artistic implications of the image. Psychological significances are not ruled out, but they must be pursued with greater caution and sophistication than Spurgeon or Armstrong display. Sixth, the derivativeness or originality of the image must be determined: the etiology of an image, or its archetypal or mythic, proverbial or topological status has interpretative consequences. Seventh, almost as fundamental in importance as the delimiting and fixing of the identity of an image is how images are chosen for study in a play or group of plays, for the simple reason that an investigator can only treat a few images, can never hope to consider or in any sense exhaust all of them. Here the problem is, which of the images can be considered to determine or contribute to the total imaginative impression left by the play? The basic inadequacy of statistical or pseudo-scientific counts and charts, of quantitative computations of occurrence is now accepted. Eighth, there is the problem of first identifying and isolating image clusters or image complexes, and then of tracing their associative links among the members of a cluster and reconstructing the associational processes of the dramatist; some of these investigations have the effect of telling us more about the psychological processes of the investigators than of Shakespeare. There is also the interweaving of several image strands and image clusters; this interlinking has also to be attended to by the commentator.

These, in brief, are some of the major interpretative problems posed by imagery in drama. I now consider the first in more detail, before discussing Spurgeon's and later commentators' views on the functions of imagery.

Imagistic critics stress the functional as distinct from the ornamental role of imagery in Shakespearian drama. Images frequently reinforce for the reader or spectator the themes or central ideas of a play. They thus act like Wagnerian *leitmotivs*, setting the mood and evoking the appropriate responses. Central thematic emphases and delicate nuances of feeling are conveyed through images and image patterns acting more or less 'subliminally' on the reader. It is one of the major ways in which Shakespeare 'contrives to make secret impressions on us' (to adopt Maurice Morgann's phrase). There has been a growing recognition of the role of imagery in furthering the dramatic processes of realisation of meanings of events, of the significance of plot-structure and plot-movement, and of the foundation and development of character and of dramatic thought. What used to be called the 'atmosphere' and background of the play and was thought to be evoked by certain references (such as the 'blood' references in *Macbeth*) is now, thanks to the focussing of attention on imagery, felt to be an essential part of the play and referred to as the 'world' of the play.[10] This world is conveyed to the reader mainly by the imagery and that is how his sense of the 'realities' of the play-world is ensured. The communication of the nature and imaginative significance of a situation, the preparation of the reader's mind for an event and the guiding of his response to it, so that he may develop the right emotional and intellectual attitude[11] to the situation and its characters, the anticipatory forecasting of action achieved by co-ordinating 'figures-in-words' and 'figures-in-action'[12] – these are some of the ways in which imagery can operate which are only occasionally highlighted by modern commentators. The correlation of imagery and action certainly deserves more attention than it has had. Image patterns lend an emotional and sometimes an intellectual unity, very often a unity of tone and mood, to a play.

Imagery is now seen to play a vital role not only in dramatic realisation of themes and plot-movement, but also in characterisation especially the playwright's manipulation of the attitudes

[10] M. H. Abrams, *The Mirror and the Lamp* (1960), (first edn 1953) gives a good account of the development of the idea of 'the Poem as Heterocosm' (pp. 272–85) during the Romantic period, of which the idea of the play's world is an offshoot.

[11] See F. R. Leavis, 'Imagery and Movement: Notes in the Analysis of Poetry', *Scrutiny*, 13 (1944–5), 119–34, esp. pp. 119–20, repr. in *The Living Principle* (1975).

[12] See Wolfgang Clemen *A Commentary on Shakespeare's Richard III* (London, 1968), on the function of foreboding performed by imagery in *Richard III*. The terms 'figures-in-words' and 'figures-in action' (verbal imagery prefiguring the same imagistic ideas subsequently recurring as part of the action of the play) are Hereward T. Price's. The co-ordination between the two is well discussed with reference to Webster by Price in 'The Function of Imagery in Webster', *PMLA*, 70 (1955), 720–39. The contribution of imagery to total dramatic effect is soberly outlined by Moody E. Prior, *The Language of Tragedy* (Bloomington and London, 1947, 1966 edn).

of one character to another, of a character to himself, and of the reader to the character. This new conception of the function of imagery in characterisation is one of the determining factors in the fresh appreciation of character in drama, which has taken the place of the early thirties' rejection of character-criticism. Imagistic clues to character take a number of forms. Not only do characters reveal themselves through their instinctive choice of imagery (images are spontaneously chosen for the character by a process of empathetic identification by the playwright; dramatic character rather than the personality of the dramatist dictates imagery), but qualitative judgements of value, or guidelines for them at least, are suggested through the kinds of imagery employed by other characters in relation to a character – animal imagery, for instance. So much of the psychological make-up, inner motivation, and unconscious aspects of personality of the character as is needed for dramatic understanding is revealed through imagery;[13] changes and exchanges of imagery in speeches, the use of imagery of a certain kind for a forensic or manipulative purpose by one character towards another, in order to make him act or speak in a particular manner, are among the finer strokes of dramatic art.

It has not often been observed that the frequency and profusion of imagery in Elizabethan drama is due as much to the dramatist's felt need to stylise, to foreshorten and to elevate dramatic speech so as to give it an aesthetic distance from normal speech, as it is to the imagistic or analogical habit of mind,[14] or delight in *discordia concors*, or the tension of discordant ideas.[15] A paradoxical function served by imagery is to deepen the concentration and so enrich the micro-context of the play, by providing it with a macro-context in the universe of thought. Una Ellis-

---

[13] Vickers, *The Artistry of Shakespeare's Prose*, uses the classificatory terms of subjective, objective and forensic imagery (pp. 19–20). K. Muir instances the 'Pity like a naked new-born babe' soliloquy as a telling example of how, through the imagery, the compunctions of Macbeth's conscience, his essential humanity, seem to show through ('Image and Symbol in *Macbeth*', *SS*, 19 (1966), 45–54, esp. 47).

[14] Prior, *The Language of Tragedy* (1947 edn.), pp. 6–18, esp. p. 6.

[15] J. A. Mazzeo, *Renaissance and Seventeenth-Century Studies* (London and New York, 1964), chapter 3 'Metaphysical Poetry and the Poetic of Correspondence', esp. pp. 54–6.

Fermor has emphasised this function of imagery, although she has not referred to its paradoxical nature.[16] By this means the play's inherent disadvantages of brevity and circumscription are overcome and a wide range of experience and thought is evoked, thus extending the frontiers of drama. Far from loosening the tension or undermining the structure of the play and providing a distraction, imagery serves only to strengthen the microcosm of the play by relating it to the macrocosm of the universe of thought and experience. It has come to be recognised in recent times that the frame of reference of the imagery in drama is the world of human experience as a whole, rather than that of intellectual discourse alone. In fact, imagery in drama is a mode of apprehending experience, thought, feeling and sensation together, as well as a mode of communication; the dramatist, and the characters through him, think and feel through images. In the experimental relationship of the playwright with his medium, images breed images through associational processes and hooked analogies – poetic charge and energy accrue in this way. The role of imagery is central to this exploratory–creative encounter, which includes and transcends the medium of words, but transcends only by inclusion.

With these general considerations in mind, I examine the work of Caroline Spurgeon and some of the other imagistic critics. Caroline Spurgeon's pioneering investigation provided the foundations for future work and inspired and challenged other investigators to strike out in new directions. She has been criticised for her assumptions, her methods, her choice and classification of images, her misunderstanding of the structure and function of the image, her failure to relate the image of its many contexts, her wrong inference-drawing, use of the biographical fallacy, 'objective fallacy', and reductive fallacy. Most of these charges are locally true, but in the consequent distrust of her preoccupations and manner of procedure, she has not been given credit for

---

[16] Una Ellis-Fermor, 'The Functions of Imagery in Drama', *The Frontiers of Drama*, pp. 80 and 85. R. A. Foakes has pointed out how such a widening of the horizons of drama results in a universalisation and intensification of a particular situation at once. Relief of tension does not preclude concentration on a situation, *The Romantic Assertion*, p. 32.

genuinely valuable findings. Her limitations of method and outlook have to be admitted; but I would suggest a historical explanation for her faults of omission and commission, in the hope that an understanding of her approach will lead to the sympathetic reading of her critical intention and achievement, which her commentary badly needs. Caroline Spurgeon's critical and scholarly orientation was derived from presuppositions and practices which were a legacy of the earlier tradition of studying imagery. She was, for the most part, working within that tradition, and could not break entirely free from it. She was also blinkered by an obsessive preoccupation with the received idea of Shakespeare as a man of character (in contrast to Frank Harris's idea of the man Shakespeare and his alleged involvement with women).[17] The positivist, inductive, quasi-scientific outlook which the scholarly-critical fashion of the twenties and early thirties called for, the inadequacies of the then traditional approaches to image study and to Shakespeare the man, the absence of any significant findings about Renaissance rhetoric and views of imagery – these factors naturally caused her false starts, misconceptions, misinterpretations, and misplaced emphasis. She succeeded only in scratching the surface of a vast subject: but it is often forgotten that she launched on a tripartite study of Shakespeare's imagery, and lived to complete only the first phase.

What of the historical conditioning of her methodology? Her interest in the light that images throw on the personality of Shakespeare, her classification of images in terms of their subject-matter, and her pursuit of the implications of idiosyncratic fields of enquiry – all of which have been denounced as a gross waste of time and energy – had ample warrant in the practice of her predecessors. Apart from Walter Whiter, John

[17] As Arthur M. Eastman (*A Short History of Shakespearean Criticism*), puts it:
So strikingly different is Spurgeon's Shakespeare from those of Harris and Lewis, so peculiarly unturmoiled, so very far from 'the expense of spirit in a waste of shame', that it has been met with some gently masculine scoffing 'Miss Spurgeon was a Lady' . . . Her Shakespeare 'a Victorian gentleman' . . . One looks in vain for clear, confident treatment of those hundreds on hundreds of items Eric Partridge catalogues in his *Shakespeare's Bawdy*. One thinks of Iago's beast with two backs and suspects Spurgeon filed it under 'Animals, Fabulous', or of Leontes' Sir Smile Fishing in his neighbour's pond and wonders, fascinated, whether it is filed under 'Daily Life, Sport' (p. 257).

Keble (*Lectures on Poetry*) was the earliest English enquirer into the imagery of a great writer. In the fourth of his five lectures, 'The Canon of Imagery' (the first is called 'The Canon of the Significant Theme'), Keble showed how Homer's personality and experiences were revealed through the imagery of his poems. The typical Romantic faith that literature is a revelation of personality is the context of this line of thinking, which governs Spurgeon's critical thought as much as it did Keble's. Keble said, 'Homer's mind and disposition can be inferred not only from his story, but from his imagery and the comparisons which he draws from every quarter, and from the choice which he makes of poetic ornament and beauty, to illustrate both the language and the subjects of which he treats'.[18] Like Keble, Spurgeon believes that Shakespeare's heart can be unlocked with the key of imagery. Keble also, quite strikingly to a student of Spurgeon, enumerated the domains or fields from which Homer draws his images and concluded that the majority of images come from nature and human life; 'There remains what is perhaps the most fruitful field of all; the many kinds of birds and beasts, tame and wild; whose sports, food, fierce contests, and whole manner and habit of living afford a rich source of splendid imagery.'[19]

Two more exponents of this, the only earlier tradition of image study, both belonging to the twentieth century and both cited by Spurgeon, show the same preoccupation with autobiographical elements, fields of image derivation and a romantic-nostalgic bias in favour of outdoor life and nature: T. Hilding Svartengren, *Intensifying Similes in English* (Lund, 1918) and Stephen J. Brown,

---

[18] *Keble's Lectures on Poetry 1832—1841*, ed. E. K. Francis (Oxford, 1912), i, 172.

[19] Keble *Lectures*, i, 190. E. Auerbach, trans. W. Trask, *Mimesis: The Representation of Reality in Western Literature* (Princeton, 1953), calls Homeric narrative 'foregrounded' (in the sense that such narrative with all its significance to the fore and on the surface, in contrast to Old Testament narrative, does not call for 'figural' explication). The profusion of images in such 'foregrounded' narrative does not demand interpretation. But, ironically, Shakespearian imagery, has elicited a disproportionate amount of comment.

Hans Sperber enunciated a semantic principle that an intense interest in a subject will result in its providing us with analogies for the description of other experiences; see his article in *Zeitschrift für deutsches Altertum*, 59 (1922) and his book, *Einführung in die Bedeutungslehre* (Leipzig, 1923). See also W. E. Collinson, *MLR* (1925), 105, and Stephen Ullmann, *Language and Style* (Oxford, 1964), p. 83.

The World of Imagery (London, 1927). Both classify images according to the sources of their subject-matter, and promptly go on to consider what the images, similes and metaphors of the English people reveal about their interests and preferences.[20]

Other critics have dismissed Spurgeon's basic approach to Shakespeare's imagery as an infallible clue to his personality and her modes of inference-drawing. Her approach has been amusingly caricatured by Lillian Hornstein, and challenged by Mario Praz.[21] Long before Spurgeon (or, for that matter, John Keble) Johnson in his *Life of Thomson*, with characteristic penetration, exposed the fallacy that a writer's imagery is some sort of personal signature (*The Lives of the Poets* (The World's Classics edition, London, 1906), 1975 reprint, vol. 2, p. 358). Clearly, Spurgeon launched on her biographical tack because she has the Romantic preconception that literature is a revelation of the writer's personality. She wrote in the days of what may be called a 'pre-Ramist' innocence in criticism and scholarship. For all the controversy over Rosemond Tuve's emphasis on Ramist influence, and her close parallel between early seventeenth-century poets and Renaissance Elizabethan rhetoric, her discoveries about Elizabethan and Metaphysical imagery have established several important characteristics. Imagery in Elizabethan and Jacobean writers is not necessarily attributable to the compulsions of the writer's personality, but also to the demands of decorum, the requirements of the subject and the logic of persuasion. The writer may be concerned with technical virtuosity and artfulness, and interested in bringing about a certain emotional and intellectual response in the reader. These purposes will be uppermost in his mind; and this will override the indulgence of personal taste.

[20] Gaston Bachelard the French critic has practised the same habit of imagistic analysis.
[21] Lillian Hornstein, 'Analysis of Imagery: A Critique of Literary Method', *PMLA*, 57 (1942), 638–53, exposes the fallacy of the connection sought by Spurgeon between imagery and the author's actual physical experience, besides drawing attention to the traditional or commonplace origins of some images taken to be personal. Mario Praz, in an important review of Spurgeon and Clemen (*English Studies*, 18 (1936), 177–9), questions with wit and force the value of the biographical inferences drawn by Spurgeon (p. 178). Bernard N. Schilling, *Dryden and the Conservative Myth* (New Haven, 1961), p. 8, has coined the expression

Spurgeon's diverting attention from the drama to the dramatist has thus been shown to be of dubious value, and the way she has drawn inferences from imagery about Shakespeare the man has provoked several kinds of criticism. Some critics have blamed her for having recourse to Freudian psychoanalytical speculation; others have blamed her for not being enough of a Freudian or Jungian.[22] Her use of the *argumentum ex nihilo* has elicited adverse comment. Above all, her gathering of images, even her identification of them, for all her painstaking labour and its illusion of exhaustiveness and scientific accuracy, have been shown to be anything but foolproof – to be guilty of many omissions, and also false classifications.

If biographical inferences are admissible at all, it is better for the interpreter to make full use of psychoanalytical principles. In the post-Freudian era, none probably can help being Freudian in some sense. But, in interpreting an iterative image, the interpreter is under no obligation to see it as a Freudian symbol, for the psychological implications of an image need not have been Freudian, and could well have been religious in a religious age. Yet, the suggestion that a recurrent image might have some symbolic suggestiveness, and the charge that Spurgeon failed to recognise this and worked out her interpretation in terms of a simple equation between image and actual experience, are valid enough. For example, it did not occur to her that fishing or angling images, frequent in Shakespeare's text, might have sprung, not from Shakespeare's fondness for angling, but from some symbolic significance which fish and fishing had for him. (But it would be unhistorical to suppose that the fish image was only a Freudian sex symbol to an Elizabethan; it could well have

'Spurgeonism' for the habit of relating imagery to the personal experience of the writer.

22 According to Lillian Hornstein, *Analysis of Imagery*, p. 649, 'Miss Spurgeon uses the Freudian method of interpretation'. S. E. Hyman, *The Armed Vision*, speaks of an unconscious debt to Freud which would probably have shocked her had she been aware of it (pp. 214–15), and almost regrets that 'she was not consciously enough Freudian' (p. 215). Norman H. Holland, *Psychoanalysis and Shakespeare*, finds Spurgeon's analysis close to psychoanalytic procedure and Armstrong 'not only psychoanalytic but devoutly so' (p. 121), but concludes, 'Neither Miss Spurgeon nor Prof. Armstrong is burdened by any particular scientific knowledge of the human mind' (p. 122).

had a primary religious significance for him.) If Spurgeon fails to recognise the quality or feature which Shakespeare might have regularly associated with a particular image, it is mainly because she does not show any awareness of its traditional origins, and associations. She betrays a belief in a thesis which is the converse of Sperber's – that the absence of imagery from a particular field is to be construed as the writer's lack of acquaintance with, or total lack of interest in, that field. How misconceived this notion is, has been pointed out. The absence of any fishing image in the other writings of 'the Compleat Angler', Izaak Walton, and the absence of any music images in the poetry of the fourteenth-century French musician, Machaut, have been adduced as exposures of the fallacy of Spurgeon's reasoning. But her failure to give due weight to certain important strains of imagery, though she included the images as they occur in one or two of the plays in her counts, is far more damning. The most remarkable of her omissions is the imagery relating to acting, the stage and the theatre. E. K. Chambers pointed out the omission; before and since other commentators have produced illuminating findings about Shakespeare's use of this imagery, to good dramatic effect, in play after play.

The categorisation of images according to the areas or subjects from which they are adopted is a convention first established by Cicero (see Christine Brooke-Rose, *A Grammar of Metaphor*, p. 8); practised by Renaissance rhetoricians and by Keble in the nineteenth century; and picked up by early twentieth-century analysts of imagery. Spurgeon was eager to preserve the identity of Shakespeare against the kind of disintegrating speculations offered by critics like J. M. Robertson and by the anti-Stratfordians, the Marlovians and, especially, the Baconians. It is only to be expected that she should start with a preconceived, a *given* image of Shakespeare the man, which is an exaggerated version of the Romantic-Victorian idea of Shakespeare's personality, and go on to find confirmatory evidence for this idea in the imagery of the plays, as though the method were strictly inductive. Stanley Edgar Hyman's description (*The Armed Vision*, p. 219) of Spurgeon's Shakespeare as the 'troop-leader of the Stratford boy scouts' is remarkably apt. If in Shakespearian imagery Spurgeon sees all too readily evidence for Shakespeare the naturalist, the gardener, the swimmer, the carpenter, bowler and angler, it is because she would have her Shakespeare a combination of the Romantic-Victorian ideal of sensitiveness and interest in nature and outdoor life, and public-school spirit and prudence. The likeness between Spurgeon's Shakespeare and Walter Bagehot's 'Shakespeare the Individual' (1853) (reprinted as 'Shakespeare the Man', *Literary Studies* (Everyman edition, 1911), I, 112–53), the 'out-of-door sporting man' with his love of dogs, is very close. (Though there is the difference that according to Spurgeon and to some of her compeers Shakespeare hated dogs![23])

Long after her first book, *Mysticism in English Literature* (1913), and fairly fresh from her edition of five hundred years of Chaucer criticism, Spurgeon started working on imagery in Shakespeare in the mid-nineteen-twenties. About this time also she discovered Keats's Shakespeare – the copies of Shakespeare that Keats apparently read, with certain lines marked and with marginal comments. Keats, with his richly sensuous imagination and the eye of a literary craftsman, preparing himself to write poetic drama, had underlined those images which struck him. Perhaps it was Spurgeon's habit of looking at Shakespeare through the eyes of Keats which led her to bestow on him overdeveloped and hence hypersensitive olfactory and auditory senses. She acknowledged her debt to J. L. Lowes's *The Road to Xanadu*. Lowes-like investigation of the source of Shakespeare's images in books, literature and art was reserved for a later volume in the set of three books she had planned. Even so, the assumption in the book that she did publish is that Shakespeare was an untutored genius who did not need the spectacles of books to look at nature and human life, and took all his images first-hand from nature. Spurgeon wrote, of course, before T. W. Baldwin, Peter Alexander, Sister Miriam Joseph, D. L. Clark, Nelson and Vickers made

---

[23] In his study of Shakespeare's use of the imagery and idiom of outdoor sports, especially blood-sports, T. R. Henn (*The Living Image: Shakespearian Essays*), refines upon William Madden, *The Diary of Master Silence* (London, 1907, 2nd edn) and points out numerous instances of Shakespeare's familiarity with the vocabularies and practices of hawking, hunting, archery and horsemanship, and also his relative lack of first-hand acquaintance with angling.

us understand how much the Elizabethan schoolboy had the opportunity to read at school – how he was only a little short of Macaulay's mythical schoolboy. One may wonder, though, whether Walter Whiter's *Specimen of a Commentary*, judging from the number of quotations from it in the notes to nineteenth-century editions of Shakespeare's plays, could have been a sealed book to her; S. E. Hyman (*The Armed Vision*, p. 214) certainly suspects that she knew it.

Given her predilections in approach and method, it is refreshing that Spurgeon did not resort to the kind of typological schemata of images which H. W. Wells constructed, or the kind of metaphor classification that was made by one of several lecturers[24] at the New Shakespeare Society in the late nineteenth century. Given too, the methods and conventions of image study which she inherited, Spurgeon cannot be blamed for inaugurating the biographical tradition or speculation about the origins of images; she was only carrying to their logical conclusion tendencies in earlier studies, and following in her footsteps came Gladys Wade, Marion B. Smith, and Theodore H. Banks,[25] who sought to apply her methods to the imagery of other sixteenth- and seventeenth-century writers such as Donne, Traherne, Marlowe and Milton.

Rosemond Tuve (*Elizabethan and Metaphysical Imagery*, pp. 27–49) among others, has shown how, in addition to the historical and aesthetic irrelevance of a preoccupation with the subject-matter of imagery and the personality of the author, Spurgeon's neglect of the interaction or interinanimation of subject-matter and object-matter or the continuum or ground of an image and,

---

[24] H. W. Wells, *Poetic Imagery Illustrated from Elizabethan Literature* (New York, 1924), classified images into seven types – the Decorative, the Sunken, the Violent or the Fustian, the Radical, the Intensive, the Expansive and the Exuberant.

Grace Latham, *Transactions of the New Shakespeare Society* (1887–92), pp. 397–427 and Emma Phipson, 'Shakespeare's References to Natural Phenomena', pp. 351–75 of the same volume, for example, employ mechanical categories in the name of analytical classification.

[25] Marion B. Smith, *Marlowe's Imagery and the Marlowe Canon* (Philadelphia, 1940); Gladys I. Wade, *Thomas Traherne* (Princeton, 1944) and Theodore H. Banks, *Milton's Imagery* (New York, 1950). But M. A. Rugoff, *Donne's Imagery: A Study in Creative Sources* (New York, 1939) is an instance of an early investigation of a writer's imagery which takes account of sources in literature and philosophy.

above all, the interrelation of image and context, is a major defect of approach and method. If, despite these and other serious inadequacies, Spurgeon was able to provide fruitful insights into the plays as poems and drama, it is because she was a critic of rare intuitive power – another example of the truth that astuteness and acuteness of perception in a critic count far more than methodology.

The predominance of birds-in-flight imagery which Spurgeon points to (pp. 48ff), is corroborated by E. A. Armstrong's findings on Shakespeare's use of ornithological images and associations. Spurgeon's emphasis on Shakespeare's fascination with the idea of movement in birds and other forms of life, and on the frequency of verbs of movement in general, is the sort of critical discovery which does illuminate the poetic technique and processes of Shakespeare's mind. It is an insight at least as useful as Fenollosa's finding (cited, for example, by Donald Davie, *Articulate Energy* (1955), p. 49) about the dominance of transitive verbs and the active voice in Shakespeare. Similarly, Shakespeare's frequent colour-changes and contrasts, noted by Spurgeon, help us to grasp the dynamism and dramatic movement in his verse. Spurgeon also draws attention to the frequent close-up of the human face, especially of its changes of colour and expression; though, characteristically, she fails to see the theatrical implications of close-ups for actors. Such close scrutiny suggests that Shakespeare wanted to bring to life on the stage the body thinking and feeling – surpassing Coleridge's idea of 'I thinking' or the Emersonian one of 'man thinking'. (There is no need in this connection to invoke the Lawrentian idea of the body mystical and to yoke it with the actor's art, as Wilson Knight does in *Principles of Shakespearian Production* .) Again, Spurgeon's identification of the instinctive habit in Shakespeare's plays of adverse reaction to noise of any kind and the keen nose for the foul smell of sin, has proved fruitful.[26] In her account of noise aversion, Spurgeon invokes, as she does on few occasions, a historical argument, and devotes an appendix (no. VIII) in her book to a catalogue of the noises of Elizabethan London, especially the

---

[26] See, for example, Richard D. Altick, '*Hamlet* and the Odor of Mortality', *SQ*, 5 (1954).

constant din of ringing bells; pointing out that conditioning by such a high level of noise perhaps bred in Shakespeare a hatred for noise in general. Other examples of Spurgeon's critical insight are how images of dirt and blackness are associated with evil, and how weeds in gardens or decay in vegetation suggest evil in men. Few of her discoveries about image strands were developed: she could only propound insights and leave others to develop and extend them.

In two chapters called 'Evidence in the Images of Shakespeare's Thought' (chapters 8 and 9), Spurgeon changes her manner of procedure, going from themes to images instead of from images to themes. She considers what images are suggested to Shakespeare by recurrent themes such as love, time, and death. This approach yields important results, so far as our response to the dramatic poetry goes. But Spurgeon does not discriminate between a cliché or hackneyed image repeated by Shakespeare and a strikingly individual image, or between the degrees of poetic 'charge' achieved by images of the same kind.

Another area of fruitful speculation opened up and charted by Spurgeon, though first discovered by Walter Whiter (1794) and raided by E. E. Kellett and George Rylands in the twenties, is 'association of ideas' (chapter 10 of her book). In this part of her study, despite the amount of attention she devotes to the practical personality of the poet-dramatist, a good deal of light is shed on his poetic personality. For example, the 'martlet' image in *Macbeth*, and the train of associations carried by it, lead Spurgeon to meditate, in an appendix with the running title 'Shakespeare and Berkeley', on when and where Shakespeare could have watched the ways of the house-martin at close quarters. This turns out to be a biographical red herring; yet Spurgeon says something useful about the way the 'martlet' image expresses the idea of being taken in by appearances, especially in Banquo's 'temple-haunting martlet' (*Macbeth*, I. vi, line 4; p. 188 of Spurgeon's book). She points out that the word 'marten' or 'martlet' was in Elizabethan usage a synonym for 'dupe', so that the introduction of the image would immediately suggest that Duncan is deceived about Macbeth's castle (pp. 188–9). The dramatic force and significance of the speech surrounding this image is well brought out, a significance which does not get proper emphasis in the classic analyses by Leavis, Wilson Knight and L. C. Knights, who may have taken it a little too much for granted.[27]

Spurgeon goes on to discuss two sets of linked ideas recurrent in Shakespeare – eyes, tears and vaults; and dogs, licking and candy – in a way which reminds one of the discussion of these and several other 'image clusters' by Whiter, Kellett, Rylands, E. A. Armstrong, Cleanth Brooks and Kenneth Muir, and the modes and criteria of interpretation they variously bring to bear. All point out that the same chain of association is set up, whichever link in the chain is the starting point; from this clue, we may reconstruct the associational processes of Shakespeare's mind against the background of his experience, life and times. Conjecturally tracing the experiential basis of such linked analogies is a legitimate interpretative activity to be sure, if one is careful to observe the limits of relevance and probability.

To take the commentators' discussion of the famous dogs–sweetmeats–flattery cluster of images as an example, they draw widely-ranging inferences. Walter Whiter discovered this image cluster, and his historical explanation of the origins of these linked ideas affords findings which modern scholars have either reached by other roads or have developed more systematically. Whiter's main interest is in a Lockean examination of the poetic psychology of association; how, in the ardour of the poet's invention, an interlinking of ideas otherwise naturally remote from one another takes place, through wordplay and associations caused by the accidents and circumstances of the theatre or Elizabethan life. Though both Whiter and Armstrong invoke historical consideration of Shakespeare's experiences in the life of his day (a practice rare with Spurgeon), these two critics are primarily concerned with the poetic and imaginative (or fanciful, to use Coleridge's distinction) processes of association in general, rather than with how Shakespeare the individual's mind works – to find out which, is Spurgeon's aim. Kellett notices the chain of associations, but does not seek an explanation for them. Rylands,

---

[27] Leavis, 'How to Teach Reading', *Education and the University*, pp. 122–5 and L. C. Knights, *Explorations*, pp. 35–6.

on the other hand, accounts for the apparently unnatural transitions in the heel – spurring – fawning – licking – flattery – sweetmeats – melting complex of ideas, taking as his point of departure the nuisance caused by licking and fawning dogs at Elizabethan tables, thus giving currency to the notion that Shakespeare disliked dogs – a notion rather wildly developed by some (Middleton Murry), and resented by others (Dover Wilson and F. P. Wilson). Spurgeon, without citing names and references, simply records that the image cluster 'has been noted by others', and offers the same explanation as Rylands (without acknowledgement to him). But her emphasis on the emotional force behind the chain of associations, as showing Shakespeare's instinctive hatred of flattery, cringing and fawning, and her recognition of the iterative image of the dog in *Timon of Athens* (a hint worked out by William Empson) are genuine interpretative contributions.

E. A. Armstrong reviews the suggestions offered by earlier commentators about the image-cluster, and concludes that the emotional link between the images in the chain is the hatred of flattery. Armstrong does not consider Whiter's historical explanation of some of the links. As Armstrong notes, Middleton Murry in his comments imagines, on the basis of the now exploded apocryphal tradition that Shakespeare was caught and punished for poaching deer in Sir Thomas Lucy's park, that Shakespeare repeatedly employs this image cluster because he had had the traumatic experience of being brought before Sir Thomas Lucy and his guests at table, and saw slobbering dogs around it. What at first sight appear to be leaps caused by quirks of association in this chain of images are explained by Armstrong in terms of subconscious, emotional links, and shown to be steps rather than leaps. Later historical scholars, however, working on the same lines as Whiter but not knowing or acknowledging him, have explained some of the transitions as stemming from literary conventions and cultural habits of the Elizabethan era.[28] But not

---

[28] James L. Jackson, 'Shakespeare's Dog-and-Sugar Imagery and the Friendship Tradition', *SQ*, 1 (1950), 260–3, traces the origin of the associations in the image-cluster to the literature of the friendship convention, in which the idea of sweet flattery appeared in the image of the fawning spaniel and the 'candied tongue' and the notion of 'melting' in conjunction with one another. Richard

all the links in the chain are explicable in this way; it may well be that some are quirks of personal association.

The most extensive contribution to cluster criticism is Armstrong's. Besides identifying some seven new recurring image clusters (that phrase, now in common currency, is his) and commenting on two or three originally discovered by Whiter, he underlines their subliminal emotional organisation, and unfolds the processes of emotional transition behind them. Using Shakespeare's associations as a test case of the ways of memory and emotion, intellect and imagination in a creative writer, Armstrong is able to show that images occur to Shakespeare in terms of the great dualisms or antinomies – life and death, love and hate, light and darkness, good and evil – a finding in line with the tendency of the now-old new critics, as well as their successors, to chart Shakespearian themes in terms of paired opposites. With wider reference to psychological and psychoanalytical theories and principles than Spurgeon (though he has been accused of psychoanalytic amateurism by thoroughgoing psychological sophisticates like Norman Holland), Armstrong has shown, using the Freudian concept of negative displacement, how a particular image may suggest an emotion which is the opposite of the one commonly associated with it. His psychological study of the processes of Shakespeare's memory and association leads Armstrong to contradict as much as to concur with Spurgeon's idea of Shakespeare the man. He shows how the psychoanalytical implications of Shakespeare's imagistic associations suggest him to be no Sir Galahad, not the exalted character Spurgeon thought him, but a man with normal abnormalities (that is, the

Harrier, 'Another Note on "Why the Sweets Melted"', *SQ*, 18 (1967), p. 67, rediscovers Walter Whiter's finding about the background to the cluster, and instances how in certain York pageants hailstones made of sweets showered on the lords and the visitors. Whiter cited Steevens and pointed out the device employed at certain royal entertainments of a rain of confects and rose-water, *Specimen of a Commentary* (1794), edited by Alan Over and Mary Bell (London, 1967), p. 159. C. H. Hobday, 'Why the Sweets Melted: A Study in Shakespeare's Imagery', *SQ*, 16 (1965), 3–17, shows that only in three of the six occurrences of this image cluster in Shakespeare does the idea of melting appear and only in one passage is there a reference to melting sweets, 'which finally disposes of Dr. Spurgeon's theory on the association of the ideas originated' (p. 14). Perhaps the common phenomenon that the dog sticks to the man who once feeds it with sweets is behind the associations.

weaknesses of the libido and ego common to most). However, the received idea of Shakespeare's mythical sorrows and his dark or tragic period died hard: Armstrong, like Spurgeon, finds in the imagery of the late middle plays and the tragedies evidence that Shakespeare experienced the horrors of the plague, venereal disease, gastric trouble, and sex-nausea.

Armstrong's application of historical information and psychological concepts to unravel the tangled skein of Shakespearian association, was an interpretative approach which suggested a number of possibilities more fully explored by later commentators. His analysis helps to show how 'material organised under a variety of different interests is brought together in a process of cross-fertilisation, for themes and images are not merely juxtaposed but interpenetrate and influence each other in a strongly fluent way so that a few contiguous words become, 'not a phrase, but a spell'. All this illuminates the process by which fancy is elevated to the level of imagination in Shakespeare, and also a great writer's exploratory-creative exploitation of the linguistic medium. Armstrong demonstrates through the religious references in *As You Like It* how verbal associations at the beginning of a play lead Shakespeare to use, in its course, ideas and images conjured up by those associations (which he describes as 'thematic' imagery).

Standard criticisms of Spurgeon are that, with her image counts, charts and graphs, she is a victim of a nineteenth-century scientific positivism, and that her conviction of the quality of what she takes to be her inductive method leads her to quantify too much. Neither the enthusiastic praise of her statistical methods by a sympathetic admirer and fellow investigator, Una Ellis-Fermor, nor the instinctive revulsion felt by most literary scholars seems to be the right attitude to statistical computations in image study. Image counts are inevitable; if, instead of tolerating them as a necessary evil, such computations were made with an eye for quality, for the relative literary-dramatic function and the weight of the images, there is an opportunity for rewarding insights. Spurgeon forgets that the impact of the dramatic positioning of an image is more important than the number of times it occurs in the course of a play. Furthermore, her habit of docketing images lends a spurious impression of unassailable accuracy, and of finality. The truth is that Spurgeon's enterprise is only a beginning, not an end; newer and newer strains of imagery are being discovered in the plays all the time.

The gravamen of the charges brought against Spurgeon's work is that she does not consider the dramatic contexts and functions of images. The criticism is valid; but a pioneer treatment of a vast theme cannot but, consciously or unconsciously, delimit itself, and sufficient allowance is not generally made for this. How imagery aids and carries forward the movement of plot and action, how the structure of a play could have an imagistic sub- or super-stratum – these are subtleties of the dramatic process beyond Spurgeon. Not that she has no sense of the function of imagery in characterisation, or of interlinking of themes and images, though her sense of the relationship between imagery and character is only fitful and her study of the articulation of themes through images does not go far enough. Of the manifold functions of imagery in characterisation, Spurgeon recognises only Shakespeare's technique of making a character employ imagery in character in his utterances. But, as Wolfgang Clemen, S. L. Bethell, and Brian Vickers (if not M. M. Morozov) have shown, Shakespeare also employs images in relation to characters as implicit value-judgements, as indications of shifts and reversals in characters, as clues to changing relationships among characters, to the forensic or manipulative intentions of one character towards another, and so on. After all, the dramatic reality that *is* a character, is conveyed to us mainly through his or her speech, imagery and diction. However, Spurgeon's demonstration that Falstaff reveals himself through characteristic images which the dramatist associates with him and, above all, that the change in the imagery associated with Falstaff between Part one and Part two of *Henry IV* reflects the change in his fortunes, is an astute reading of character through imagery and vice versa. As for the exposition of theme through imagery, this tradition was established by Spurgeon, and all later studies follow her lead.

In the second part of her book, in her analysis of the dominant strains of imagery in the plays, Spurgeon offers brilliant insights of fundamental importance in determining their motifs. The imagery of growth in vegetation or, in particular, of the tree in the history plays; the disease imagery in *Hamlet*; the clothes imagery in *Macbeth*; the imagery relating to the body in *King Lear*; the animal imagery in *Coriolanus* – she identified them all and interpreted them thematically. If Clemen in this, as in other respects, has improved upon her approach and findings, it is by exploring *new* interconnected strains of imagery, and by doing this with an awareness of Shakespeare's evolution from dramatic poet responding to poetic conventions to masterful poet-dramatist whose imagery, in his mature plays, is increasingly organic and thematically relevant. Clemen thus explores a number of aspects which Spurgeon left untouched.

The theatrical context of imagery, which she ignored, has been brought out well by others; one might almost describe the evolution of image criticism as moving from a study-oriented to a theatre-oriented analysis. If the need to correlate image study with our knowledge of Elizabethan rhetorical traditions has been emphasised as a corrective to Spurgeon's methodological inadequacies, even more emphasis has been put on the need to relate imagery to its dramatic context and to the probable intentions of stage embodiment. Even Clemen, for all the comprehensiveness with which he considers aspects of imagery, considers only the dramatic, and not the actual *stage*-implications of imagery. It is only in his later studies that he displays a constant awareness of the theatrical as well as the rhetorical implications of image and style (*English Tragedy before Shakespeare, Shakespeare's Dramatic Art,* and *A Commentary on 'Richard III'*). The fundamental differences between imagery in drama and imagery in lyric or nondramatic poetry in general have been pointed out by R. A. Foakes, Ronald Peacock, Edward Partridge and Maurice Charney, among others. It is only by doing full justice to the theatrical dimension of imagery that a greater appreciation of Shakespeare's art can be achieved. Imagery may be a convenient way of entering into the mind and art of Shakespeare; but only in relation to its stage context, as John Lawlor has shown in a paper in *Shakespeare Quarterly*, can we see how Shakespeare's mind and art went together ('Mind and Hand: Some Reflections on the Study of Shakespeare's Imagery', *SQ*, 8 (1957), 179–93). It is through visualising imagery in its stage context that Maurice Charney, Kenneth Muir and Nigel Alexander provide a fuller account of imagery in plays, Charney on images in the Roman plays and *Hamlet*, and all three on the imagery of weapons and arms in *Hamlet*. Three further studies have stressed the non-verbal, presentational characteristics of Shakespeare's imagery – those of Clifford P. Lyons, Alan S. Downer and Rudolf Stamm.[29] It is not surprising, given Spurgeon's entirely literary orientation, that she fails to note the theatrical dimensions of images – the inspiration for imagery which might have come to Shakespeare from the physical features and circumstances of the stage and the theatre. The image of the play, or the player acting on the stage of the world, is so well exploited by Elizabethan dramatists, by Shakespeare above all, that it is not surprising that Spurgeon's omission has been made good in a number of studies. Shakespeare may have been aware of the neoplatonic significance and implications of the trope on 'all the world's a stage'; but one wonders whether he was actively conscious of, and meant to convey, this significance. He might have used this strand of imagery to suggest the nature of illusion, how 'real' an illusion could appear, so introducing the Platonic theme of a contrast between illusion and reality, a difference so difficult to grasp and experience existentially.[30]

[29] Clifford P. Lyons, 'Stage Imagery in Shakespeare's Plays', *Essays on Shakespeare and Elizabethan Drama*, edited by Richard Hosley (London, 1963), pp. 261–74; Alan S. Downer, 'The Life of Our Design: The Function of Imagery in the Poetic Drama', *The Hudson Review*, 1949, pp. 242–60, rpt. in L. F. Dean, ed. *Shakespeare: Modern Essays in Criticism*; and Rudolf Stamm, *The Shaping Powers at Work* (Heidelberg, 1967), Part 1, 'The Theatrical Physiognomy of Shakespeare's Plays', pp. 9–84. Also, Alan C. Dessen, 'Hamlet's Poisoned Sword: A Study in Dramatic Imagery', *Shakespeare Studies* 5 (1969), 53–69; David J. Houser, 'Armor and Motive in *Troilus and Cressida*', *Renaissance Drama*, n.s. 4 (1971), 121–34; Dieter Mehl, 'Visual and Rhetorical Imagery in Shakespeare's Plays', *Essays and Studies* (1972), 83–100, and Inga Stina-Ewbank, ' "More Pregnantly than Words": Some Uses and Limitations of Visual Symbolism', *SS*, 24 (1971), 13–18.
[30] Anne Righter comments on this sense of an interplay between illusion and reality created through the use of the play image in Elizabethan plays like *The Spanish Tragedy* (*Shakespeare and the Idea of the Play* (1967 edn.), pp. 71–8). So do Philip Edwards (*Thomas Kyd and Early Elizabethan Tragedy* (London, 1966), pp. 31–3) and E. W. Talbert (*Elizabethan Drama and Shakespeare's Early Plays* (1963), p. 73). E. K. Chambers, 'William Shakespeare: An Epilogue', *Shake-*

Thanks to the recent closer relationship of theatre perform-
ances, theatrical studies and imagistic criticism of Shakespeare,
most critics would now consider that figurative senses were
grasped immediately by Elizabethan audiences. The audiences
would not work out meanings as a modern critic does. The point
of modern criticism is that through the images a subliminal
communication is established between the stage and the text,
the spectator and the reader, and complex impressions are conveyed to the reader, who receives them as Shakespeare's intention.

The full subtleties and complexities of this dramatic–poetic
communication were bound to be missed by a first explorer of the
territory. Spurgeon ignores connections between one strand of
imagery and another, or between clusters of images, and fails to
note the moral and artistic effects brought about by the contradic-
tion between the covert suggestion of the imagery in a passage
and the character's overt statement of ideas and feelings. It is
delicate areas such as these that are explored by Leavis and L. C.
Knights.

---

spearean Gleanings, pp. 43–50, notices Spurgeon's omission and makes a list of
passages in which Shakespeare uses the play image. The occurrences of the
theatrum mundi metaphor in Shakespearian and other Elizabethan plays are
traced by T. B. Stroup, *Microcosmos: The Structure of an Elizabethan Play* (Lexington, Ky, 1965). Shakespeare's self-consciousness about his art of poetry and
drama, and his artistic exploitation of that self-consciousness, have been
studied by J. L. Calderwood, *Shakespearean Metadrama* (Minneapolis, 1971).
Among studies of Shakespeare's use of the play metaphor the most speculative
and the most comprehensive is Jackson I. Cope, *The Theater and the Dream: From
Metaphor to Form in Renaissance Drama* (Baltimore, 1973). Other significant
studies of Shakespeare's use of the image of the world as theatre are V. Y.
Kantak, 'An Approach to Shakespearian Tragedy: The Actor Image in *Macbeth*',
SS, 16 (1963), 42–52; Harold Fisch, 'Shakespeare and "The Theatre of the
World"', *The Morality of Art*, edited by D. W. Jefferson (London, 1969),
pp. 76–86; James Winny, *The Player King* (London, 1968); L. F. Dean, '*Richard II*:
The State and the Image of the Theatre', *PMLA*, 67 (1952), 211–18; Maynard Mack,
'Engagement and Detachment in Shakespeare's Plays', *Essays on Shakespeare
and Elizabethan Drama in Honor of Hardin Craig*, edited by Richard Hosley (London, 1963); and Charles R. Forker, 'Theatrical Symbolism and Its Function in
Hamlet', *SQ*, 14 (1963). Richard Bernheimer, 'Theatrum Mundi', *The Art Bulle-
tin*, 38 (1956), 225–47; E. R. Curtius, translated by W. R. Trask, 'Theatrical
Metaphors', *European Literature and the Latin Middle Ages* (New York, 1953),
138–44, and Frances A. Yates, *The Theatre of the World* (London, 1969), between
them, provide a full account of the history and background of the *theatrum
mundi* idea.

It seems unjust to blame Spurgeon for her disinclination to raise the question of the sources, background, context, and inspiration of images, or her failure to consider whether an image is derivative or original, when she deliberately reserved these aspects for a later volume which was never written. But her failure to recognise the sources of certain images does prevent her fully grasping their function and quality. This shows that 'source-hunting', carried out with a strict sense of relevance is a necessary aid to criticism and interpretation. Shakespeare's use and manipulation of the sources of his imagery reveal major aspects of his dramatic art.

It is possible that a Shakespearian image or strand of imagery has reference to these background sources; literature; rhetorical conventions, *topoi*, iconology or iconography, the emblem convention, traditions of pageantry, the art of mnemonics, arithmetical, astronomical, or astrological notions, heraldry, proverb-lore, Renaissance colour-and-flower-symbolism and, above all, the physical circumstances of the Elizabethan stage, or those of the Morality tradition.

These traditions and backgrounds and their relationships to specific Shakespearian images have by now been thoroughly explored by scholars. Hornstein, in her penetrating article on Spurgeon's fallacies and omissions, 'Analysis of Imagery: A Critique of Method', and J. E. Hankins, *Shakespeare's Derived Imagery* (Lawrence, Kansas, 1953), provide two examples of investigation into the sources of Shakespeare's imagery in literature, including popular and ephemeral literature. Sister Miriam Joseph, *Shakespeare's Use of the Arts of Language*, Brian Vickers, *The Artistry of Shakespeare's Prose*, and Nicholas Brooke, *Shakespeare's Early Tragedies* (London, 1968), and Maurice Charney in his *Style in 'Hamlet'* (1969), take account of the rhetorical basis of imagery in Shakespeare. The work of E. R. Curtius on the *topoi* of late medieval and Renaissance literature (*European Literature and the Latin Middle Ages*, New York, 1953) has facilitated understanding of the topological basis of some strands of imagery (see 'The Book as Symbol in Shakespeare', pp. 332–40). Though a few studies of Shakespeare's use of commonplaces have been made (e.g. John L. Harrison, *'Measure for Measure* and the Convention of Tongue and Heart', *SQ*, 5 (1954)), there is room for many more. J. W. Lever and J. B. Leishman have pointed out the origins in classical literature, and analogues in Renaissance literature, of themes and images in the sonnets.

The iconographic background of Shakespearian imagery, an important aspect, is ripe for investigation, thanks to the work of Erwin Panofsky, Edgar Wind, Samuel C. Chew, Howard R. Patch, and other studies emerging from the Warburg and Courtauld Institute of London. In *English Dramatic Form* and *Shakespeare the Craftsman*, M. C. Bradbrook has drawn attention to stage icons such as the severed head which are repeatedly used in the plays; imagery has a close reference to such stage presences. Visual conventions of the popular and the learned cultural traditions have close bearing on Shakespeare's imagery. Among these are the popular shows and civic pageants and processions of his day, the convention of the emblem books, and the pictorial convention of arras and tapestry paintings. Alice Venezky, *Pageantry on the Shakespearian Stage* (New York, 1951) shows the relationship of a number of scenes and images in Shakespeare to the Elizabethan pageants. Thanks to the monumental accounts compiled by J. G. Nichols of the progresses of Queen Elizabeth and King James I, and to the relationships seen by Janet Spens and C. L. Barber, for example, between the plays and popular traditions of ritual pageant and festivity, we may suppose that inspiration for a number of the images in the plays came from these traditions of pageantry and 'game', including the Lord Mayors' shows, and the aristocratic masques and *impresas*. (A comprehensive account of the municipal pageants of those times is now available in David Bergeron, *English Civic Pageantry 1558–1642*, London, 1971.)

The relationship of Shakespeare to the emblem convention was crudely exaggerated by Henry Green.[31] But it has since been examined with varying degrees of caution by Rosemond Tuve, Russell A. Fraser, Rosemary Freeman,[32] and, particularly with

---

[31] *Shakespeare and the Emblem Books*.

[32] Rosemond Tuve, *Allegorical Imagery* (Princeton, 1966); Russell A. Fraser, *Shakespeare's Poetics in Relation to 'King Lear'*; Rosemary Freeman, *English Emblem Books* (London, 1948).

reference to the stage, by Martha Hester Golden, Dieter Mehl and Glynne Wickham.[33]

The medieval and Renaissance reinterpretation in allegorical form of the classical myths surrounding Orpheus, Hercules, Diana, Venus, and also Isis, for instance, may not have influenced Shakespearian drama and its imagery as much as it did Spenser's or Milton's poetry and Chapman's drama. But that some of these syncretist allegorical interpretations of mythology could have had some influence on Shakespeare, is shown by Richard P. Cody, *The Landscape of the Mind* (Oxford , 1969), D. C. Allen in his interpretation of *The Tempest*, *Image and Meaning in Five Poems of the Renaissance* (Baltimore, 1960), J. M. Steadman 'Falstaff as Actaeon: A Dramatic Emblem', *SQ*, 14 (1963), 231–44, and Richard Knowles, 'Myth and Type in *As You Like It*', *ELH*, 33 (1966), 1–22.

It is possible that some images have a heraldic significance (see W. W. Scott-Giles, *Shakespeare's Heraldry* (London, 1950)) or an astronomical or astrological one (F. R. Johnson and S. K. Heninger, Jr have sketched the background). Some images may have something to do with colour symbolism or with symbolic or theoretical music (see L. J. Ross, 'Shakespeare's "Dull Clown" and Symbolic Music', *SQ*, 17 (1966)). These give the background to a restricted number of images. The same holds true for the memory systems, the meditative paradigms and the arithmetical or numerological conventions which seem to have affected certain writers of the sixteenth and seventeenth centuries. (Memory systems, of which there is an account in Frances A. Yates, *The Art of Memory* (London, 1966), may have bearing on the choice of imagery to accord with rhetorical practice, in non-dramatic rather than dramatic literature. Much the same is the case with the meditative paradigms outlined by Louis Martz, *The Poetry of Meditation* (New Haven, 1954), and Harold Fisch (*RES*, 1949), and

---

[33] Martha Hester Golden (Fleischer), 'Stage Imagery in Shakespearean Studies', *Shakespeare Research Opportunities*, 1 (1965), 10–20 (also in O. J. Campbell and E. G. Quinn, eds, *A Shakespeare Encyclopaedia* (London, 1966)) and her *The Iconography of the English History Play* (Salzburg, 1974); Dieter Mehl, 'Emblems in English Renaissance Drama', *Renaissance Drama*, n.s. 2 (1969), 39–57, and Glynne Wickham, *Early English Stages 1300–1600* (London, 1963), vol. II, part I, pp. 206–44.

the arithmetical systems of literary structure and composition discovered by Alastair Fowler, Kent Hieatt, and Marie Sofen-Rostvig.)

But two sources which richly contributed to Shakespeare's imagery are the tradition of the theatre, acting, actors and the drama, already touched on, and the tradition of popular speech and proverbs. It is striking that in Tilley's dictionary many of the examples of proverbs current in Elizabethan times come from Shakespeare. Shakespeare's use of proverbial utterance is well illustrated by F. P. Wilson ('The Proverbial Wisdom of Shakespeare' and 'Shakespeare and the Diction of Common Life', *Shakespearian and Other Studies* (London, 1969), edited by Helen Gardner), and also by Charles G. Smith, *Shakespeare's Proverb Lore* (Cambridge, Mass., 1963), and Robert Weimann, *Shakespeare and the Popular Tradition in the Theater*, editor Robert Schwartz (Baltimore, 1978, revised English edition of the original German work of 1967). Hilda M. Hulme has proved in her annotations of a number of expressions in Shakespeare, *Explorations in Shakespeare's Language* (London, 1962), that dialectal uses and idioms may be behind certain images in the plays.

One of Spurgeon's major expectations about the possibilities of image study was that it could be used as an all-but-infallible test of authorship. The belief follows as a corollary from her assumption that imagery is a personal signature of the writer; as it does also from the allied notion of E. A. Armstrong that a particular collocation of image themes into clusters is a telling personal characteristic of a writer's memory, see the appendix in Armstrong, *Shakespeare's Imagination* (London, 1946). Spurgeon thought that with the master-key of image study, the mysteries of authenticity and attribution surrounding the plays of doubtful or disputed authorship, as well as of personal identity, could be unlocked, and doubts about the canon and the apocrypha resolved once and for all. Spurgeon was fighting an indirect, but running battle against the disintegrators on the one hand and the Baconians and the Anti-Stratfordians on the other. It was only natural that she planned to devote a whole volume to this question.

Sanguine hopes for imagery as a test of authorship were entertained by her fellow-investigators, such as Una Ellis-Fermor, who tried to establish Tourneur's authorship of *The Revenger's Tragedy* on the basis of its imagery. Kenneth Muir has attempted to determine the Shakespearian elements in plays in which he is suspected to have had a chief hand, such as *Sir Thomas More, Edward III, The Two Noble Kinsmen*, and also *Henry VIII*, through the detection of characteristic image clusters. Karl Wentersdorf tries to authenticate *The Taming of the Shrew* by identifying a number of typically Shakespearian image sequences in the play. As Moody E. Prior points out in his rejoinder dramatic imagery is partly governed by the themes and conventions of Elizabethan drama, and hence cannot be considered as a personal signature. He instances the likeness between the night–darkness imagery of the original version of Kyd's *The Spanish Tragedy* and the same imagery in the additions to the play, which are known to have been made by a later hand. While we grant that imagery can be derivative and can come from any of the sources already mentioned, it remains true that individuality can be detected in the nuances of imagery manipulation or combination.[34] For instance, as Walter Whiter showed in most Elizabethan tragedies imagery of night, darkness and hell (a dark place of privation) is conventional – perhaps a stage convention to call up the atmosphere of night in night-scenes played in the afternoon. But an original and paradoxical use of the imagery of light and darkness, with subtle interchanges between the two elements as in *Romeo and Juliet*, is Shakespearian, whereas Chapman, with his interest in occult-

---

[34] Una Ellis-Fermor, 'The Imagery of *The Revenger's Tragedy*, and *The Atheist's Tragedy*', *MLR*, 30 (1935), 281–301. Inga-Stina Ekeblad (Ewbank), 'An Approach to Tourneur's Imagery', *MLR*, 54 (1959), 489–98. R. W. Chambers, 'The Expression of Ideas – Particularly Political Ideas – in the Three Pages', *Shakespeare's Hand in the Play of 'Sir Thomas More'*, edited by A. W. Pollard (Cambridge, 1923); Kenneth Muir, *Shakespeare as Collaborator* (London, 1960); Kenneth Muir, 'Image and Symbol in Shakespeare's Histories', *BJRL*, 50 (1967), 103–23 tries to show that the test of imagery excludes the dual authorship of *Henry VIII*. Karl Wentersdorf, 'The Authenticity of *The Taming of the Shrew*', *SQ*, 5 (1954); M. E. Prior, 'Imagery as a Test of Authorship', *SQ*, 6 (1955). Also Karl Wentersdorf, 'Imagery as a Criterion of Authenticity: A Reconsideration of the Problem', *SQ*, 23 (1972), 231–59. MacD. P. Jackson, 'Shakespeare and *Edmund Ironside*', *N&Q*, n.s. 10 (1963), 331–2, detects the presence in Shelley's poem 'The Boat on the Serchio' of the beetle–crow–mouse cluster regarded by Armstrong as uniquely Shakespearian.

ism, uses the light–darkness contrast with an underlying esoteric neo-platonist symbolism.

Clemen's study, *The Development of Shakespeare's Imagery* (London, 1951) (the German version was published as early as 1936), is generally, and justly, regarded as exemplary, for he emphasises the influence that imagery in Shakespearian drama has on the other aspects of the play and brings to bear, in his analysis of imagery, a wide variety of the speculative instruments of scholarship. Though Clemen does not aim at exhaustiveness, he provides, in his comprehensive terms of reference, an outline of the manifold uses of image study in the illumination of the plays. Moreover, he examines imagery from a single consistent point of view – that of Shakespeare's development – and charts an evolution from a conventional, decorative or 'amplificatory' use of imagery to a concentrated, dramatic, and thematic use of it; in short, the increasing correlation between imagery, character, plot and situation. Whereas in the earlier plays it is the 'aggregative and associative' power of fancy that is behind imagery, in the middle and late plays images exhibit the 'moving and shaping' power of the creative imagination.[35] The function of dramatic presaging performed by imagery, the emotional unity into which images, through their interconnections, can knit a play, and 'subliminal' communication through imagery, are among the points Clemen makes. But he does not entertain the notion that the imagery of a play is autonomous. If images deepen and reinforce significances, or at times act as the main conveyors of dramatic meaning and effect, they do so not in isolation from, but in close cooperation with, the traditionally recognised major components of drama, such as plot and character. This is clear when Clemen's analysis of *King Lear* is compared with Robert Heilman's,[36] who considers that images and image clusters communicate independently of the other elements in the play and interweave only their own patterns of meaning and significance. If one feels that most of the time Clemen succeeds in relating an image to its immediate dramatic context of plot-

---

[35] An early illustration of this was provided by Madeleine Doran, 'Imagery in *Richard II* and *Henry IV*', *MLR*, 37 (1942), 113–22.
[36] *This Great Stage: Image and Structure in 'King Lear'*, (Baton Rouge, La., 1948).

situation or character, but fails to relate it to the impression made by the play as a whole, it is largely because he has naturalistic conceptions of character or considers imagery as only mediatorial in function on behalf of plot, character and central ideas. Clemen would not (as Heilman does) regard the play as a reification of images, but as a whole, with imagery as only one of its several constituent elements.

Heilman assumes that *King Lear* is a hypostasis of images, and not a dramatic reality with action and character made manifest. Understandably, this brought a caustic comment from the Chicago critic, W. R. Keast, in his lengthy review (*MP*, 47 (1949)). Heilman's concentration on the recently discovered, but not deeply-enough realised truth of the subliminal communication established by the dramatist in and through imagery, was bound to give the impression of an imagistic autonomy. The weight he places on images as theme-carriers, not mere theme-supporters, in *King Lear*, is meant to be no more than an emphasis on the organic integration of imagery with the themes and other elements of the play. In other words, it is only a way of saying that vital significances of the play could be communicated only through the impact of the imagery. If Heilman had gone further into the relationship of the imagery to the other major components of drama such as action and plot development, as Keast urged, his book would have become unmanageably big. Heilman's concern is with the importance and interrelationship of the functions of imagery in *King Lear*; his fixed attention to this concern, illuminating as it is, gives a sense that images exist independently of plot and action, ironically creating a curious literalness of interpretation – which Keast exposes – for all the subtlety of the commentary. Little purpose is served by invoking the analogy of a lyric, and calling the whole play an image, as C. Day Lewis called a poem as a whole an image, except perhaps by way of suggesting that the play is something which we *see* on the stage or at least in the theatre of the mind (see also appendix, p. 197).

This outline of approaches to Shakespeare's imagery will have given readers an idea of the size and complexity of the subject. As Armstrong remarked, the study of Shakespeare's imagery is nothing less than the study of humanity. While no single mind can ever hope to offer a completely integrated study covering all its aspects the need for critical and scholarly alertness and for eclecticism is plain enough; it is in that direction that most recent studies of imagery tend. The more conscious the interpreter is that imagery is a way of evoking a total response to drama, the greater the integration of his imagistic criticism to a full apprehension of the play. This is the first of the two general lessons one draws from the study. The second is that the more actively the critic brings historical conceptions to bear on his analysis of imagery, the sounder and the more illuminating his interpretation. In no other field of Shakespearian investigation is it more forcefully borne in upon us that soundness of response and of judgement are secured by remaining at once true to the total impression of elements in a play and applying, in an informed and sensitive way, the tools of historical knowledge.

It is customary in studies of Shakespeare's imagery to regard G. Wilson Knight as one of the pioneer interpreters. But as he pointed out in his preface to the 1953 edition of *The Shakespearian Tempest*, his intentions and ways of proceeding are totally different from those investigators like Spurgeon; and if he talks of a play as an autonomous pattern of images, or of the whole canon as a pattern of music–storm oppositions, conveying an order–disorder antithesis, this is an incidental consequence of his spatialised apprehension of a play or the whole canon.

7

Conclusion

If my appraisal of the commentaries of the leading critics of the school of poetic interpretation has brought out some of the theoretical and methodological implications of their approaches, their basic attitudes, assumptions and practices, it will have served its purpose. Seen in their context the commentaries of Wilson Knight, L. C. Knights and Caroline Spurgeon find their place in the developing twentieth-century tradition in Shakespeare studies, and reveal their own innovative character. The ambivalent relationship between Shakespeare criticism and scholarship is also a theme of this study. There have been so many indirect and direct channels of communication between criticism and scholarship that there is no need to postulate a dichotomy. A critic may have a preference in theory for the 'liberty of interpreting', or a belief in the principle of the 'now-meaning' of Shakespeare; but in practice, consciously or unconsciously, he often uses historical findings to interpretative effect or intuitively arrives at interpretative findings which confirm those of historical scholarship. Of course, one sometimes wishes the dialogue had been closer, but there has been considerable interplay, and almost, in recent years, an unconscious collaboration between the two apparently opposed camps. In a sense the criticism can be called the harvest of the scholarship.

The history of the Shakespearian criticism of any age may not inappropriately be called an epitome of the cultural and literary history of that age. New approaches to Shakespeare replace or modify the old, as 'shifts of sensibility' occur from generation to generation and as new modes of literature are created as a result.

The truth of this, that Shakespeare criticism is a sensitive area in which shifts of taste are reflected, so that it serves as a true barometer of taste, is amply illustrated by the predominance of the poetic approach to Shakespeare between the twenties and, say, the sixties of this century. The great Shakespeare critics of the past, such as Johnson and Coleridge, were themselves masters of creative literature, whereas the important Shakespearian commentators since Bradley have been critics, pure and simple, and academic critics at that. Nonetheless, they have been in touch with the main current of literature, perhaps without being conscious of it.

In conclusion, I comment on two general questions: the controversy between those critics who favour a 'literalist' interpretation of Shakespeare and those who prefer to unfold 'allegorical' or moral significances in the plays; and the alleged insubstantiality of the theoretical framework beneath the different approaches to Shakespeare.

A convenient way of distinguishing between the approach of poetic interpreters such as Wilson Knight and commentators of the neo-Aristotelian school, such as Elder Olson, or an independent critic such as John Holloway, would be to invoke the distinction between the 'literalist' and 'allegorical' interpretations. The difference is, at times, expressed in an extreme form, as though the two were poles apart:

So far as this [the conflict between literalists and allegorists] is merely party politics it need not interest us; but at bottom it is something more. It is an eternal see-saw between two basic and apparently permanent attitudes of the human mind. Literal and allegorical interpretations spring from two radically different ways of looking at the world, themselves probably based on an irreducible psychological difference (Jung would call it the difference between extroverts and introverts). In extreme cases it is therefore fundamentally irreconcilable . . . And nothing very sensible can be said about this, except that the best interpretative critics have managed to avoid both positivism and obscurantism.

      Graham Hough, *An Essay on Criticism* (London, 1966), pp. 73–4

There is an important qualifier, however:

But there are not too many extreme cases, it is frequently possible and always desirable that the two types of criticism should complement each other.   (p. 74)

The problem of literalists versus allegorists in modern literary interpretation is seen not only in the study of Renaissance literature and Shakespearian drama, but in classics like *Beowulf*, in Chaucer and Langland and in some of the Middle English romances and religious poems. The controversy bears a number of resemblances to the medieval and Renaissance disputes about the allegorical or typological interpretation of the Bible, especially the question of the relative importance of the literal and spiritual senses. It may be relevant to remind ourselves that St Augustine and the early Christian fathers such as Origen thought it necessary to lay stress on the spiritual or anagogical levels of meaning in the Scriptures, that Aquinas insisted on the equal importance of the spiritual and the literal sense, and that Luther and the Protestant theologians emphasised the literal sense of the Bible, if only because the challenges of their respective religious and cultural situations demanded it. In a similar way, the poetic interpreters of Shakespeare in our century – Wilson Knight, L. C. Knights and R. B. Heilman – accent the non-literal elements of Shakespearian drama so heavily, at least in their theoretical statements, that one is left wondering whether *Macbeth* can be read exactly as we read *The Waste Land*, or whether *King Lear* can be understood as a hypostatisation of images and image patterns. Fortunately, in practice, Wilson Knight and L. C. Knights do not generally lose touch with the human realities embodied in dramatic form in the plays. If R. B. Heilman seems to be not mindful enough of the primary facts and plot progression of *King Lear* it is not out of ignorance. In his concern with the metaphorical structure of the play, he could take these more obvious elements for granted and assume that the metaphors and images could communicate on their own not merely as analogies or figures of speech, but as embodiments of experience in their own right. However, his study produces an undesirable dichotomy between image and metaphor on the one hand and plot and character-in-action on the other. Images *do* lend significance to each other, but they must be seen in the total context of the play, which includes character, action and plot.

If the imagistic or poetic structure of a Shakespearian play is repeatedly demonstrated to be a unity in modern criticism, that

structure, we have to remember, entails, and is sustained by, the
unity of action. John Holloway's strictures on the failure of our
leading Shakespearian critics to accord due attention to the 'literal' elements in the play, and their tendency to treat plays as
though they were primarily remarkable for the knowledge they
afford about problems of value include a complaint about the
critics' frequent resort to the language of metaphors (a complaint
echoed by Barbara Everett, P. R. Grover and William Righter[1]).
While this may be a sign that the critic has locally lost his grip on
the essential, literal happenings in the play, one is not justified in
supposing that the use of metaphor or, for that matter, the use of
the 'allegorist' made of interpretation results in total loss of contact with what happens; nor should the critic be forbidden to use
metaphorical expressions (as Elder Olson wished, *'Hamlet* and
the Hermeneutics of Drama', *MP*, 61 (1963–4), 232).

There is a safeguard against any 'pan-allegorical school' of
criticism. The basic truth and interest of the plays, and our resulting imaginative involvement with them are so potent that the
impact of the plays is bound to act as the solid centre of our
interpretation. Perhaps the balance of emphasis between the
literal and the allegorical, which Aquinas advocated, is not so
very difficult to achieve. In typological, as distinct from allegorical exegesis, as Charles Donahue points out,[2] the original, literal
meaning is not overwhelmed by the divine or spiritual meaning:
the two coexist and communicate with equal force. For instance,
in the episode of Noah in the Bible, or in the medieval mystery
plays, the literal comic reality of Noah's drunkenness or his
hen-pecked state is no less true, and brought home with no less
vividness, than the significance of the figure and his building the
ark as a typological anticipation of Christ, the true servant of
God and the embodiment of patience. Whatever the excesses of
Robertsonianism in expounding late medieval literary texts with
its assumption that all that is written is doctrine in 'dark conceits',
in Elizabethan drama, thanks to the force of the flesh and blood

[1] Everett, 'The Figure in Professor Knights' Carpet', 171–2; Grover, 'The Ghost of
Dr. Johnson: L. C. Knights and D. A. Traversi on *Hamlet'*, 143–57; and Righter,
Logic and Criticism (London, 1963), p. 38.
[2] 'Patristic Exegesis: Summation', *Critical Approaches to Medieval Literature: English
Institute Papers*, ed. Dorothy Bethurum, New York, 1960, p. 71.

realities, the living, suffering human beings represented by the actors, the critic is called back from his allegorist flights by what may be called the reality principle.

This need for a proper balance of emphasis between the literalist and allegorist interpretations has been expounded with clarity by Helen Gardner, with special reference to the poems of Donne.[3] In the same context, she reverses a warning by Janet Spens about Spenser, and exhorts us not to read Shakespeare as though he were a Spenserian allegorist (p. 134). She also finds fault with Cleanth Brooks for missing, in his preoccupation with the babe image in the 'Pity like a naked new born babe' speech in *Macbeth*, the fact that Macbeth is feeling conscience-stricken and horrified at the prospect of the whole world spontaneously revolting against him and his crime. Here, again, it is not so much a question of literal versus allegorical, as a matter of formulation by the critic. One supposes that Brooks took the obvious meaning of the speech for granted.[4] But his failure to give sufficient weight to the primary import of the passage detracts from the value of his interpretation. On the other hand, evidence about the continuity of the late medieval dramatic traditions into the Elizabethan age (though it is sometimes exaggerated), about the closeness of Jacobean drama to the masque tradition and the closeness of both Elizabethan and Jacobean drama to the tradition of pageantry, seems to make it likely that symbolic and allegorical meanings were indeed built into the plays and have not merely been read into them by modern critics. We assume that the Elizabethan's analogical habit of mind and his capacity to see the world as a set of correspondences were ingrained; and our distrust of the neatness of the so-called 'Elizabethan world picture' does not lead us to deny Elizabethan habits of mind. Ultimately, the critic's tact, his sense of proportion and relevance are the best criteria.

It has sometimes been said that serious approaches to Shakespeare are undermined by the insubstantiality of their theoretical framework, and that, because no approach can be self-sustained,

---

[3] *The Business of Criticism*, 127–57.
[4] For which he has been blamed by E. E. Stoll, in 'Symbolism in Shakespeare', 9–23 and O. J. Campbell, 'Shakespeare and the New Critics', pp. 81–97.

critics have inevitably resorted to eclecticism (for instance, L. J. Ross, in his review of N. Rabkin, ed., *Approaches to Shakespeare*, in *SQ*, 16 (1965), 359). Critical eclecticism and pluralism are not necessarily a sign of the poverty of any individual approach or method. Nor need one insist that every critical approach come complete with the panoply of an aesthetic, an ethic and a metaphysic. So far as theoretical or general soundness goes, all one expects is that the critic's initial postulates about Shakespeare's drama should not be too narrow and should have a certain validity. Underlying these assumptions, there may well be unvoiced concepts which imply a latent aesthetic, ethic or metaphysic. Discussion of any literary or dramatic criticism has to draw the line somewhere. Perhaps one service performed by analytical philosophy in our time is its lesson that logical analysis of basic concepts is likely to show that no system is invulnerable to charges of unsoundness, or lack of objectivity or consistency in practice. Any branch of knowledge has to start and end with some kind of 'hypothesis-making'. This is particularly the case in literary criticism; hence the importance of directing attention to the critic's method of hypothesis-making and of considering his implicit or explicit initial postulates.

This has been acknowledged by some recent commentators such as R. S. Crane, and by Morris Weitz in his study of the modern criticism of the most commented-upon of Shakespeare's plays, *Hamlet*. Here are two statements by Weitz:[5]

We do not find, it seems to me, the spiritual reality of a play by any mode of apprehension. Instead, what we do when we interpret a play, is formulate a hypothesis about what is central, and then use this hypothesis to clarify everything else.   (p. 34)

Interpretation, hence, is not a theory but a maxim, not a true statement of the essence of this drama, but a recommendation to look at Shakespearian drama in a certain way.   (p. 35)

The statements may appear extreme, the products of an over-severe analytical scepticism. Nor need we agree with this view of the function of criticism. Yet there is one basic truth in the state-

---

[5] *'Hamlet' and the Philosophy of Literary Criticism*.

ments; namely, that the idea of the Shakespeare play with which the critic starts is based on his interest in that aspect of the play. Instead of supposing that all Shakespeare critics of all generations are in an eternal symposium, raising and discussing the same questions about the plays, we should remind ourselves that, reflecting changing concerns and tastes, the questions asked of Shakespeare vary from age to age, and that the discussion's frame of reference keeps shifting and changing. Weitz divides questions asked into four categories: those of description, explanation, evaluation, and theorising. Significantly, the first three kinds of question are put and answered in a way which is heavily dependent on how the fourth kind is asked.[6] That is, whether or not the critic overtly theorises about the nature of Shakespearian drama, or a particular genre like comedy, he assumes a hypothesis, an idea about the play. When it comes to deciding the kind of validity the hypothesis has, the criterion has to be one of usefulness. Vague and too inclusive as the expression may seem *usefulness* determines the value of a critical approach.

It is acceptable, then (and inevitable), that the critic should isolate one or more aspects of Shakespearian drama for concentrated attention; his commentary can provide a viewpoint from which one can see the plays with greater understanding and appreciation than before, so long as he and we do not lose sight of the composite wholeness of the drama. If the same choice of aspects is critically highlighted over an extended period of time, there is a chance that those aspects are built into the general critical consciousness. This does not mean that there is simple progress in Shakespeare criticism. It is impossible for all the available insights to be held in a single mind; but it is quite possible, and indeed common in practice, for the intelligent reader to make his own synthesis of them, according to his trained taste and capacity. It is, after all, the vitality and inexhaus-

---

[6] Elder Olson, '*Hamlet* and the Hermeneutics of Drama', pp. 225–37, divides interpretative propositions into three categories: basic propositions (merely factual); inferential propositions; and evaluative propositions. He makes the point that it is not words, but verbal action the critic should be concerned with in drama, not so much the significance of what is said in the play but the significance of someone saying it. (The ' "language" of action – . . . does not give us "Hamlet is speaking", but *Hamlet speaking*' (p. 229).

tibility of Shakespearian drama that has enabled Shakespeare criticism to propose so many hypotheses. If, as T. J. B. Spencer pointed out some time ago, in his British Academy lecture, there has been no challenge to modern Shakespearian criticism in the form of a vigorous attack on Shakespeare's reputation,[7] one may say that this absence has been a different kind of challenge. Because the reputation is beyond question, a multiplicity of critical approaches could be made.

However, no one approach – and that includes the poetic approach – can be regarded as self-sufficient, still less infallible. I suggest that it is desirable and necessary to use several valid approaches in suitable combination, so that they may act as reflectors and illuminate the plays to the utmost. At any rate, in the multiplicity of critical approaches there is safety not only for the interpreter but for the reader.

[7] T. J. B. Spencer, 'The Tyranny of Shakespeare', reprinted in *Studies in Shakespeare: British Academy Lectures*, ed. Peter Alexander (London, 1964).

Appendix

Play, image and critic: some examples of developments

To give an idea of the refinements that have evolved in imagistic criticism since Spurgeon, we may look at the approaches of critics such as Clemen, Kenneth Muir, Heilman, and Maurice Charney to three plays – *Richard II*, *Hamlet* and *Macbeth* – whose imagery was first outlined suggestively by Spurgeon. We may also make a useful comparison between Spurgeon's method and findings and those of later commentators by considering the specific image strains relating to disease, animals and clothes which they all discuss.

In *Richard II*, Spurgeon (*Shakespeare's Imagery and What It Tells Us*, pp. 233–43) identifies the tree image as conveying the idea of descent in the royal family, the image of the garden used to denote the state, the sun–king analogy, and the jewel image. Clemen (*The Development of Shakespeare's Imagery*, pp. 53–62) notes the abundance of imagery and the resulting emotional unity given to the play which, as Pater pointed out, is like the harmony of a musical composition. Clemen shows how Richard II is characterised by the imagery he uses, not only as poet and dreamer but as actor: at once a player-king and one who plays the king – an early example of how imagery is a means of characterisation. He observes that to the reflective king an abstract idea appears as a concrete embodiment. The recurrent use of words such as 'tongue', 'mouth', 'speech' and 'word' by Richard II and other characters in the play, indicates the king's trait of excessive verbalising, and Shakespeare's concern with the efficacy of the word. Clemen notes how frequent the sun image is used in references to the king, and the dramatic image of the crown which is also a stage-property. So Clemen offers – unlike Spurgeon – a reading of character and of dramatic structure and themes through imagery.

Richard D. Altick unravels a number of interwoven strands of imagery, which give a symphonic unity to the play and aid its movement.[1] Altick also examines the imagery of tongue–mouth–speech and word; the ideas of the crown, tears, grief; and the key notions of earth, ground, land and garden, blood, pallor of the face, sin, tears, snake-venom, stain and sourness. He points to the ambiguous use of the idea of earth–ground–land; to the figurative meanings of inheritance, descent and familial pride suggested by 'blood'; and to the idea of evil or guilt as a blot or stain on a clean surface which cannot be washed away (an idea used later in *Hamlet* and *Macbeth*). Among Altick's findings are the metonymic use of the crown idea common to all the histories; the synaesthetic use of the image of taste ('sour', 'sourness'); and the foreshadowing of imagery to come through anticipatory hints (e.g. the occurrence of the image motif of 'bankruptcy' in I.i.151–2, III.ii.148–52 and III.ii.147–53 prefiguring the climactic use in IV.i.267 and IV.i.309).

However, it is the sun image (which Altick merely notes as the most famous motif in the play), which has promoted the most numerous and substantial studies. Samuel Kliger criticises Spurgeon for her failure to see the obvious – that the sun–king image is used in the play to make clear the idea of the tragic reversal (peripeteia) of the hero, Richard II.[2] S. K. Heninger Jr[3] stresses the 'essentiality of the sun–king image in the thematic structure of the play' (p. 321), and concerns himself with its double significance as Shakespeare uses it. Besides lending a cosmological context to the action of the play, the image serves to point up the ideal of order and, at the same time, the deviation from the norm shown both in Richard and Bolingbroke. Thus a conventional image, through Shakespeare's original treatment, turns out to be more than a representation of the political commonplace about kingly supremacy; it supplies the mode through

---

[1] 'Symphonic Imagery in *Richard II*', *PMLA*, 62 (1947), 339–65.
[2] 'The Sun Image in *Richard II*', *SP*, 45 (1948), 196–202.
[3] 'The Sun-King Analogy in *Richard II*', *SQ*, 11 (1960), 319–27.

which the dramatist carries out 'an agonized investigation into the morality of both Richard and Bolingbroke' (p. 325). It unifies, in dramatic terms, the two halves of the deposed despot's personality; it brings home to us the personal abasement, the political–historical failure, and the martyr-like end of Richard II, thus making the play at once a moral history and personal tragedy. Kathryn Montgomery Harris shows how the sun–king image is part of a larger dynamic image carrying forward the movement of the play, suggesting an analogy between the confrontation of the elements and the confrontation of Richard and Bolingbroke.[4] Spurgeon does not relate the sun–king analogy to the scheme of correspondences in the Elizabethan world-picture.[5]

Similarly, Spurgeon does not consider the emblematic, heraldic and genealogical background and origin of the image of the tree (it commonly denotes royalty, royal birth and descent) in drama; nor, unfortunately, does she extend her discussion of the traditional currency of the stage-as-garden idea (Thomas Elyot in his *Governor* gave it a famous formulation) beyond that bare statement. Consideration of the intercommunication of the ideas of decay and the imagery of weeds in this play and in the *Sonnets* and *Hamlet* would have resulted in illuminating perceptions. An example of how usefully Spurgeon's idea that the suggestions of decay and corruption in the weed-imagery in Shakespeare may be developed is to be found in Arthur Mizener's analysis of the images of flowers, canker and weeds in the *Sonnets*.[6] Spurgeon does not relate these strands of imagery to the motif of rise and fall[7] which pervades the play, and is noted by later commentators. Those who, like Clemen, have looked at Shakespeare's imagery for signs of development in his poetic-dramatic powers, have invariably found *Richard II* and *King John* to be crossroads.

---

[4] 'Sun and Water Imagery in *Richard II*: Its Dramatic Function', *SQ*, 21 (1970), 157–65.
[5] That the analogy came naturally to the Elizabethan mind was shown later by Tillyard in his *Elizabethan World Picture*.
[6] 'The Structure of Figurative Language in Shakespeare's Sonnets', *The Southern Review*, 5 (1940), 730–47, reprinted in Barbara Herrnstein, ed., *Discussions of Literature: Shakespeare's Sonnets* (Boston, 1964).
[7] Walter Suzmann, *SQ*, 7 (1956), 355–70, and Paul A. Jorgensen, 'Vertical Patterns in *Richard II*', *SAB*, xxiii, 119–34.

As Madeleine Doran tried to prove,[8] the imagery of *Richard II* primarily displays Shakespeare's associative fancy while, in contrast, that of *Henry IV* exhibits the moving and creative power of the maturing playwright. But, as Clemen shows, the imagery in *Richard II* is for the most part in character, and the relationships between image strands point forward to the tight organisation of the mature plays. The studies I have mentioned above, with a few others,[9] have also demonstrated that image patterns are a unifying factor in the play, and that imagery, for all its essential role in building and conveying the play's significance, is correlated to action and character.

Some of the most striking developments in methods and results of imagistic study of a Shakespeare play can be seen in successive treatments of *Hamlet*, the touchstone of Shakespeare criticism. Spurgeon spots the sickness images in the play, and shows that their cumulative impression is of the world of the play as corrupted. Hamlet, for Spurgeon, is in a *condition* for which he cannot be held guilty or personally responsible, and Shakespeare at the beginning of his Tragic period was obsessed with the idea of disease. Clemen uses Spurgeon's discovery as a point of departure, and shows how Hamlet's imagery reveals the character of the hero and serves to correct popular misconceptions about Hamlet as 'a man who could not make up his mind'. Clemen also brings out the communication between the image themes of disease and the image motifs and corruption, decay and poison; and makes clear the links between these pervasive image strands and two seminal events before the play opens: the murder of Hamlet's father and the incestuous remarriage of Gertrude with Claudius. Clemen also shows how the images of Fortune and the death of a king, so dominant in the player's speech, refer to the whole play.

More recent studies of the play have found new image motifs of the first importance, have corrected the overemphasis on disease imagery, and enlarged our understanding of the function of this

[8] Madeleine Doran, 'Imagery in *Richard II* and *Henry IV*'.
[9] J. A. Bryant, Jr, 'The Linked Analogies of *Richard II*', *SR*, 65 (1957), 420–33.

imagery in relation to other strands. Kenneth Muir[10] called attention to the imagery of war, weapons and violence as one of the dominant image groups. That Hamlet's world is a world of words (and also a world of puns) mainly because Shakespeare, through Hamlet, seeks to explore the efficacy of words and the relationship between word and deed, has come to be recognised;[11] ironically enough, at about the same time, the richness of the action and of the imagistic suggestion of action in the play has come to be acknowledged. Nigel Alexander in his *Poison, Play and Duel: A Study in 'Hamlet'* (London, 1971), has stressed both the imagery of war and arms, and the theatrical imagery of the play and its references to acting, actors and their profession, ignored by Spurgeon. Commentators such as Martin Holmes and Maurice Charney[12] have underlined the theatrical functions as well as the concrete theatrical representation of the images in the play. Images of secrecy and poison, and a claustrophobic sense of confinement, have also been discovered to underlie the play. All this imagistic evidence shows the increasing tendency to regard the play as the working-out of a fight between Hamlet and Claudius, or as a duel which crystallises into an overt stage-fight at the end, and to see Hamlet as in a state of war with his enemy. At least, it serves as a corrective to the vision of Hamlet as tainted and corrupt.[13] The complexity of the interpenetrating image motifs is now acknowledged, thanks to the partial isolation of skeins of imagery.

Macbeth is another play from which a rich harvest of imagery has been reaped. Dowden and Bradley, much maligned for their apparent neglect of the poetic effects of the plays, did comment on the imagery of blood and darkness in this play. They were not

[10] K. Muir, *Hamlet*, Studies in English Literature Series, General Editor, D. Daiches (London, 1964).

[11] M. M. Mahood, *Shakespeare's Wordplay*; Jorgensen, *Redeeming Shakespeare's Words*, and C. B. Hungerford, 'Hamlet: The Word at the Centre', *Tri-Quarterly*, 8 (1968), 69–89 and Terence Hawkes, '*Hamlet*: The Play on Words', *Shakespeare's Talking Animals* (London, 1973), 105–26

[12] Maynard Mack, 'The World of *Hamlet*', and in *Tragic Themes in Western Literature* (New Haven, 1956); C. R. Forker, 'Theatrical Symbolism and its Function in *Hamlet*'; Anne Righter, *Shakespeare and the Idea of the Play*; M. Charney, *Style in Hamlet*; Martin Holmes, *The Guns of Elsinore* (London, 1964).

[13] Peter Alexander, *Hamlet: Father and Son* (Oxford, 1955): Nigel Alexander, *Poison, Play and Duel: A Study in 'Hamlet'*.

so literal-minded as to suppose that the story of murders committed in the dark of night alone evoked this imagery. Kolbë considers the play as dealing with 'a crime of sleep, blood and darkness, and its corresponding Nemesis, as one episode in the universal war between sin and peace'. Spurgeon singles out for special attention the clothes motif in the play, and conjectures that Shakespeare visualises Macbeth the usurper as a man who wears garments too large for him, as a pigmy in giant's robes. Spurgeon emphasises Macbeth's small stature, countering Bradley's, Coleridge's (and Lascelles Abercrombie's) belief in his dimension of greatness. In a challenging essay, which has provoked a good deal of hostile comment, Cleanth Brooks extends the possibilities of interpretation of the clothes reference, and elaborates on the babe images in the play. According to Brooks, the point of the clothes image is that Macbeth tries to shine in borrowed feathers, and adopts manliness as a cloak to cover his guilt and sin – to such an extent that the behaviour and character of Macbeth is one more variation on the Shakespearian theme of appearance and reality. The babe images are a symbol of the future dispensation which Macbeth dreads and desperately tries to manipulate in his favour. Kenneth Muir looks upon the play's imagistic structure and movement as a complex of the babe images and the associated important (though generally unnoticed) 'sucking' or 'breast-feeding' images; 'sickness and medicine' images; and 'light–darkness' images – through all of which a juxtaposition of opposites such as good and evil, heaven and hell, and truth and falsehood, is suggested. Reginald Foakes rediscovered the imagery of sleep in the play, and pointed out how this strain of dramatic imagery embodies in itself, as both visual and verbal motif, the significance of the forces of life.[14]

Animal imagery is an easily recognisable category in Shakespeare, isolated and interpreted by commentators from many standpoints. Spurgeon highlights this imagery in *Othello*, notes

[14] Spurgeon, pp. 324–35. Cleanth Brooks, 'Shakespeare as a Symbolist Poet'; Brooks's essay is commented on by O. J. Campbell, 'Shakespeare and the "New Critics" ', E. E. Stoll, 'Symbolism in Shakespeare'; Helen Gardner, *The Business of Criticism* pp. 53–61; K. Muir, 'Image and Symbol in Macbeth', *SS*, 17 (1966), 45–54; R. A. Foakes, 'Suggestions for a New Approach to Shakespeare's Imagery'.

its presence in *King Lear*, *Julius Caesar*, and the *Henry VI* plays, points to the bird imagery in *Cymbeline*, but fails to notice it in other plays. Nor does she consider the implications of these images in the plays, except perhaps in the case of *Othello*. Clemen has interpreted the functions of animal imagery in *Richard III*, and J. C. Maxwell and Maurice Charney the animal images in *Coriolanus*. Charney has also discussed those in *Julius Caesar* and *Hamlet*, distinguishing the different purposes they serve in the different plays. Audrey Yoder[15] outlines the relationship of the animal imagery in the plays to traditional animal and bird symbolism, especially the indications for moral evaluation of characters. Armstrong, in his description of the associative links between the bird and insect images in several image clusters, shows how Shakespeare by no means confines himself to the attributes and values pertaining to animals and birds in the physiologus or bestiary tradition, but uses these images in ways which reflect his first-hand experience. As Wilson Knight points out, the animal and bird imagery is often linked with storm or music symbolism. Probably of greater importance than the communication between this strand of imagery and others is its use in conveying 'subjective' and 'objective' characterisation, for manipulative purposes and, above all, for deepening the effect of particular dramatic actions and situations.

These functions of animal imagery have long been recognised. In the examination of animal imagery by more recent commentators, such as Brian Vickers, it is the situational suggestion and effect of this imagery that has received emphasis. The situation of hunting, snaring or trapping a character is well suggested by an accumulation of animal imagery, as in the utterances of Iago in relation to Roderigo or Othello, or in the remarks of Sir Toby and his crew about Malvolio and his gulling in *Twelfth Night*.[16]

Strands of disease imagery have been noticed in several plays, and have provided some remarkable interpretative clues.

---

[15] *Animal Analogy in Shakespeare's Character Portrayal* (New York, 1948).
[16] The animal imagery in *King Lear* attracted the attention of some late nineteenth-century Shakespearians; among the earliest investigations of Shakespeare's images presented to the New Shakespeare Society is a paper on this theme (The Rev. Joshua Kirkman, 'Animal Nature *vs.* Human Nature in *King Lear*', *New Shakespeare Society's Transactions* (1879)). It seeks to discover in the pattern of animal references in the play an anticipation of the Darwinian idea of evolution from the lower forms of creation to man.

Spurgeon detects this imagery in *Troilus and Cressida* – where it occurs in conjunction with images of food, as in *Hamlet*, and also in *Coriolanus*. She pays little attention to the way in which this imagery links with body references in some of the plays, which she was the first to isolate; nor does she consider the manifold implications of the body-politic image. Clemen notes the effects of this imagery in *Julius Caesar* (in the original version of his work; the chapter is omitted in the English translation), in *Hamlet*, of course, and in *Timon of Athens*. The body-politic image emerges from the background of an age-long tradition that the country is the mystical body of the king, and the troubles of the realm are the illnesses of the king, and anti-national or anti-social individuals diseased limbs. If the body images are numerous in *King John*, *King Lear*, and elsewhere, and become associated with sickness or ulcer images, it is because in a play like *King Lear* especially, the dramatist is preoccupied with the sufferings of the person of the king, a microcosm of the nation and the world. That may be the drive behind the images of torture which abound in *King Lear* and which are noted by Spurgeon.[17] While such conjectures may be worth pursuing, direct correspondences between references to disease or physio-psychological terms and Elizabethan physiology, psychology and medicine cannot be confidently established. At best, some indirect links can be seen. There is no need to suppose that Shakespeare fashioned his characters in terms of the theory of humours,[18] or that Hamlet is a victim of melancholy, that Shakespeare got his knowledge of the symptoms from Timothy Bright's *Treatise of Melancholy*, or that the melancholics who appear in the plays are case-studies.

The clothes motif isolated by Spurgeon in *Macbeth* has been spotted by other commentators in other plays, though the background and significance of this strand of imagery have not been adequately explored. Arthur Sewell makes an incidental comment that this imagery in *King Lear* symbolises social institutions

---

[17] Ernst Kantorowicz, *The King's Two Bodies: A Study in Medieval Political Theology*, is an account of this significance of the body-politic idea. David G. Hale, 'Coriolanus: The Death of a Political Metaphor', *SQ*, 22 (1971), 197–202, finds signs of a decline of the body-politic idea around the time of writing of *Coriolanus*.

[18] As is assumed by John W. Draper, *The Humors and Shakespeare's Characters*.

which sustain and are in turn sustained by man. Robert B. Heilman regards the clothes motif in *King Lear* as dominant, whereas Maynard Mack, in a classic essay on *Hamlet*, finds the garments idea to be of central import in that play, especially as it accentuates the contrast between appearance and reality. At the simplest level, the idea of costumes and garments is likely to have been ever-present in the mind of a man of the theatre like Shakespeare, particularly in the context of the Elizabethan love of dress and the realistic use of costume on the otherwise non-naturalistic Elizabethan stage. Apart from the fact that dress carried a symbolism of its own in Elizabethan daily life, dress was a social convention (an idea dramatised in Medwall's *Nature*, and which brings to mind Carlyle's speculations in *Sartor Resartus*).[19] If, according to Spurgeon, Shakespeare conceived Macbeth as a man in ill-fitting kingly robes, it may be that he took the suggestion from seeing actors in ill-fitting garments (probably bought from a noble household); or it may be that he was inspired with the idea in Elyot's *Governor*[20] that honour is like a costly garment inherited from one's forefathers, which has to be preserved and worn well.

Spurgeon's comments on the light-darkness imagery in *Romeo and Juliet* have been perceptively developed by Moody E. Prior (pp. 62–8). Whiter, here as elsewhere anticipating Spurgeon, intuitively suggested that the image of the gunpowder-flash had seized Shakespeare's imagination while writing this play. Prior, like Clemen, emphasises the great variety of styles and skeins of imagery that Shakespeare employs. Prior shows the dramatically paradoxical purport of the imagery of light and darkness in the balcony scene, and the striking reversal in the suggestions of this imagery, which is consummated in the scene in the chamber. He also notes the star imagery, as well as the imagery of voyaging (pp. 68–70).

The image of the world in *Antony and Cleopatra*, the 'purchase',

[19] Arthur Sewell, *Character and Society in Shakespeare* (Oxford, 1951), p. 110; Heilman, *This Great Stage*; pp. 67–87; Maynard Mack, 'The World of *Hamlet*'; Dean Frye, 'The Context of Lear's Unbuttoning', *ELH*, 32 (1965), 17–31; and Thelma N. Greenfield, 'The Clothing Motif in *King Lear*' *SQ*, 5 (1954), 281–6. See also W. Clemen, *Shakespeare's Dramatic Art*, p. 181.
[20] Sir Thomas Elyot, *The Book Named the Governor*, edited by S. E. Lehmberg (London, 1962), p. 105.

'value' and money images in *Cymbeline*, and the idea of life, growth and sap in vegetation and nature in *The Winter's Tale*, are also among Spurgeon's leading perceptions. What Spurgeon called 'purchase' and 'value' imagery has come to be called legal or economic imagery and has been discovered in plays other than *Cymbeline* and in Shakespeare's poems. A. A. Stephenson and F. C. Tinkler considered this strand of imagery to be more prominent in *Cymbeline* than Spurgeon believed, and their impression has, in turn, been challenged.[21] Legal and economic imagery, as well as religious imagery, are recurrent strands of Shakespearian imagery, and they need to be examined with close reference to the legal background of Shakespeare's age.[22]

A curious category of images discussed by Spurgeon is what she calls 'topical' images. She finds several of these in *As You Like It*, *The Merry Wives of Windsor* (p. 266) and *Twelfth Night* (p. 269). But they are no more than allusions to features of Elizabethan life, and it is rather strange that, while she uses the historical knowledge available to her to explicate these imagistic allusions, she does not draw upon this kind of knowledge to study, for example, images about time, and to point out the Elizabethan iconographical attributes of Time personified. Apart from her refusal to invoke the aid of historical scholarship as frequently as she could have done, a now old-fashioned notion that 'poetical' images are qualitatively superior to images from daily life or grotesque or artificial or ugly and crooked images, handicaps her in her treatment of Shakespeare's imagery.

---

[21] A. A. Stephenson, 'The Significance of *Cymbeline*', *Scrutiny*, 10 (1942), 329–38; F. C. Tinkler, '*Cymbeline*', 7 (1939), 5–19. Leavis, 'Criticism of Shakespeare's Last Plays: A Caveat', 10 (1941–2), 339–45 questions the qualitative importance of this imagery in the play.

[22] W. L. Rushton, *Shakespeare's Legal Maxims* (1859); Sir Dunbar Planket, *Links between Shakespeare and the Law* (1929) (reprinted New York, 1971); G. W. Keeton, *Shakespeare's Legal and Political Background*; and, also, O. Hood Phillips, *Shakespeare and the Lawyers* have sketched the background in detail.

Select Bibliography

G. WILSON KNIGHT

'Brutus and Cassius', *The Adelphi*, 4 (1927), 555–8, reprinted in *Shakespeare and Religion*.

'Henry VI and Macbeth', *The New Adelphi*, 1 (1927), 69–73, reprinted in *The Sovereign Flower*.

'The Principles of Shakespeare Interpretation', *The Shakespeare Review*, 1 (1928), 347–80, reprinted in *The Sovereign Flower*.

Myth and Miracle. An Essay on the Mystic Symbolism of Shakespeare (London, 1929), reprinted in *The Crown of Life*.

The Wheel of Fire: Essays in Interpretation of Shakespeare's Tragedies (London, 1930; revised and enlarged 1949).

The Imperial Theme: Further Interpretations of Shakespeare's Tragedies, Including the Roman Plays (London, 1931, 1951 edn).

The Shakespearian Tempest (London, 1932, 1953 edn with a 'Chart of Shakespeare's Dramatic Universe').

The Christian Renaissance with Interpretations of Dante, Shakespeare and Goethe and a Note on T. S. Eliot (Toronto, 1933; revised edn 1962).

Shakespeare and Tolstoy, The English Association Pamphlet 88 (London, 1934), reprinted in *The Wheel of Fire* as 'Tolstoy's attack on Shakespeare' (1949 edn).

'The Vision of Jupiter in *Cymbeline*', *TLS* (21 November 1935), 958.

Principles of Shakespearian Production (London, 1936; revised and enlarged as *Shakespearian Production*, 1964).

'The Shakespearian Integrity', *The Burning Oracle* (London, 1939), reprinted in *The Sovereign Flower*.

'A Note on Henry VIII', *The Criterion*, 15 (1936), 228–36, reprinted in *Shakespeare and Religion*.

Chariot of Wrath (London, 1942).

The Olive and the Sword (London, 1944), reprinted in part in *The Sovereign Flower*.

The Crown of Life. Essays in Interpretation of Shakespeare's Final Plays (London, 1947, reprinted in 1948).

'The New Interpretation *EC*, 3 (1953), 382–95 and also a response by Gāmini Salgādo and Allan Rodway, *EC*, 4 (1954), 217–22 and by F. W. Bateson, *EC*, 4 (1954), 430–1.

The Laureate of Peace: On the Genius of Alexander Pope (London, 1954).

The Mutual Flame: On Shakespeare's Sonnets and the Pooenix and the Turtle (London, 1955).

The Sovereign Flower: On Shakespeare as the Poet of Royalism together with Related Essays and Indexes to Earlier Volumes (London, 1958).

The Starlit Dome (London, 1959).

'Timon of Athens and its Dramatic Descendants', *A Review of English Literature*, 2 (1961), 9–18, reprinted in *Shakespeare and Religion*.

The Golden Labyrinth: A Study of British Drama (London, 1962), reissued 1965.

'J. Middleton Murry', *Of Books and Humankind: Essays and Poems Presented to Bonamy Dobrée*, edited by John Butt (London, 1964), 149–63.

'Scrutiny and Criticism', *EC*, 14 (1964), 32–6.

'Shakespeare and Theology: A Private Protest', *EC*, 15 (1965), 95–104, reprinted in *Shakespeare and Religion*.

'T. S. Eliot: Some Literary Impressions', *SR*, 74 (1966), 239–55, reprinted in *T. S. Eliot: The Man and His Works* (London, 1967).

'Symbolism', *A Shakespeare Encyclopedia*, edited by O. J. Campbell and E. G. Quinn (New York, 1966), reprinted in *Shakespeare and Religion*.

Shakespeare and Religion (London, 1967).

Neglected Powers: Essays on Nineteenth and Twentieth Century Literature (London, 1971), preface, pp. 1–19.

'Gloucester's Leap', *EC*, 22 (1972), 279–82.

Shakespeare's Dramatic Challenge, a collection of lectures (London, 1977).

L. C. KNIGHTS

How Many Children Had Lady Macbeth? (The Minority Press, 1932).

'Education and the Drama in the Age of Shakespeare', *The Criterion*, 11 (1932), 599–625.

'Notes on Comedy', *Scutiny*, 1 (1932–3), 356–67, reprinted in *Determinations*, edited by F. R. Leavis (1934).

'Shakespeare's Sonnets', *Scrutiny*, 3 (1934–5), 133–60, reprinted in *Explorations*.

'Shakespeare and Profit inflations', *Scrutiny*, 5 (1936–7), 48–60.

Drama and Society in The Age of Jonson (London, 1937).

'Prince Hamlet', *Scrutiny*, 9 (1940–1), 148–60, reprinted in *Explorations*.

'The Ambiguity of *Measure for Measure*', *Scrutiny*, 10 (1941–2), 222–33.

'Shakespeare and the Elizabethan Climate', *Scrutiny*, 12 (1943–4), 157–62.

Explorations (London, 1946).

Poetry, Politics, and the English Tradition (1954), reprinted in *Further Explorations*.

'Historical Scholarship and the Interpretation of Shakespeare', *SR*, 63 (1955), reprinted in *Further Explorations*.

Shakespeare's Politics: with some Reflections on the Nature of Tradition, *PBA*, (1957), reprinted in *Further Explorations*.

'The question of character in Shakespeare', *More Talking of Shakespeare*, edited by John Garrett (London, 1959), reprinted in *Further Explorations*.

Some Shakespearean Themes (London, 1959).

with Basil Cottle, editors, *Metaphor and Symbol* (London, 1960).

An Approach to 'Hamlet' (London, 1960).

'Shakespeare's Imagery', *The Living Shakespeare*, edited by R. Gittings (London, 1960).

William Shakespeare: The Histories (London, 1962).

'Shakespeare, the Language and Ourselves', *The Spectator* (17 April 1964), 509–11.

'Imaginative Energy or Why Read Shakespeare', *New Theatre Magazine*, vol. 5 (1964), no. 2, 26–8.

'Theology and Poetry', *Theology and the University*, edited by John Coulson (London, 1964), 207–19.

Further Explorations (London, 1965).

Some Shakespearean Themes and An Approach to 'Hamlet' (Harmondsworth, 1966).

'Thought in Shakespeare', *The Hidden Harmony: Essays in Honor of Philip Wheelwright*, edited by Oliver Johnson (New York, 1967) reprinted in *Explorations 3*.

'Shakespeare's Tragedies and the Question of Moral Judgment', *Shenandoah*, 19 (1968) reprinted in *Explorations 3*.

'Timon of Athens', *The Morality of Art: Essays Presented to G. Wilson Knight* (London, 1969), pp. 1–17.

'The Teaching of Shakespeare', *The Use of English*, 19 (1967), 3–16 (also printed in *Manner and Meaning in Shakespeare: Stratford Papers*, 1965–7 (Shannon, 1969), 1–20).

'Shakespeare', *Public Voices: Literature and Politics with Special Reference to the Seventeenth Century* (London, 1971), pp. 30–51.

Explorations 3 (London, 1976); contains reprint of 'Integration in *The Winter's Tale* between Nature and Grace', first published in *SR*, 84 (1976), 595–613.

'Shakespeare and History', *SR*, 86 (1978).

210 *Select bibliography*

CAROLINE F. E. SPURGEON

Keats's Shakespeare: A Descriptive Study (Oxford, 1928), reprinted 1966 and 1968.
Leading Motives in the Imagery of Shakespeare's Tragedies (London, 1930).
'Imagery in the More Fragment', *RES*, 6 (1930), 257–70.
'Shakespeare's Iterative Imagery' (1931), *Aspects of Shakespeare*, edited by J. W. MacKail (Oxford, 1932), 255–86.
Shakespeare's Imagery and What It Tells Us (Cambridge, 1935).

II

Abercrombie, Lascelles. 'A Plea for the Liberty of Interpreting' (1930), reprinted in *Aspects of Shakespeare*, edited by J. W. MacKail (Oxford, 1932), 227–54.
Abrams, M. H. *The Mirror and the Lamp: Romantic Theory and the Critical Tradition* (London, 1953, 1960 edn).
Adams, J. C. *The Globe Playhouse: Its Design and Equipment* (Cambridge, Mass., 1942).
'The Original Staging of King Lear', *J. Q. Adams Memorial Studies*, edited by J. G. McManaway, *et al.* (Washington, D.C, 1948).
Adams, J. Q. *Shakespearean Playhouses* (Boston and London, 1917).
Adams, R. M. *Strains of Discord: Studies in Literary Openness* (Ithaca, New York, 1958).
Alden, R. M. 'The Lyrical Conceit of the Elizabethans', *SP*, 14 (1917).
Alexander, Nigel. *Poison, Play and Duel: A Study in Hamlet* (London, 1971).
Alexander, Peter., 'Restoring Shakespeare: The Modern Editor's Task', *SS; 5* (1952). *Hamlet: Father and Son* (Oxford, 1955), editor. *Studies in Shakespeare: British Academy Lectures* (London, 1964).
Altick, Richard D. 'Symphonic Imagery in *Richard II*', *PMLA*, 62 (1947). '*Hamlet* and the Odor of Mortality', *SQ*, 5 (1954).
Anderson, Ruth. *Elizabethan Psychology and Shakespeare's Plays* (Iowa City, 1927).
'The Pattern of Behaviour Culminating in *Macbeth*', *SEL*, 3 (1963).
Armstrong, E. A. *Shakespeare's Imagination: A Study of the Psychology of Association and Inspiration* (London, 1946), revised edn, Gloucester, Mass., 1963.
Babb, Lawrence. *The Elizabethan Malady: A Study of Melancholia in English Literature from 1580 to 1642* (Michigan, 1951).
Babcock, R. W. *The Genesis of Shakespeare Idolatry: 1766–1799* (Chapel Hill, 1931).
'Mr Stoll Revisited Twenty Years After', *PQ*, 28 (1948), 289–313.
'Historical Criticism of Shakespeare', *MLQ*, 13 (1952), 6–20.

Badawi, M. M. 'Coleridge's Formal Criticism of Shakespeare's Plays', *EC*, 10 (1960).
Coleridge: Critic of Shakespeare (Cambridge, 1973).
Baldwin, T. W. *'Shakespeare's Small Latine and Lesse Greeke'* (Urbana, 1944).
Shakespeare's Five-Act Structure (Urbana, 1947).
Bamborough, J. B. *The Little World of Man* (London, 1952).
Barber, C. L. *Shakespeare's Festive Comedy: A Study of Dramatic Form and Its Relation to Social Custom* (Princeton, 1959).
Barfield, Owen. *Poetic Diction: A Study in Meaning* (London, 1928).
Barnet, Sylvan. 'Some Limitations of A Christian Approach to Shakespeare', *ELH*, 22 (1955), 81–92, reprinted in Norman Rabkin, editor, *Approaches to Shakespeare* (McGraw-Hill, 1964).
Baskervill, C. R. 'Dramatic Aspects of Medieval Folk Festivals in England', *SP*, 17 (1920), 19–87.
Bateson, F. W. *English Poetry: A Critical Introduction* (London, 1950).
Essays in Critical Dissent (London, 1972).
Battenhouse, Roy W. *'Measure for Measure* and the Christian Doctrine of the Atonement', *PMLA*, 61 (1946).
'The Ghost in *Hamlet* – A Catholic Lynchpin?', *SP*, 48 (1951).
Shakespearean Tragedy: Its Art and Its Christian Premises (Bloomington, 1969).
Berry, Francis. 'Wilson Knight: Stage and Study', *The Morality of Art*, edited by D. W. Jefferson, the Wilson Knight *Festschrift* (London, 1969).
Bethell, S. L. *Shakespeare and the Popular Dramatic Tradition* (London, 1944).
The Winter's Tale – A Study (London, 1947).
The Cultural Revolution of the Seventeenth Century (London, 1951).
Shakespeare's Imagery: 'The Diabolic Images in *Othello'*, *SS*, 5 (1952).
Bowers, F. T. *Elizabethan Revenge Tragedy* (Princeton, 1940).
'Hamlet as Minister and Scourge', *PMLA*, 70 (1955).
Bradbrook, M. C. *Elizabethan Stage Conditions* (Cambridge, 1932).
Themes and Conventions of Elizabethan Tragedy (Cambridge, 1935, 2nd edition, 1980)
English Dramatic Form (London, 1965).
Shakespeare the Craftsman (London, 1969).
Bradbury, M. and Palmer, D. J., eds. *Contemporary Criticism: Stratford-upon-Avon Studies*, 12 (London, 1970).
Bradley, A. C. 'Henry V', *The Fortnightly Review* (1902).
Shakespearian Tragedy: Lectures on 'Hamlet', 'Othello', 'King Lear', 'Macbeth' (London, 1904, 1957, paperback edn).
Oxford Lectures on Poetry (London, 1909).
A Miscellany (London, 1929).

Bridges, Robert. 'The influence of the Audience on Shakespeare's Drama' (1907), *Collected Essays* (Oxford, 1927).

Britton, John. 'A. C. Bradley and Those Children of Lady Macbeth', *SQ*, 12 (1961), 349–51.

Brooke, Nicholas. 'The Characters of Drama', *CQ*, 6 (1964), 72–82.
Shakespeare's Early Tragedies (London, 1968).

Brooke-Rose, Christine. *A Grammar of Metaphor* (London, 1958).

Brooks, Cleanth. 'Shakespeare as a Symbolist Poet', *Yale Review* (Summer, 1945), reprinted as 'The Naked Babe and the Cloak of Manliness', *The Well Wrought Urn* (London, 1947).

Brower, Reuben A. *The Fields of Light: An Experiment in Critical Reading* (New York, 1951).

Brown, Arthur. *Edmond Malone and English Scholarship* (1963).

Brown, John Russell. *Shakespeare's Plays in Performance* (London, 1966).
'The Theatrical Element of Shakespeare Criticism', *Reinterpretations of Elizabethan Drama: English Institute Papers*, edited by Norman Rabkin (New York, 1969), 177–95.

Brown, Stephen J. *The World of Imagery* (London, 1927).

Bush, Geoffrey. *Shakespeare and the Natural Condition* (1956).

Butler, Francelia. *The Strange Critical Fortunes of Shakespeare's 'Timon of Athens'* (Iowa City, 1966).

Campbell, Lilly B. *Shakespeare's Tragic Heroes: Slaves of Passion* (London, 1930).
Shakespeare's Histories: Mirrors of Elizabethan Policy (San Marino, 1947).

Campbell, O. J. 'Shakespeare and the "New Critics" ', *J. Q. Adams Memorial Studies*, edited by James G. McManaway *et al.* (Washington DC, 1948), 81–97.

Campbell, O. J. and Quinn, E. G., editors, *A Shakespeare Encyclopaedia* (London, 1966).

Casey, John. *The Language of Criticism* (London, 1966).

Chambers, E. K. *The Elizabethan Stage* (Oxford 1923), 4 vols.
Shakespeare: A Survey (1900) (London, 1925).
William Shakespeare (Oxford, 1930), 2 vols.
Shakespearean Gleanings (Oxford, 1944).

Charlton, H. B. *Shakespeare, Politics and Politicians*, English Association Pamphlet no. 72 (Oxford, 1929).
Shakespearian Tragedy (Cambridge, 1948), introduction.

Charney, Maurice. *Shakespeare's Roman Plays: The Function of Imagery in Drama* (Cambridge, Mass., 1961).
Style in 'Hamlet' (Princeton, 1969).

Clark, Richard C. 'Shakespeare's Contemporary Relevance', *A Review of National Literatures: Shakespeare and his England*, edited by J. G. McManaway, 3 (1972), 185–97.

Clemen, Wolfgang. *The Development of Shakespeare's Imagery* (London, 1951), original German version *Shakespeare's Bilder* (Bonn, 1936).

'Anticipation and Foreboding in Shakespeare's Early Histories', *SS*, 6 (1953).

English Tragedy Before Shakespeare, translated by T. S. Dorsch (London, 1961).

A Commentary on Shakespeare's 'Richard III' (London, 1968).

Shakespeare's Dramatic Art: Collected Essays (London, 1972).

Coates, J. B. *The Crisis of the Human Person: Some Personalist Interpretations* (London, 1949).

Coghill, Nevill. 'The Basis of Shakespearian Comedy', *E&S*, 3 (1950).

Shakespeare's Professional Skills (Cambridge, 1964).

Coleridge's Shakespearean Criticism, edited by Raysor, T. M. (Cambridge, Mass., 1930); 2 vols revised and reprinted in Everyman's Library (London, 1960).

Coleridge on Shakespeare (Harmondsworth, 1969), edited by Terence Hawkes.

Coleridge's Lectures on Shakespeare, edited by R. A. Foakes (London, 1971).

Cooke, Katharine. *A. C. Bradley and His Influence in Twentieth-Century Shakespeare Criticism* (Oxford, 1972).

Cope, Jackson I. *The Theater and the Dream: From Metaphor to Form in Renaissance Drama* (Baltimore, 1973).

Cormican, L. A. 'The Medieval Idiom in Shakespeare', *Scrutiny*, 17 (1950–1).

Crane, R. S. *The Languages of Criticism and the Structure of Poetry* (Toronto, 1953).

ed. *Critics and Criticism* (Chicago, 1952).

Crow, John. 'Deadly Sins of Criticism, or, Seven Ways to Get Shakespeare Wrong', *SQ*, 9 (1958), 301–6.

Curry, W. C. *Shakespeare's Philosophical Patterns* (Baton Rouge, 1937).

Danby, J. F. *Shakespeare's Doctrine of Nature* (London, 1949).

David, R. W. *The Janus of Poets* (Cambridge, 1935).

Dean, L. F. ed. *Shakespeare: Modern Essays in Criticism* (New York, 1957, revised edn. 1967).

Dessen, Alan C. 'Hamlet's Poisoned Sword: A Study in Dramatic Imagery', *Shakespeare Studies*, 5 (1969), 53–69.

Dobrée, Bonamy. 'On (Not) Enjoying Shakespeare', *E&S*, 9 (1956) 39–55.

Doran, Madeleine. 'Imagery in *Richard II* and *Henry IV*', *MLR*, 37 (1942), 113–22.

Endeavors of Art (Madison, 1954).

Dowden, Edward. *Shakespeare: His Mind and Art* (London, 1875).

'The Elizabethan Science of Psychology', *Essays Modern and Elizabethan* (1910).

Draper, John W. *The Humors and Shakespeare's Characters* (Durham, NC, 1945).

Duthie, George Ian. *Shakespeare* (London, 1951).

Durham, W. H. '*Measure for Measure* as Measure for Critics', *Essays in Criticism: University of California* (Berkeley, 1929), 113–32.

Eastman, Arthur M. *A Short History of Shakespearean Criticism* (New York, 1968).

Edwards, Philip. *Thomas Kyd and Early Elizabethan Tragedy* (London, 1966).

Eliot, T. S. 'Ulysses, Order and Myth', *The Dial*, 5 (1923), reprinted in *Forms of Modern Fiction*, edited by William O'Connor (Minneapolis, 1948).

Selected Essays (London, 1932, 1934 edn).

'Shakespeare Criticism I: From Dryden to Coleridge', *A Companion to Shakespeare Studies*, edited by Harley Granville-Barker and G. B. Harrison (Cambridge, 1934), 287–99.

On Poetry and Poets (London, 1957).

To Criticize the Critic and Other Essays (London, 1965).

Selected Prose, edited by John Hayward (Harmondsworth, 1953).

Ellis-Fermor, Una. *Christopher Marlowe* (London, 1927).

Some Recent Research in Shakespeare's Imagery, Shakespeare Association Pamphlet (Oxford, 1937).

The Frontiers of Drama (London, 1945).

'Shakespeare and his World: The Poet's Imagery', *The Listener*, vol. 42 (July 1949).

'English and American Shakespeare Studies, 1937–1952', *Anglia*, 71 (1952), 1–49.

Shakespeare the Dramatist and Other Papers, edited by K. Muir (London, 1961).

Elyot, Sir Thomas. *The Book Named the Governor*, edited by S. E. Lehmberg (London, 1962).

Empson, William. *Seven Types of Ambiguity* (London, 1930).

The Structure of Complex Words (London, 1951).

'Hamlet When New', *SR*, 61 (1953), 15–42 and 185–205.

Milton's God (London, 1961).

Correspondence in *CQ*, 7 (1965).

Empson, William and Garrett, George. *Shakespeare Survey* (1936).

Enright, D. J. *Shakespeare and the Students* (London, 1970), esp. introduction.

Everett, Barbara. 'The Figure in Professor Knights' Carpet', *CQ*, 2 (1960), 171–2.

'The New King Lear', *CQ*, 2 (1960), 325–39.

'Reflections on the Sentimentalist's Othello', *CQ*, 3 (1961), 127–39.

Ewbank, Inga-Stina. ' "More Pregnantly than Words": Some uses and Limitations of Visual Symbolism', *SS*, 24 (1971), 13–18.

Farnham, Willard. *The Medieval Heritage of Elizabethan Tragedy* (Berkeley, 1936).

Shakespeare's Tragic Frontier (Berkeley, 1950).

The Shakespearean Grotesque: Its Genesis and Transformations (Oxford, 1971).

Fisch, Harold. 'Shakespeare and "The Theatre of the World" ', *The Morality of Art*, edited by D. W. Jefferson (London, 1969), 76–86.

Foakes, R. A. 'Suggestions for a New Approach to Shakespeare's Imagery', *SS*, 5 (1952), 81–92.

The Romantic Assertion (New Haven, 1958).

Forest, L. C. Turner. 'Caveat for Critics against Invoking Elizabethan Psychology', *PMLA*, 61 (1946), 651–72.

Forker, Charles R. 'Theatrical Symbolism and Its Function in *Hamlet*', *SQ*, 14 (1963).

Frank, Joseph. 'Spatial Form in Modern Literature' (1945), reprinted in *Criticism: the Foundations of Modern Literary Judgement*, edited by Mark Schorer, Josephine Miles and Gordon McKenzie (New York, 1948), 379–92.

Fraser, Russell A. *Shakespeare's Poetics in Relation to 'King Lear'* (London, 1962).

Frazer, Ray. 'The Origin of the Term "Image" ', *ELH*, 27 (1960), 149–61.

Friedman, Norman. 'Imagery: From Sensation to Symbol', *JAAC*, 12 (1953), 25–37.

Frye, Dean. 'The Context of Lear's Unbuttoning', *ELH*, 32 (1965), 17–31.

Frye, Northrop. *The Anatomy of Criticism* (Toronto, 1957).

A Natural Perspective (New York, 1965).

Frye, Ronald Mushat. *Shakespeare and Christian Doctrine* (Princeton, 1963).

Furbank, P. N. 'Do We Need the Terms *Image* and *Imagery*?', *CQ*, 9 (1967), 335–45.

Reflections on the Word 'Image' (London, 1970).

Gardner, Helen. 'The Noble Moor', *PBA*, 42 (1956).

The Business of Criticism (London, 1963 edn).

'Shakespeare in the Age of Eliot', *TLS* (23 April 1964), 335–6.

'*Othello*: A Retrospect 1900–67', *SS*, 21 (1968).

ed. F. P. Wilson's *Shakespearian and Other Studies* (London, 1969).

Golden, Martha Hester (Fleischer). 'Stage Imagery in Shakespearean Studies', *Shakespeare Research and Opportunities*, 1 (1965), 10–20.

Grace, W. J. *Approaching Shakespeare* (New York, 1964).

Granville-Barker, Harley. *Prefaces to Shakespeare*, five series (London, 1927–48).

Granville-Barker, Harley and Harrison, G. B., editors, *A Companion to Shakespeare Studies* (Cambridge, 1934).

Grebstein, Sheldon Norman. editor, *Perspectives in Contemporary Criticism* (New York, 1963).

Green, Henry. *Shakespeare and the Emblem Books* (London, 1870).

Greenfield, Thelma N. 'The Clothing Motif in *King Lear*', *SQ*, 5 (1954), 281–6.

Grover, P. R. 'The Ghost of Dr Johnson: L. C. Knights and D. A. Traversi on Hamlet', *EC*, 17 (1967), 143–57.

Hale, David G. '*Coriolanus*: The Death of a Political Metaphor', *SQ*, 22 (1971), 197–202.

Halliday, F. E. *Shakespeare and His Critics* (London, 1953).
  The Poetry of Shakespeare's Plays (London, 1954).

Hankins, J. E. *Shakespeare's Derived Imagery* (Lawrence, Kansas, 1953).

Hapgood, Robert. 'Shakespeare and the Ritualists', *SS*, 15 (1962).

Harbage, Alfred. *Shakespeare's Audience* (New York, 1941).
  Shakespeare and the Rival Traditions (New York, 1952).
  Theatre for Shakespeare (Toronto, 1955).
  As They Liked It (New York, 1947, paperback edn. 1961).
  William Shakespeare: A Reader's Guide (New York, 1963).
  'Shakespeare and the "Myth of Perfection" ', *SQ*, 15 (1964).
  Conceptions of Shakespeare (Cambridge, Mass., 1966).

Harding, D. W. *Experience into Words* (London, 1963).

Hardy, Barbara. ' "I Have a Smack of Hamlet": Coleridge and Shakespeare's Characters', *EC*, 8 (1958).

Harrier, Richard. 'Another Note on "Why the Sweets Melted" ', *SQ*, 18 (1967).

Harrison, John L. '*Measure for Measure* and the Convention of Tongue and Heart', *SQ*, 5 (1954).

Hart, Alfred. *Shakespeare and the Homilies* (London, 1934).

Hastings, W. T. 'The New Critics of Shakespeare: An Analysis of the Technical Analysis of Shakespeare', *SQ*, 1 (1950).

Hawkes, Terence. *Shakespeare and the Reason* (London, 1964).
  Shakespeare's Talking Animals (London, 1973).

Heilman, Robert B. *This Great Stage: Image and Structure in 'King Lear'* (Baton Rouge, La., 1948).
  Magic in the Web: Action and Language in 'Othello' (Lexington, Ky., 1956).
  'Historian and Critic: Notes on Attitudes', *SR*, 73 (1965), 426–44.

Henn, T. R. *The Harvest of Tragedy* (London, 1956).
  The Living Image: Shakespearian Essays (London, 1972).

Herford, C. H. *A Sketch of Recent Shakespearian Investigation* (London, 1922).

Hirsch, E. D., Jr. 'Objective Interpretation', *PMLA*, 75 (1960).
  Validity in Interpretation (New Haven, 1967).

Hobday, C. H. 'Why the Sweets Melted: A Study of Shakespeare's Imagery', *SQ*, 16 (1965), 3–17.

Hodges, C. Walter. *The Globe Restored* (London, 1968, 2nd edn).

Holland, Norman N. *Psychoanalysis and Shakespeare* (New York, 1964).

Holloway, John. *The Charted Mirror* (London, 1960).
  The Story of the Night (London, 1961).
  'Criticism – 20th Century', *A Shakespeare Encyclopaedia*, edited by O. J. Campbell and E. G. Quinn (London, 1966).

Holmes, Elizabeth. *Aspects of Elizabethan Imagery* (Oxford, 1929).

Hornstein, Lillian. 'Analysis of Imagery: A Critique of Literary Method', *PMLA*, 57 (1942), 638–53.

Hosley, Richard. 'The Discovery-space in Shakespeare's Globe', *SS*, 12 (1959).

'The Gallery over the stage in the Public Playhouse of Shakespeare's Time', *SQ*, 14 (1963).

'The Origins of the Shakespearian Playhouse', *SQ*, 15 (1964).

'The Origins of the So-called Elizabethan Multiple Stage', *The Drama Review*, 12 (1968), 28–50.

Hotson, Leslie L. *Shakespeare Versus Shallow* (Boston, 1931).

William Shakespeare (London, 1937).

Shakespeare's Sonnets Dated (London, 1949).

The First Night of 'Twelfth Night' (London, 1954).

Shakespeare's Wooden O (London, 1959).

Mr W. H. (London, 1964).

Hough, Graham. *Image and Experience* (London, 1960).

Houser, David J. 'Armor and Motive in *Troilus and Cressida*', *Renaissance Drama*, n. s. 4 (1971), 121–34.

Howarth, Herbert. *The Tiger's Heart: Eight Essays on Shakespeare* (London, 1970).

Hughes, Merritt Y. 'Meditations on Literary Blasphemy', *JAAC*, 15 (1955).

Hungerford, C. B. 'Hamlet: The Word at the Centre', *Tri-Quarterly*, 8 (1968) 69–89.

Hyman, Stanley Edgar. *The Armed Vision: A Study in the Methods of Modern Criticism* (New York, 1952).

'The Imagery of Shakespeare: Dr Clemen and Walter Whiter', *TLS*, 35 (1936), 701–2.

Jackson, James L. 'Shakespeare's Dog-and-Sugar Imagery and the Friendship Tradition', *SQ*, 1 (1950), 260–3.

Jackson, MacD. P. 'Shakespeare and *Edmund Ironside*', *N&Q*, n.s. 10 (1963), 331–2.

James, D. G. *Scepticism and Poetry* (London, 1937).

The Dream of Learning (Oxford, 1951).

The Dream of Prospero (Oxford, 1967).

Jarrell, Randall. *Poetry and the Age* (New York, 1955).

Jefferson, D. W., editor. *The Morality of Art: Essays presented to G. Wilson Knight* (London, 1969).

Johnson, F. R. 'Elizabethan Drama and the Elizabethan Science of Psychology', *English Studies Today*, edited by G. Bullough and C. L. Wrenn, 1st series (London, 1951).

Jones, Howard Mumford. *The King in 'Hamlet'* (Austin, Texas, 1918).

Jones, John. 'Shakespeare and Mr Wilson Knight', *The Listener*, vol. 52 (1954), 1011–12

Jorgensen, Paul A. *Shakespeare's Military World* (Berkeley, 1956).
 Redeeming Shakespeare's Words (Berkeley, 1962).
Joseph, Sister Miriam. *Shakespeare's Use of the Arts of Language* (New York, 1947).
 'Discerning the Ghost in *Hamlet*', *PMLA*, 76 (1961).
Jump, John D. 'Shakespeare's Ghosts', *CQ*, 12 (1970).
Kantak, V. Y. 'An Approach to Shakespearian Tragedy: The Actor Image in *Macbeth*', *SS*, 16 (1963), 42–52.
Kantorowicz, Ernst H. *The King's Two Bodies: A Study in Medieval Political Theology* (Princeton, 1957).
Keble, John. *Lectures on Poetry, 1832–41*, vol. I, edited by E. K. Francis (Oxford, 1912).
Keeton, George W. *Shakespeare's Legal and Political Background* (London, 1967).
Kellett, E. E. 'Some Notes on a Feature of Shakespeare's Style', *Suggestions* (Cambridge, 1923).
Kernodle, George R. *From Art to Theatre: Form and Convention in the Renaissance* (London, 1944).
King, T. J. *Shakespearean Staging, 1599–1642* (Cambridge, Mass., 1971).
Kirsch, Arthur C. *Jacobean Dramatic Perspectives* (Charlottesville, 1972).
Kitto, H. D. F. *Form and Meaning in Drama* (London, 1956).
Knowlton, E. C. 'Nature and Shakespeare', *PMLA*, 51 (1936), 719–44.
Knox, R. S. 'Recent Shakespearean Criticism', in R. S. Harris and R. L. McDougall, eds. *The Undergraduate Essay* (Toronto, 1958).
Kökeritz, H. *Shakespeare's Pronunciation* (New Haven, 1953).
Kolbë, Mgr. F. C. *Shakespeare's Way: A Psychological Study* (London, 1930).
Krieger, Murray. *A Window to Criticism* (Princeton, 1964).
Lawlor, John. 'On Historical Scholarship and the Interpretation of Shakespeare: A Reply to L. C. Knights', *SR*, 64 (1956), 186–206.
 'Mind and Hand: Some Reflections on the Study of Shakespeare's Imagery', *SQ*, 8 (1957), 179–93.
 The Tragic Sense in Shakespeare (London, 1960).
Lawrence, W. J. *The Elizabethan Playhouse and Other Studies* (Stratford-on-Avon, 1912–13).
 The Physical Conditions of the Elizabethan Public Playhouses (Cambridge, Mass., 1927).
 Pre-Restoration Stage Studies (New York, 1927).
 Those Nut-Cracking Elizabethans (London, 1933).
 Speeding Up Shakespeare: Studies in the Bygone Theatre and Drama (London, 1937).
Lawrence, W. W. *Shakespeare's Problem Comedies* (New York 1931).
Leavis, F. R. *Education and the University* (London, 1943, 1948 edn) incorporating *How to Teach Reading* (1931).
 New Bearings in English Poetry (London, 1932, revised Harmondsworth, 1963).

'*Antony and Cleopatra* and *All for Love*: A Critical Exercise', *Scrutiny*, 5 (1936–7), 158–69.

Revaluation (London, 1936).

'Diabolic Intellect and the Noble Hero: A Note on *Othello*', *Scrutiny*, 6 (1937–8), 259–83.

'Criticism of Shakespeare's Late Plays: A Caveat', *Scrutiny*, 10 (1941–42), 339–45.

'The Greatness of *Measure for Measure*', *Scrutiny*, 10 (1941–2), 234–47.

'Tragedy and the "Medium" ', *Scrutiny*, 12 (1943–4), 249–60.

' "Thought" and Emotional Quality', *Scrutiny*, 13 (1944–5), 52–71.

'Imagery and Movement: Notes in the Analysis of Poetry', *Scrutiny*, 13 (1944–5), 119–34.

'Reality and Sincerity: Notes in the Analysis of Poetry', *Scrutiny*, 19 (1950–1), 90–8. These three essays are reprinted in *The Living Principle*.

The Common Pursuit (London, 1952) (incorporating several of the *Scrutiny* essays).

Letter to *TLS* (9 July 1954) 441.

The Living Principle (London, 1975).

ed. *Towards Standards of Criticism* (essays from *The Calendar of Modern Letters*) (London, 1932).

ed. *Determinations* (London, 1934) (essays from *Scrutiny*).

Leech, Clifford, ed. *Shakespeare: The Major Tragedies. A Collection of Critical Essays* (Chicago, 1965).

Legouis, Pierre. 'Some Remarks on Seventeenth Century Imagery', *Seventeenth Century Imagery*, edited by E. Miner (Los Angeles and London, 1970), 187–97.

Lerner, L. D., ed. *Shakespeare's Tragedies: An Anthology of Modern Criticism* (Harmondsworth, 1963).

Lever, J. W., ed. *Measure for Measure* (New Arden Shakespeare) (London, 1965).

Levin, Harry. 'The Primacy of Shakespeare', *SQ*, 26 (1975), 99–112.

Levin, Richard. 'Some Second Thoughts on Central Themes', *MLR*, 67 (1972), 1–10.

'Thematic Unity and the Homogenization of Character', *MLQ*, 33 (1972), 23–9.

Lewis, C. S. 'Hamlet: The Prince or the Poem' (1942), reprinted in *Studies in Shakespeare: British Academy Lectures*, edited by P. Alexander (London, 1964).

Lodge, David. *The Language of Fiction* (London, 1966).

Lovejoy, Arthur O. 'Nature as Aesthetic Norm', *MLN*, 42 (1927), 444–50.

'The Gothic Revival and Return to Nature', *MLN*, 47 (1932), 419–446.

Lyons, P. Clifford. ' "It appears so by the story": Notes on Narrative-Thematic Emphasis in Shakespeare', *SQ*, 9 (1958), 287–94.

'Stage Imagery in Shakespeare's Plays', *Essays on Shakespeare and*

Elizabethan Drama in Honor of Hardin Craig, edited by R. Hosley (1963), 261–74.

Mack, Maynard. 'The World of *Hamlet*' (1952), reprinted in L. F. Dean, *Shakespeare: Modern Essays in Criticism* (New York, 1957, 2nd edn. 1961).
'The Jacobean Shakespeare', *Jacobean Theatre* (Stratford-upon-Avon Studies, i), edited by J. R. Brown and Bernard Harris (London, 1960).
'Engagement and Detachment in Shakespeare's Plays', *Essays on Shakespeare and Elizabethan Drama in Honor of Hardin Craig*, edited by R. Hosley (1963).

Mackail, J. W. *The Approach to Shakespeare* (Oxford, 1933).

Madariaga, Salvador de. *On Hamlet* (1948).

Mahood, M. M. *Shakespeare's Wordplay* (London, 1957).

Marder, Louis. *His Exits and His Entrances* (London, 1964).

Marcus, Philip. L. 'T. S. Eliot and Shakespeare', *Criticism*, 9 (1967), 63–79.

Matthews, Honor. M. V. *Character and Symbol in Shakespeare* (Cambridge, 1962).

Mazzeo, J. A. *Renaissance and Seventeenth-Century Studies* (London and New York, 1964).

Mehl, Dieter. 'Emblems in English Renaissance Drama', *Renaissance Drama*, n.s. 2 (1969), 35–57.
'Visual and Rhetorical Imagery in Shakespeare's Plays', *Essays and Studies* (1972), 83–100.

Milward, Peter S. J. *Shakespeare's Religious Background* (London, 1973).

Mizener, Arthur. 'The *Scrutiny* Group', *Kenyon Review*, 10 (1948), 344–360.

Morozov, Mikhail M. 'The Individualization of Shakespeare's Characters through Imagery', *SS*, 2 (1949).

Morris, Ivor. *Shakespeare's God* (London, 1972), esp. Appendix C.
'The Interpretation of Tragedy through Poetic Imagery', 461–77.

Moulton, R. G. *Shakespeare as a Dramatic Artist* (Oxford, 1892).

Muir, Edwin. *Essays on Literature and Society* (London, 1949).

Muir, Kenneth. 'Fifty Years of Shakespearian Criticism', *SS*, 4 (1951).
'Changing Interpretations of Shakespeare', *The Age of Shakespeare: The Pelican Guide to English Literature*, vol. 2 edited by Boris Ford (Harmondsworth, 1955).
'Shakespeare's Imagery – Then and Now', *SS*, 18 (1965), 34–46.
Shakespeare the Professional (London, 1973).

Muir, Kenneth and Schoenbaum, S., editors *A New Companion to Shakespeare Studies* (Cambridge, 1971).

Murray, P. *The Shakespearian Scene* (London, 1969).

Murry, J., Middleton. *The Problem of Style* (Oxford, 1922).
Countries of the Mind (London, 1922).
Shakespeare (London, 1936).

'A. C. Bradley: The Surrender to Poetry', *TLS* (25 May 1936) (unsigned).

Heaven-and-Earth (London, 1938).

John Clare and Other Studies (London, 1950).

Myrick, K. O. 'The Theme of Damnation in Shakespearian Tragedy', *SP*, 38 (1941), 221–45.

Narayana Menon, C. *Shakespeare Criticism: An Essay in Synthesis* (London, 1938).

Newton, J. M. *'Scrutiny's* Failure with Shakespeare', *Cambridge Quarterly*, 1 (1965–6), 144–77.

Nicoll, Allardyce. *Shakespeare* (London, 1954).

Nuttall, A. D. 'The Argument about Shakespeare's Characters', *CQ*, 7 (1965), 107–20.

Two Concepts of Allegory: A Study of Shakespeare's 'Tempest' and the Logic of Allegorical Expression (London, 1967).

O'Connor, William. *An Age of Criticism: 1900–1950* (Chicago, 1952).

editor. *Forms of Modern Fiction* (Minneapolis, 1947).

Olson, Elder. *Tragedy and the Theory of Drama* (Detroit, 1961).

'Hamlet and the Hermeneutics of Drama', *MP*, 61 (1963–4).

Ong, J. Walter. *Ramus, Method, and the Decay of Dialogue* (Cambridge, Mass., 1958).

Ornstein, Robert. *The Moral Vision of Jacobean Tragedy* (Madison, 1960).

Osborne, Harold. *Aesthetics and Criticism* (London, 1955).

Palmer, D. J. 'G. Wilson Knight', *The Critical Survey*, vol. 3 (Summer 1965).

Panichas, A. George. 'G. Wilson Knight: Interpreter of Genius', *English Miscellany*, 20 (1969), 291–312.

Parker, M. D. H. *The Slave of Life* (London, 1955).

Partridge, Edward. *The Broken Compass: A Study of the Major Comedies of Ben Jonson* (London, 1958).

Patch, Howard R. *The Goddess Fortuna in Medieval Literature* (Cambridge, Mass., 1927).

Peacock, Ronald. *The Art of the Drama* (London, 1957).

Phillipps, E. James. *The State in Shakespeare's Greek and Roman Plays* (New York, 1940).

Phillips, O. Hood. *Shakespeare and the Lawyers* (London, 1972).

Prescott, F. C. *The Poetic Mind* (New York, 1922).

Poetry and Myth (New York, 1927).

Price, T. Hereward. 'The Function of Imagery in Webster', *PMLA*, 70 (1955), 720–39.

Price, J. G. *The Unfortunate Comedy: A Study of 'All's Well' and Its Critics* (Liverpool, 1968).

Prior, Moody, E. *The Language of Tragedy* (Bloomington and London, 1947, 1966 edn).

Prosser, Eleanor. *Hamlet and Revenge* (Stanford, 1967).

222   *Select bibliography*

Purdom, C. B. Correspondence on Wilson Knight in *The Listener*, vol. 52, 23 December 1954.
Rabkin, Norman. *Shakespeare and the Common Understanding* (New York and London, 1967).
Ralli, Augustus. *A History of Shakespearian Criticism* (Oxford, 1932), 2 vols.
Raleigh, Sir Walter, editor *Shakespeare's England* (Oxford, 1916), 2 vols.
Ramsey, Jarold. 'Timon's Imitation of Christ', *Shakespeare Studies*, 2 (1966), 162–73.
Reese, M. M. *The Cease of Majesty: A Study of Shakespeare's History Plays* (London, 1961).
Reynolds, G. F. *The Staging of Elizabethan Plays at the Red Bull Theatre, 1605–25* (New York, 1940).
  On Shakespeare's Stage, edited by R. K. Knaub (Boulder, 1967).
  'The Staging of *Troilus and Cressida*', *J. Q. Adams Memorial Studies*, edited by J. G. McManaway (1948).
  'Some Principles of Elizabethan Staging', *MP*, 2 (1904–5), 581–614 and *MP*, 3 (1905–6), 69–97.
  'Trees on the Stage of Shakespeare', *MP*, 5 (1907–8), 153–68.
  'Two Conventions on the Elizabethan Stage', *MP*, 17 (1919–20), 35–43.
  'Was There a "Tarras" in Shakespeare's Globe?' *SS*, 4 (1951), 97–100.
Ribner, Irving. 'Shakespeare Criticism: 1900–1964', *Shakespeare: 1564–1964*, edited by E. A. Bloom (Brown University Press, 1964), 194–208.
  Patterns in Shakespearian Tragedy (London, 1960).
  The English History Play in the Age of Shakespeare (Princeton, 1957).
Rickword, Edgell. 'A Note on Fiction', *The Calendar of Modern Letters*, March 1925 – July 1927, vols. III and IV (new impression in two vols., London, 1966), II, 226–33.
Ricks, Christopher. 'The Tragedies of Webster, Tourneur and Middleton: Symbols, Imagery, and Conventions', *English Drama to 1710: The Sphere History of Literature in the English Language*, edited by C. Ricks (London, 1971), 306–51.
Ridler, Anne (Bradby), ed. *Shakespeare Criticism: 1919–1935* (London, 1936).
  ed. *Shakespeare Criticism: 1935–1960* (London, 1963).
Riggs, M. David. *Shakespeare's Heroical Histories: The Henry VI Plays* (Cambridge, Mass., 1971).
Righter, Anne. *Shakespeare and the Idea of the Play* (London, 1962, Harmondsworth paperback edn 1967).
Righter, William. *Logic and Criticism* (London, 1963).
Rossiter, A. P. *Angel with Horns*, edited by G. Storey (London, 1961).
Rowse, A. L. *William Shakespeare* (London, 1963).
Rylands, George. *Words and Poetry* (London, 1928).
  'Shakespeare's Poetic Energy', *PBA* 37 (1951), 99–119.

Sale, Roger. 'G. Wilson Knight', *MLQ*, 29 (1968), 77–83.

Sanders, Wilbur, L. *The Dramatist and the Received Idea* (Cambridge, 1968).

Schücking, Levin, L. *Character Problems in Shakespeare's Plays* (1919), English translation (London, 1922).

Schwartz, Elias. 'The Idea of the Person in Shakespearian Tragedy', *SQ*, 16 (1965), 39–47.

Sen, S. K. *Capell and Malone, and Modern Critical Bibliography* (Calcutta, 1960).

'A Neglected Critic of Shakespeare: Walter Whiter', *SQ*, 13 (1962).

Sen Gupta, S. C. *Towards a Theory of the Imagination* (Calcutta, 1959).

'Shakespeare's Craft of Verse', *TLS* (2 July 1954), 424.

Siegel, Paul. 'In Defence of Bradley', *College English*, 9 (1948), 250–6.

'The Damnation of Othello', *PMLA*, 68 (1953), 1068–78.

Sirluck, Ernest. Introduction to *Complete Prose Work of Milton*, vol. II (New Haven, 1959), 12–52.

Sisson, C. J. *Le Goût Public et le Théâtre Élisabéthain Jusqu'à la Mort de Shakespeare* (Dijon, 1922).

'The Mythical Sorrows of Shakespeare' *PBA* (1934), reprinted in *Studies in Shakespeare: British Academy Lectures*, edited by P. Alexander (London, 1964), 9–32.

Smith, Grover. 'The Naked New-Born Babe in *Macbeth*: Some Iconographical Evidence', *Renaissance Papers* (1964), 21–7.

Smith, D. Nichol. *Shakespeare in the Eighteenth Century* (Oxford, 1928).

ed. *Shakespeare Criticism: A Selection 1623–1840* (Oxford, 1916), revised edn 1963.

Smith, M. Robert. 'Interpretations of *Measure for Measure*', *SQ*, 1 (1950), 208–18.

Speaight, Robert. *Nature in Shakespearean Tragedy* (London, 1955).

Spencer, T. J. B. 'The Course of Shakespeare Criticism', *Shakespeare's World*, edited by J. Sutherland and J. Hurstfield (London, 1965), 172–93.

Spencer, Theodore. *Shakespeare and the Nature of Man* (Cambridge, Mass., 1942).

Spens, Janet. *Shakespeare and the Tradition* (London, 1916).

Stallman, R. W. 'The New Critics', *Critiques and Essays in Criticism*, edited by R. W. Stallman (New York, 1949).

Stamm, Rudolf. *The Shaping Powers at Work* (Heidelberg, 1967).

Stavisky, Aron Y. *Shakespeare and the Victorians: The Roots of Modern Criticism* (Oklahoma, 1969).

Stead, C. K. *The New Poetic* (London, 1964).

Stein, Walter. *Criticism as Dialogue* (Cambridge, 1969).

Stewart, J. I. M. *Character and Motive in Shakespeare* (London, 1949).

Still, Colin. *Shakespeare's Mystery Play: A Study of 'The Tempest'* (London, 1921), expanded into *The Timeless Theme* (London, 1936).

Stoll, E. E. *Shakespeare Studies* (New York, 1927).
  Poets and Playwrights (Minneapolis, 1930).
  Art and Artifice in Shakespeare (Cambridge, 1933).
  Shakespeare and Other Masters (Cambridge, Mass., 1940).
  From Shakespeare to Joyce (Garden City, New York, 1944).
  'Symbolism in Shakespeare', *MLR*, 42 (1947), 9–23.
Strachey, Lytton. 'Shakespeare's Final Period' (1904), reprinted in *Books and Characters* (London, 1922) and *Literary Essays* (London, 1948).
Stroup, T. B. *Microcosmos: The Structure of an Elizabethan Play* (Lexington, Ky, 1965).
Talbert, E. W. *The Problem of Order: Elizabethan Political Commonplaces and an Example of Shakespeare's Art* (Chapel Hill, NC, 1962).
  Elizabethan Drama and Shakespeare's Early Plays (Chapel Hill, NC, 1963).
Tillyard, E. M. W. *Shakespeare's Last Plays* (London, 1938).
  The Elizabethan World Picture (London, 1943).
  Shakespeare's History Plays (London, 1944).
  Shakespeare's Problem Plays (London, 1950).
Tomlinson, T. B. *A Study of Elizabethan and Jacobean Tragedy* (Cambridge, 1964).
Traversi, Derek A. *An Approach to Shakespeare* (3rd edn in two vols 1968), introduction in vol. I on 'Modern Shakespeare criticism', 9–22.
Trousdale, Marion. 'The Question of Harley Graville-Barker and Shakespeare on Stage', *Renaissance Drama*, n.s. 4 (1971).
Tuve, Rosemond. *Elizabethan and Metaphysical Imagery* (Chicago, 1947).
Ullmann, Stephen. *Language and Style* (Oxford, 1964).
Venezky, Alice. *Pageantry on the Shakespearian Stage* (New York, 1951).
Vickers, Brian. *The Artistry of Shakespeare's Prose* (London, 1968).
  ed. *Shakespeare: The Critical Heritage* (London, 1974), vol. I.
Viswanathan, S. ' "Illeism with a Difference" in Certain Middle Plays of Shakespeare', *SQ*, 20 (1969).
  'A Shakespearian Device: The Scene within the Scene', *Anglia*, 90 (1972).
  ' "The School of Night" Reopened', *ES*, 54 (1973).
  Review of Patrick Murray, *The Shakespearean Scene* (London, 1969), *SQ* (Summer 1973).
  ' "Time's Fickle Glass" in Shakespeare's Sonnet 126', *ES*, 57 (1976).
  ' "The Medlar in the Forest of Arden', *Neuphilologische Mitteilungen*, 77 (1976).
  ' "This Fell Sergeant Death" Once More', *SQ*, 29 (1978).
  'Sleep and Death: The Twins in Shakespeare', *Comparative Drama*, 13 (1979).
Vyvyan, John. *The Shakespearean Ethic* (London, 1959).
Waith, Eugene M. *The Herculean Hero in Marlowe, Chapman and Shakespeare* (London, 1962).

Walkley, A. B. 'Professor Bradley's *Hamlet'*, *Drama and Life* (London, 1907), 148–55.

Watson, George. *The Literary Critics* (Harmondsworth, 1962).

Weisinger, Herbert. 'The Study of Shakespearian Tragedy since Bradley', *SQ*, 6 (1955).

'The Myth-and-Ritual Approach to Shakespearian Tragedy' (1957), originally published in *The Centennial Review of Arts and Sciences* and reprinted in *Perspectives in Contemporary Criticism*, edited by Sheldon Norman Grebstein (New York, 1968).

Weiss, Samuel A. ' "Solid", "Sullied" and Mutability: A Study in Imagery', *SQ*, 10 (1959).

Weitz, Morris. *Hamlet and the Philosophy of Literary Criticism* (Chicago and London, 1964).

Wellek, René. *Concepts of Criticism* (New York and London, 1963).

'The Criticism of F. R. Leavis', *Literary Views: Critical and Historical Essays*, edited by Caroll Camden (Chicago, 1964).

Wellek, René and Warren, Austin. *A Theory of Literature* (New York, 1942).

Wells, H. W. *Poetic Imagery Illustrated from Elizabethan Literature* (New York, 1924).

'Indian Drama and the West', *The Journal of Commonwealth Literature*, no. 1, September 1965.

Wells, Stanley. 'Shakespeare Criticism since Bradley', *A New Companion to Shakespeare Studies*, 249–61.

Wentersdorf, Karl. 'The Authenticity of *The Taming of the Shrew*', *SQ*, 5 (1954), 11–32.

'Imagery as a Criterion of Authenticity: A Reconsideration of the Problem', *SQ*, 23 (1972), 231–59.

West, Rebecca. *The Court and the Castle* (London, 1958).

West, H. Robert. *Shakespeare and the Outer Mystery* (Lexington, 1968).

Whitaker, Virgil K. *Shakespeare's Use of Learning* (San Marino, California, 1953).

The Mirror up to Nature (San Marino, California, 1965).

Whiter, Walter. *Specimen of a Commentary on Shakespeare* (1794), edited by Alan Over and Mary Bell (London, 1967).

Williams, Charles. *The English Poetic Mind* (Oxford, 1932).

Reason and Beauty in the English Poetic Mind (Oxford, 1933).

Wilson, F. P. *Elizabethan and Jacobean* (Oxford, 1945).

Wilson, S. Harold. 'Commentary', *SQ*, 9 (1958), 307–10.

Wimsatt Jr. W. K. and Beardsley, M. C. *The Verbal Icon* (Lexington, 1954).

Wimsatt, W. K. and Brooks, C. *Literary Criticism: a Short History* (New York, 1957).

Woodhouse, A. S. P. 'Nature and Grace in *The Faerie Queene*', *ELH*, 16 (1949), 194–228.

'The Argument of Milton's *Comus*', *UTQ*, 11 (1941), 46–71.

Wright, Louis B. *Middle Class Culture in Elizabethan England* (London, 1935).
Yates, Frances A. *The Art of Memory* (London, 1966).
The Theatre of the World (London, 1969).
Shakespeare's Last Plays – A New Approach (London, 1975).
Yoder, Audrey. *Animal Analogy in Shakespeare's Character Portrayal* (New York, 1948).

Index

Index   231

India, 56
interpretation and criticism, the
    distinction between, 66–7,
    112–15, 120–1.
Isaacs, J., 6 n.5, 74 n.24

Jackson, James L., 174 n.28
Jackson, MacD. P., 185 n.34
James, D. G., 24 n.45, 50 n.19,
    52 n.24, 104 n.11, 115, 147
James I, King, 26 n.52, 76 n.32
James, Henry, 53–4 and n., 129 n.9,
    143 n.23
Jameson, Anna, vii
Japan, 56
Jeffares, A. Norman, 54 n.29
Jefferson, D. W., 96 n.1
Johnson, E. D. H., 8 n.9
Johnson, F. R., 22 and n., 183
Johnson, Oliver, 154 n.32
Johnson, Samuel, 24–5, 53 n.28,
    143 n.23, 166, 190
Jones, Howard Mumford, 83 n.41
Jones, John, 29 n.60, 62 n.1
Jonson, Ben, 116
Jorgensen, Paul A., 17 n.26, 158 n.8
Joseph, Bertram, 34 n.80
Joseph, Sister Miriam, 23 n.41,
    26 n.51, 169, 181
Julius Caesar, 68, 96–7 and notes,
    141–2, 202–3, 204
Jump, John D., 23 n.41
Jung, Carl, 58–9, 190
Jusserand, J. J., 52 n.24

Kabuki plays, the, 56 n.33
Kantak, V. Y., 179n.30
Kantorowicz, Ernst H., 17 n.23,
    204 n.17
Keast, W. R., 187
Keats, John, 169
Keble, John, 164, 165
Keeton, George W., 17 n.26, 206 n.22
Kellett, E. E., 158 n.8, 172, 173
Kelly, H. A., 17 n.23
Kermode, Frank, 45 n.7, and n.9
Kernodle, George R., 33
Kierkegaard, Soren, 72, 140 n.22
King John, 102–3, 141, 199, 204
King Lear, 88–92, 132–7, 147, 148–9,
    150–1, 178, 186–7, 191–2, 202–3,
    204–5
Kirkman, the Rev. Joshua, 203 n.16
Kirsch, Arthur C., 116
Kirschbaum, Leo, 37 n.83

Kitto, H. D. F., 29 n.60, 56 n.36
Kittredge, George Lyman, 28 and n.
Klein, David, 34 n.80
Kliger, Samuel, 198 and n.
Klingopulos, G. D., 45 n.9
Knight, George Wilson, **62–95,
    96–121,** and viii, ix, 27, 35, 47,
    48, 51, 123, 125, 131, 143 n.23,
    157–8, 159, 171, 173, 189, 190,
    191
his theory of interpretation, 63–70;
    influences on, 66–72; Wilson
    Knight and the 'New Criticism',
    47–8, 75, 112–13; on *Measure for
    Measure*, 73–6, 79; on *Troilus and
    Cressida*, 76–8, 79; on *All's Well
    That Ends Well*, 78–9; on *Timon of
    Athens*, 79–81; on *Hamlet*, 81–6;
    on *Othello*, 86–8; on *King Lear*,
    88–92; on *Macbeth*, 92–5; on
    Julius Caeser, 96–7; on *Coriolanus*,
    97–8; on *Antony and Cleopatra*,
    98–102; as pioneer of the new
    interpretation of the history
    plays, 102–3; on the last plays,
    103–7; on the comedies, 107–8;
    on imaginative solidities or
    direct poetic symbolism, 108–9;
    on his so-called Christianising
    interpretation, 51, 109–10; critical
    response to his interpretation,
    110–15, 118–19; his interpretation
    and its relation to historical
    scholarship, 116–18; his
    Shakespeare productions and
    acting experience and their
    impact on his interpretation, 79,
    81, 83, 92, 94, 95, 102 n.9, 103,
    108, 108–9, 119–21, 159; as an
    imagistic critic so-called, 108–9,
    188
Knights, Lionel Charles, **122–55,** and
    viii, ix, 4 n.4, 9, 16 n.22, 25, 38,
    40 n.1, 41 n.2, 48, 53 n.28, 75 n.26,
    77 n.33, 78 n.34, 84 n.44, 173, 180,
    189, 191
his emergence as Shakespeare
    critic and influences, 122–7; his
    critical methods and response to
    historical scholarship, 127–31,
    132–7, 140–1, 142–6, 151–4; on
    Macbeth, 126–7, 128–32; on *King
    Lear*, 132–7; on four major
    Shakespearian themes, 137–42;
    his 'personalist' bias, 139–43; his

moral values, interpretation in terms
of, 24–5, and n., 36–7, 46–7 and
notes, 68–70, 142–3 and n.,
145–7, 153
Morgann, Maurice, 161
Morozov, M. M., 177
Morris, Ivor, 51–2
Muir, Edwin, 8 n.9, 16 n.22, 91 n.48,
133
Muir, Kenneth, 1 n.2, 11 n.14,
74 n.35, 162 n.13, 173, 185 n.34,
197, 201 and n., 202 and n.
Murray, Gilbert, 35 and n.
Murray, Patrick, 13, 14–15
Murry, John Middleton, 2 n.3,
18 n.27, 27 and n., 51 n.20,
63 n.3, 73 n.22, 103 n.10, 104 n.11,
123 and n., 174
Mysteries, the, 25
Myrick, Kenneth O., 51 n.23
Myth, ritual, symbol and archetype,
approaches through, 32–3, 50–1,
64–5, 67–9, 103–7, 111–14,
115–18, 190–3

Nagarajan, S., 76 n.31
Nature, by Henry Medwall, 135 n.15
nature and naturalism, 90, 91, 94,
99–100, 105–6, 129–30, 131–6 and
notes
nature and grace, 105–6, 131–6 and
notes
Neimann, Fraser, 47 n.15
Nelson, Norman, 169
✳ 'new criticism', assumptions of, 42–7,
60
George Wilson Kinight and, 47–8,
75, 112–13
'new sciences', their relation to
Shakespeare criticism, 32, 57–9
New Shakespeare Society, 170
Newton, John, 154 and n.
Nichols, J. G., 182
Nichols, R., 83
Nicoll, Allardyce, 1 n.2, 71 n.19
Nietzsche, F. W., 70 n.14, 71, 83 n.40
Nōh Plays, 56 n.33
Nuttall, A. D., 37 n.83, 116, 117 n.28,
123 n.3, 149–50

Olson, Elder, 43 n.4, 159 n.9, 190, 195
and n.
Olson, Paul, 26 n.52
organicism, 41, 124–5

origins of drama, arguments about,
56–7
Ornstein, Robert, 17 n.23, 24 n.45
Osborne, Harold, 157 and n.
✳ *Othello,* 85–8, 119, 142–4, 202–3,
48 n.16
Over, Alan, 174 n.28

Palmer, D. J., 114 n.23, 126 n.6
Palmer, John, 36
Panichas, George A., 118
Panofsky, Erwin, 116 and n., 182
Parker, M. D. H., 24 n.44, 51 n.23
Parkes, H. B., 133
Partridge, A. C., 29
Partridge, Edward, 157 n.4, 178
Patch, Howard R., 117, 134 n.14, 182
Patrides, C. A., 134 n.12
Peacock, Ronald, 158 n.7, 178
Pericles, 104–5, and n.
Personality and the Person, attitudes
to and their impact on
Shakespeare criticism, 60–1,
68–9, 74–5, 82–3, 85–6, 93–4,
127–8, 142–6, 153–4
Phillips, James E., 210 n.23
Phillips, O. Hood, 6 n.5, 206 n.22
Phillips, Stephen, 54
Phipson, Emma, 170 n.24
Pickard-Cambridge, A. W., 56 and n.
Planket, Sir Dunbar, 206 n.22
Poe, Edgar Allan, 122 n.1
Poel, William, 70 and n.
Poetic Drama, the revival of and
assumptions about, 40–2, 54–5,
81–2, 124–5
Pollard, A. W., 185 n.34
Pope, Elizabeth M., 76 n.30
Poulet, Georg, 67 n.10
Pound, Ezra, 45, 49, 60
Powell, Chilton L., 76 n.31
Praz, Mario, 166 and n.
Prescott, F. C., 32–3, and n., 58
Price, Hereward T., 161 n.12
Prior, Moody E., 10 n.11, 161 n.12,
162 n.14, 185 and n., 205
problem comedies, interpretation, *see*
comedies
Prosser, Eleanor, 23 n.41, 84 n.44,
143 n.23
Psychology, influence on
Shakespeare criticism, 57–9
Purdom, C. B., 70 n.16

Quiller-Couch, Arthur, 75 n.27